Democracy: A History of Ideas

Boris DeWiel

Democracy: A History of Ideas

UBCPress · Vancouver · Toronto

321.8
D43
2000

Printed in Canada on acid-free paper ∞

ISBN 0-7748-0801-2

Canadian Cataloguing in Publication Data

DeWiel, Boris, 1956-
  Democracy

  Includes bibliographical references and index.
  ISBN 0-7748-0801-2

  1. Democracy – History. I. Title.

JC421.D48   2000   321.8'09   C00-910653-7

This book has been published with the help of a grant from the Humanities and Social Sciences Federation of Canada, using funds provided by the Social Sciences and Humanities Research Council of Canada.

UBC Press acknowledges the financial support of the Government of Canada through the Book Publishing Industry Development Program (BPIDP) for our publishing activities.

Canada

We also gratefully acknowledge the support of the Canada Council for the Arts for our publishing program, as well as the support of the British Columbia Arts Council.

Set in Stone by Artegraphica Design Co. Ltd.
Printed in Canada by Friesens
Copy editor: Joanne Richardson
Proofreader: Darcy Cullen

UBC Press
University of British Columbia
2029 West Mall, Vancouver, BC V6T 1Z2
(604) 822-5959
Fax: (604) 822-6083
E-mail: info@ubcpress.ubc.ca
www.ubcpress.ubc.ca

Contents

Acknowledgments / vi

1 Democracy and Value Pluralism / 3

2 What Is the People? A Conceptual History of Civil Society / 11

3 From Ancient Virtues to Modern Values: Positive Liberty and the Creative Will / 23

4 The Teleology of Modern Time: Negative Liberty and Human Nature / 43

5 Splitting the Individual: The Subatomic Values of Liberalism / 72

6 Conservatism and the Temporal Order / 91

7 Socialism and the Power of Social Unity / 117

8 Democracy as a Pattern of Disagreement / 142

Notes / 181

Bibliography / 191

Index / 198

Acknowledgments

I would like to thank Stan Stein, Roger Gibbins, Rainer Knopff, and, especially, Tom Flanagan. With their talents above my own, they raised the standard of possibility for me.

The greatest influence on this book came from the ideas of Isaiah Berlin, whom I never met. I have taken liberties with his work, drawing them out in ways he may not have liked. Berlin had little need for linear stories and should not be faulted for these ones.

From Berlin's writing, I learned two great things. The first is that moral sympathy comes before understanding. Only by looking for their ideas of goodness can we know what others mean. The second is the self-understanding that comes from accepting the fact of value pluralism. By shading us from the blindingly enlightened hope for harmony among them, it allows us to know our common values more fully.

A longer version of Chapter 2 appeared as 'A Conceptual History of Civil Society: From Greek Beginnings to the End of Marx,' in *Past Imperfect* 6 (1997): 3-42.

My greatest thanks is to the citizens who, through the Social Sciences and Humanities Research Council of Canada and various universities, supported me in the privilege of enquiring into their beliefs. This book is an attempt to be truer to them.

Democracy: A History of Ideas

1
Democracy and Value Pluralism

Why do people disagree about politics? One reason is that interests collide, but this explanation is too easy. Why do honest, unselfish people differ in their conceptions of the good society? Why is there no consensus among theorists who specialize in these questions? Why, for example, is it so easy to identify right-wing and left-wing positions across political issues? Why are these differences recognizable in the politics of every modern democracy? Why do they reach across historical eras? A pattern of dissensus seems entrenched in democracy. As issues change, left-right conflicts may retrench, but reports of their demise, whether hopeful or despairing, are exaggerations. Why is democracy so fractious?

The purpose of this book is to challenge the notion that ideological conflict is a contest between good ideas and bad ones – one's own and those of others, as it always turns out; instead, this book attempts to discover the political implications of value pluralism, the thesis that our ultimate values, or ideas about the good, conflict with each other. By identifying the common but conflicting values underlying the left-right political spectrum, we can begin to outline the inherently conflictual nature of democracy. As members of modern democracies, we share values, but, because they conflict, we prioritize them differently. We are divided by our commonalities. Democracy is an irresolvable contest of priorities among common values. Were we able to remove all the sources of venality, stupidity, and nastiness in politics, democracy would still cleave in familiar ways.

On one level, the claim that values conflict is a truism. We are happy to admit the conflict among the values we hold dearest, but we are quick to draw the line of legitimacy according to our own priorities. Value pluralism is quickly forgotten when our priorities run hard up against another's. The fact of deep disagreement is unpleasant, and so we tend to associate with those who see things more or less as we do. Most political arguments are intramural because that is the level at which discussion occurs. Because we argue mostly with those who have views close to our own, it is easy to pull the circle of legitimacy too closely. Respectful dialogue rarely crosses ideological borders. The truly deep differences among us are across camps, and this dissensus is rarely recognized as legitimate.

If we accept value pluralism at a deeper level, it could change the way we think about ethics and politics. Such a revolution would be analogous in Western theology to the overthrow of monotheism. What if there were more than one God, and what if Their commands were to conflict? Or, putting the metaphor slightly less heretically, what if God gave irreconcilable commands? Value pluralism is the uncomfortable theory that the good is not unitary, that our common goods conflict, and that there is no right answer when goods ultimately collide.

Is value pluralism a form of moral relativism? The suggestion here is that it is not, although mono-ethicists may disagree. Relativism is the doctrine that every person or group is the source of unique subjective values. In the theological analogy, relativism means that we each have our own unitary God. Pluralism is the doctrine that human beings share common values but that these conflict with each other. To say it in a culturally sensitive way, value pluralism is the theory that the expanding culture of modernity provides each of us with shared conceptions of the good but that these conceptions are irreconcilable. For relativists, each person (or group) is mono-ethical, and their divergent values never meet. For pluralists, the monoculture of modernity is multi-ethical, and our common values collide within each of us.

Relativism is an unsophisticated variant of one of the great concepts of liberty, which holds that to be free is to be the source of one's own defining ends. Relativists hold that we create our own good – that we are our own God. They believe, more literally than others, that, as each person is the source of value, whatever one values is good. Because it trivializes the good as a mere subjective preference, relativism is inadequate as an ethical theory. Yet it arises from a deeply important ethical belief – that each person is the source of value. The history of this idea, and its ongoing importance in democracy, is one of the stories that will be told here.

In contrast to relativists, value pluralists do not believe that we each create our own good *ex nihilo*. Rather than trivializing the idea of goodness as subjective, pluralism recognizes both the legitimacy and the commonality of values. Every normal person can understand the ultimate importance of values like liberty, equality, justice, and so on. To be normal in this sense is to have common norms. We do not just tolerate these values in others, we share them. However, because we have no ultimate criteria to rank competing goods, our priorities inevitably differ.

In politics there are not many pluralists. Politics is about what we should do together, a question that demands that a choice be made. Politicians do not merely suggest options, they are proponents of a certain set of priorities. Political theorists, to the extent that they come to practicable evaluative conclusions, are politicians of the best sort. They work to sort out evaluative ideas as best they can, and they attempt to convince others that their own priorities are best. To the extent that the priorities of social scientists and humanists in general are reflected in their work, they are politicians too. From politicians we will not find a pluralist theory. The proponents of a normative order must reduce the breadth of pluralism by narrowing the range of legitimate disagreement. To do politics is to reject competing options, whether the practitioner is a theorist or an electoral candidate. The true meaning of pluralism has been missed by political theorists and social scientists, whose calling is to resist the political complexity of ordinary people. Philosophers who seek to change the world in certain ways are driven to misunderstand it.

And yet we cannot do without political philosophies and ideologies. As defined in this book, ideologies are honest attempts to make the best possible sense of an insoluble evaluative problem, the ultimate conflict of our shared values. More than other people, ideological thinkers seek consistency and rational justifications for their priorities. This leads them to dismiss or diminish some values, while defining others in ways that can be synthesized into a single normative story. A value like equality, for example, begins as something we share but comes to be defined to fit within a story about what we should do together. For socialists, the just society is one in which positive liberty should be shared, while negative liberty is of diminished importance. For economic libertarians, on the other hand, equality is not about shared power but about common rules of competition, while negative liberty is given a high priority. Other ideological thinkers find their own ways to prioritize values in consistent ways.

Ideological thinkers are necessary to political practice because they present us with rational options. They show us how to put political values into action. We cannot do without them because they alone show us how to do some good. When we move towards one good, we move away from another, but the alternative is to do no good at all. Ideological politics is politics at its very best, a contest of ideas about the good. Without ideology, politics becomes the pursuit for power as its own reward. In pre-modern eras, politics was about power alone. Today, it is a competition of goods. The political mode of modernity is democratic, and democratic politics is a permanent ideological contest.

Does the contest of democracy have an underlying structure? Democracy may be essentially contestable, but does it involve a regular pattern of disagreement? This book traces the history of a few political values about which people disagree today, and it searches for deep continuities and patterns. If persistent differences can be discovered in the values of modernity as they developed, then the underlying contest of modern politics will become clearer. We will be able to specify the values embedded in the familiar, but ill-defined, model of the left-centre-right political continuum. The political centre, we will see, is not a zone of confusion or wishy-washy trade-offs; rather, it is defined by the dominant, though contested, ideology of modernity.

The historical approach to the study of political ideas is justified by the epistemological theory that the only immediate source of our ideas is other ideas. Direct knowledge of truth is not available to us, and so we all begin with the competing ideas of our time. Our perceptions are important but not sufficient; only through ideas can we make sense of our sensations. Ideas are theories about what our perceptions mean. They are attempts to fit the sense data of our lives into some kind of meaningful whole so that we can know what to do. In this sense, our ideas are always normative. They are neither innate nor perceived but are communicated to us by others. We try to reconcile our own life-data – our private perceptions, reflections, emotions, and desires – using the various theories taken from our culture. Occasionally, ideas may be put together in interesting ways, and new variants of old ideas will be passed on to new thinkers. A culture changes over generations, but its geniuses must begin with the ideas of their time. The changes in our theories about how to live are incremental, modest, and never entirely original. The source of our ideas is cultural, and the culture of modernity is deeply rooted. Our ideas are very old, and their sources and substance can be traced to other ideas.

Our values come from our culture, and the culture of democracy has antecedents that reach across millennia. At the core of democracy, this book will argue, is a definable pattern of disagreement. The conflicts among our values are as deeply rooted as our ideas themselves. Apart from the epistemological postulate that ideas come from ideas, there is no overriding theory of cultural progress, no end of history, to be found in these pages. The only universal lesson is that people have always argued about the good.

The process by which we separate truth from falsehood remains controversial and will not be discovered here. In particular, we have no uncontested way to decide the contest of values. Moral and political philosophers just disagree. Rather than entering into philosophical arguments about whether certain values are better than others, the approach will be to understand our values sympathetically by tracing their emergence. The goal is to present, in the end, an overview of the structure of competing values and ideologies without becoming lost in the rivalry among them. These values will be described with the hope that a fair-minded reader will see them as truly valuable, but a full philosophical defence is not available.

Our political values are not mere subjective preferences but belong to an old common culture. They are objective in the sense that they are things in themselves, objects of exchange among persons. They may change very gradually in the process, but they belong to no one alone. Our values are highly condensed abstractions, each of which summarizes a long braid of normative ideas. Political values, such as liberty, equality, or justice, encapsulate theories about what it means to live a good life. Each of our political values – and every contending version of each value – represents a long normative background story that belongs to our culture. These stories tell us who we are, the first step to knowing what we ought to do. Why do we value freedom? Because we understand ourselves as the sorts of beings who cannot live a good life, individually and together, unless we are free.

The contending versions of these background stories, we will see, conflict with each other. Our culture is composite, complex, and convoluted. Distilled into a single word like 'liberty' is a set of competing theories about the good. Because we lack an overriding normative story in which these conflicts are resolved – because value pluralism is true – politics is endlessly contentious. The conflicts of values, like the contending meanings of liberty, are what drives democratic politics. Democracy is not a single theory or ideal; it is a quarrel driven by the clash of ideals. It is not the quest for united self-determination, equality, and the common good. Democracy is not an egalitarian super-story but a multi-sided shouting match in which egalitarians are not the only legitimate voice. If value pluralism is true, then democracy is an argument that can never be won. It is about a terrible clash of goods, analogous to a civil war in heaven. Democracy is not the triumph of the common good but an unwinnable war of good against good against good.

Egalitarians have their own version of pluralism, according to which human differences should be recognized so that the powerless can be made equal. Everyone should be equally self-determining, say egalitarians; equality of power is the prerequisite to true democracy. Unfortunately, this story of the good society is one that most people do not accept as the best; and a conception of democracy that leaves out most of the people is, by definition, wrong. The priorities of the people tend to be different than those of egalitarians not because the people are the dupes of social forces or confused in some other way, but because equality is not the highest value of our culture. The culture of democracy has no single highest value.

Pluralism has a larger meaning, in which the priority of equality is contested. No one can deny that equality is among our ultimate values, but it conflicts with some of them. To take a quick example, equality necessarily conflicts with excellence. We cannot deny the reality of this conflict without abandoning the meaning of the concepts involved. If we pretend that everyone can be equally excellent, then the idea of excellence is flattened into meaninglessness. If we feign that equality requires only that everyone should have the same chance to excel, then we have misunderstood what equality means. To excel is to become unequal, and to be equal is not to excel.

People normally believe in the value of both equality and excellence, and yet these two concepts conflict in their very meaning. As ultimate values, they belong to different stories about what it means to live a good life together. The themes of these stories make sense to all of us – they are stories that belong to the common culture of democracy – and yet they are not reconcilable. Forced to decide among goods, we differ inevitably over our priorities. In what respects should excellence be relevant to social life? To what extent and in what forms should it be rewarded with wealth and social power? Should we be allowed to empower our own children more than others so that they have a better chance to excel? What is the minimum owed to those who are left behind while others excel? Depending on one's priorities, the answers to questions like these will vary.

Politics is more complex than this example suggests, but it illustrates the nature of our common dilemma. Nor does our future hold an evaluative consensus to be found through new moral understandings. A new morality, or a new set of values, would only increase the complexity of our cultural story by adding another layer of competing ideas. Pluralism cannot be eliminated by addition.

The long run of moral philosophy in our culture is disputational, and the hope for final agreement is unreal. People will always differ in how they prioritize competing values, and democracy will always be a contest of priorities. Those who believe we cannot have democracy until we have more equality, or until any other value triumphs finally, are not for the people but against them. The people are neither a monolith nor clay to be reshaped in better ways; rather, they are complex evaluators, dealing with the deep dilemma of democracy as best they can. The simplicities of political theory do not belong to them.

Between ultimate values there is no best trade-off because there is no super-value by which we can measure and judge. Ultimate values are not just different like apples and oranges, but like apples and opals, opals and idols, idols and ideals. They differ not in their *quantity* of goodness but in their defining *quality*. Goodness is not a single thing. If compromises are necessary, there is no way to find the best balancing point because there is no common scale of measurement. The best we can do is to argue forever. We find our way by following a path for a while, while disagreeing endlessly about the true way to go. We backtrack in confusion, we go in circles, we head off in all directions, and we come apart. True democracy will always be an ethical mess.

It is a mess, however, with a recognizable shape. Democracy is more than a conflict between equality and excellence, but its complexity is not infinite. By identifying a few ultimate values, we can begin to sketch the outlines of democratic disagreement. The ubiquitous left-right political metaphor, we will see, is useful and enduring because it captures a core of central value conflicts. Wherever democracy arises, this theory suggests, broadly similar ideological differences will arise. Local differences are also important, but these add to, rather than diminish, the divisiveness of democratic politics.

In summary, this book makes two general points. First, democracy is not a political philosophy but a battle of philosophies. We have no super-philosophy to settle this contest; we never had one and we never will. Second, there is a permanent pattern to the disagreement of democracy, which we can outline minimally by recognizing the conflict between two great traditions of liberty, for individuals and for communities. The resulting ideological model of democracy is parsimonious and could be expanded by adding additional values. Democracy may be more disputational but not less so.

The culture of democracy, sometimes called Western civilization or simply the West, began about three millennia ago. The theories about the good taught by Plato and Aristotle led, in time, to competing ideas among the medieval Scholastics, which emerged into contending traditions in early modernity before coming to us in ways familiar today. On one side is the belief that there is a deep teleology to human affairs, which may be understood as a causal flow or a natural order. On this side are those who see human purposes in terms of the pursuit of economic happiness and those who see society as structured by an invisible hand of moral order. On the other side are those who believe that the truest liberty is in the power to create our defining ends, that the human will is not just the locus but the source of value. Whether this freedom is vested in individuals or in society as a progressive whole, goodness is in the human will, a power exercised most fully as moral self-determination.

From this clash of ancient philosophies, each of which was modernized over millennia, arose the familiar pattern of ideological disagreement that characterizes democratic politics. Both stories are deeply embedded in the culture of modernity, and most people, unless ideologically committed to a comprehensive philosophy, know the value of both. For most people, democracy is an ongoing dilemma. We tend to lean in certain ways, with varying degrees of consistency, but the value of foregone alternatives always retains its appeal.

The people rule, but we have no single voice. It is not just that we differ about solutions to our problems, it is that we differ about what our problems are. The obstacles to our attainment of the good, and the threats to the good we have attained, inevitably vary with our conflicted understanding of what constitutes the good. To be democratic is to be divided by common ideas – understandings we share but that are not reconcilable with each other. To understand politics, therefore, we must understand the conflict among our values. The meaning of democracy can be found in the history of its competing ideas.

2
What Is the People?
A Conceptual History of
Civil Society

Democracy is the rule of the people, but what do we mean by the people? In politics, we mean something more than an aggregate of individuals. When we speak of the people of a nation, we invoke ideas of cultural wholeness and particularity. This conception belongs only to the modern idea of democracy. For the ancient theorists, the idea of the people as a cultural unity did not exist. They did not think of the people as a single whole, united by common history, mores, and beliefs. Peoples, cultures, and nations are overlapping modern notions, essential to the modern idea of democracy. For the ancient and early modern writers, civil society was a synonym for political society, while today it is understood as the realm of public institutions apart from the state. For us, democracy is the rule of the people, and the people is a singular organized entity conceptually distinct from the state. To understand modern democracy, we must begin by tracing this idea of the people as an autonomous entity. How did civil society come to be seen as separate from the political order?

Ancient Roots and Early Modern Branches
The first known attempts to answer the basic questions of political philosophy were those of the Sophists in the fifth century BC. These itinerant teachers were united less by a set of common beliefs than by their vocation and methods, but they did share the revolutionary doctrine that virtue could be taught. This meant that anyone with a suitable education could be entrusted with political power. The Sophist Protagoras appears to have been the first to discuss the underlying tenets of democratic theory. Another Sophist innovation was the idea of progress, in contrast to the prevailing Hellenistic doctrine that history was cyclical or, alternatively, that the golden age lay in the past. The idea of progress led Critias, who was a Sophist and a student of Socrates, to the belief that humankind could emerge from savagery only through the legal sanctions of the civil state, a view that would reappear much later with Hobbes.

Aristotle is credited with the first usage of the term 'civil society,' although his meaning has been distorted subtly in the translation from Greek to Latin and then to English. The Greek phrase used by Aristotle, at the outset of his *Politics*, was *koinonia politikē*.[1] The noun, *koinonia*, was translated by Liddell and Scott as 'communion, association, partnership'[2] and, according to Riedel, 'means nothing else than association, union.'[3] The common rendering into Latin was *societas* or *communitas*. With this transition, the word began to take on new shades of meaning, becoming somewhat closer to what we today mean by society or community. But it is important to note that these words in their Greek and Latin meaning, and in their early English usage as discussed below, did not have the sense of 'the people' as a cultural group as we understand it today. For the ancients, the idea of culture in this sense did not exist, as we will see, and was not implied by words like *koinonia* and *societas*.

The adjective *politikē* is a derivative of *polis*, a Greek city-state. Thus we have words like metropolis, or mother city. Originally, the *polis* referred only to the citadel at the centre of the Greek city, like the Athenian Acropolis, while the residential area surrounding it was the *asty*. But *polis* in time came to refer to the inhabitants of the city and its close environs as a single political unit. The adjectival form of *polis*, *politikē* 'signifies the theory (or rather the art) of the common life of the *polis* and the betterment of that life.'[4] In the Latin translation, *politikē* became *civilis*, an adjective pertaining to a member of a city or, originally, a resident of a citadel; hence the word citizen. This mirrors the Greek derivation, so the translation into Latin was without change of meaning.

Koinonia politikē was translated into Latin as *societas civilis* and, thus, in English became 'civil society.' But a more literal translation of Aristotle's phrase would be 'political community' or 'political association.' Indeed, Benjamin Jowett's translation[5] of his *Politics* used the first of these alternatives, while Ernest Barker's used the second. Barker's term, 'association,' better captured Aristotle's belief that politics was the deliberate and purposeful activity of self-organization in the effort to achieve common ends. For this reason, Aristotle's *koinonia politikē* is best translated directly into English as 'political association.'

As its etymology indicates, 'civil society,' for Aristotle, was identified with the *polis* itself. He saw the political organization of the *polis* as natural, arising through the intermediate stages of the household and the village. Man, for Aristotle, was naturally a political animal, but the adjective had none of today's pejorative sense. He wrote that there was 'an immanent impulse in all men towards an association of this order'[6] – the order of the *polis* in which human life has reached its highest social form.

If, for Aristotle, civil society was inherently political, the distinction between state and society also had ancient seeds. Religious faith would become important as a locus of resistance to the state, for example, in the European religious wars that followed the Reformation. An intimation of this resistance appeared in Jesus' answer to the Pharisees' question about whether it was right to pay Roman taxes. His reply – 'Render therefore unto Caesar the things which are Caesar's; and unto God the things that are God's' – implied that church and state involve separate realms of life. This distinction would be formalized by Aquinas as the *sacerdotum* and *regnum*, respectively, the jurisdictions of the sacred and the secular, within the *respublica christiana*, or Christian republic. For Aquinas, while these categories were conceptually distinct, if their interests should conflict, the state should be subordinate to the church: the emperor should bow to the pope. Religious authority, in contrast to state authority, would become central to the natural law doctrine of Locke.

Early usage of 'society' had none of the modern sense in which we might speak of 'the norms of Victorian society' or 'the history of Western society,' denoting a *particular* people joined by a common culture. In early usage, society meant association with one's fellows, as in the phrase, 'We desire the society of others.' Still in its early form, it also came to mean a collectivity of persons, as in, 'We desire to create a society.'[7] But in these usages there was none of the modern sense of a society as 'a people,' a singular entity defined by common culture, language, geography, history, and so on. This new connotation can be seen in the original agricultural meaning of the word 'culture,' suggesting organic, orderly growth. Every people, each society, is a single entity arising naturally from its own historical soil.[8] The modern idea of a society, a people, and a culture as an orderly whole, self-organized according to its own unique mores and customs, was the necessary precursor to the contemporary idea of civil society as distinct from the state. These related ideas did not enter the lexicon of political debate until the eighteenth century.

For early writers, the adjective 'civil' distinguished the political community from other purposeful forms of association – civil simply meant political, as it had for Aristotle. The *Oxford English Dictionary* gives Shakespeare's prologue to *Romeo and Juliet* as the first English usage of civil in the relevant sense,[9] closely followed by Richard Hooker's *Laws of Ecclesiastical Polity*: 'Civil Society doth more content the nature of man than any private kind of solitary living.'[10] The Aristotelian sense of man as a political or social animal remained in Hooker's usage: 'But forasmuch as we are not by ourselves sufficient to furnish ourselves with competent store of things needful for such a life as our nature doth desire, a life fit for the dignity of man; therefore to supply those defects and imperfections which are in us living single and solely by ourselves, we are naturally induced to seek communion and fellowship with others. This was the cause of men's uniting themselves at the first in politic Societies.'[11]

Hooker defended the Anglican Church against Puritan dissenters. The latter's political claims were illegitimate, argued Hooker, because they relied on divine revelation to the exclusion of natural law. Secular government was the embodiment of natural law, just as the church was the embodiment of the revealed law of God. Because positive and natural law were combined in the eternal law of God – the *lex aeterna* – church and state should be congruent. Thus Hooker could defend the Anglican monarchies of Henry the Eighth and his daughter Elizabeth while denying the claims of extreme Puritan sects. Hooker, writing in support of a popular queen, did not envision the need to revolt against tyrants. But Locke would later make explicit the conclusion that Hooker's argument seemed to imply: any government that fails to embody natural law must, thereby, be illegitimate. While the separation of church and state was not compatible with Hooker's political goals, his defence of natural law set the stage for later dissenters against the Crown.

In Hobbes's *Leviathan*, political and civil society were the same thing. Yet some of the modern meaning of civil society began to emerge, as in the approbative sense of the adjective 'civilized.' Thus for Hobbes the character of life in the state of nature was entirely uncivilized. Before civil society there was only, in his famous phrase, 'War, where every man is Enemy to every man ... And the life of man, solitary, poor, nasty, brutish and short.'[12] For Hobbes, natural law was minimal prior to the social contract, so whatever order existed in the world was due to the sanctions of positive law.

Locke too began by considering humanity's lot in the state of nature, though that state for him was very different from the one described by Hobbes. Locke's *Second Treatise of Government* suggests that we need to understand the origins of political society (which was, for Locke, civil society) before we can understand its true nature: 'To understand political power right, and derive it from its original, we must consider, what estate all men are naturally in, and that is, a state of perfect freedom to order their actions, and dispose of their possessions and persons, as they think fit, within the bounds of the law of nature, without asking leave, or depending upon the will of any other man.'[13] Locke went on to quote a long passage from Hooker on the obligations of justice and charity implied by humanity's natural equality. Thus natural law, for Locke, continued to have force even after civil, or political, society had been established.

Unlike Hobbes, Locke was true to the Aristotelian vision of humanity as naturally sociable. Like Hooker, he believed that human nature was divinely given and included the impetus to form social groups. 'God having made man such a creature, that in his own judgment, it was not good for him to be alone, put him under strong obligations of necessity, convenience, and inclination to drive him into society.'[14] This vision of human nature led to

Locke's idea of political, or civil, society: 'Those who are united into one body, and have a common established law and judicature to appeal to, with authority to decide controversies between them, and punish offenders, are in civil society one with another; but those who have no such common appeal, I mean on earth, are still in the state of nature ... Where-ever there-fore any number of men are so united into one society, as to quit every one his executive power of the law of nature, and to resign it to the public, there and there only is a political, or civil society.'[15]

While Hobbes had been a supporter of Charles the First against the Puritan Revolution, Locke was born on the side of the Puritans (his father was a captain in Cromwell's army). Hobbes was patronized by Charles the Second following the Restoration, while Locke's patron was the first earl of Shaftesbury, whom he followed into Dutch exile after a conspiracy against Charles. Hobbes's goal was to defend royal power as the embodiment of law and order, but Locke's goal was more complex. Following Shaftesbury, Locke supported the Glorious Revolution that brought William and Mary to power in 1689. Thus Locke had at once to justify the overthrow of one monarch while defending the right to rule of another. Arguments like Robert Filmer's thesis that kings had a divine right to rule because they were the direct descendants of Adam, or Hobbes's defence of whatever ruler could best maintain order, were inadequate for Locke's purposes; instead, he found his model in Hooker's ideas of legitimacy and consent.

Locke rejected Hobbes's view of a belligerent state of nature and followed Hooker in arguing that human beings, while naturally peaceful and socia-ble, were none the less partial to their own interests. This meant that life and property could not be secure unless an impartial authority existed to mediate disputes. But an absolute ruler does not fit this criterion because a ruler with unrestricted power would be partial to his or her own interests. 'And hence it is evident, that absolute monarchy, which by some men is counted the only government in the world, is indeed inconsistent with civil society, and so can be no form of civil government at all. For the end of civil society, being to avoid, and remedy those inconveniences of the state of Nature, which necessarily follow from every man's being judge in his own case, by setting up a known authority ... which every one of the society ought to obey.'[16]

Thus, for Locke, civil government was compatible not with absolute mon-archy, as Hobbes had claimed, but with something like a constitutional monarchy. In Locke's usage, civil society was political society, but it was a specific kind of political society – one in which the powers of the state were carefully limited. Locke endorsed an idea implicit in Hooker – that govern-ment is a trust granted on the sufferance of the people. Locke took the step that Hooker did not: a ruler who violates the people's trust may be deposed.

Natural law and positive law are distinct, and natural law gives people natural rights, discoverable by reason. Where rulers contravene the natural rights of their subjects, they may be overthrown.

While the idea of the English people as a culture was not explicit in either Locke or Hooker, the revolution their theories seemed to justify was driven by an early form of nationalism. In the early seventeenth century the idea of a nation was primarily racial in that one belonged to a group – one was native – not by culture but by blood. The word came into English from the Latin *nātus*, a participle derived from *nascor,* 'to be born.' This racial concept began to change with the idea of an English birthright based on political freedoms. Thus John Milton would write pamphlets supporting the Puritan Revolution by extolling the liberties of the English people. This new idea was partly religious, following the paradigm of the Chosen People of Israel, but it also invoked mythic conceptions of political rights such as those thought to be implied by documents like the Magna Carta. The English people was constituted not by blood but by political and religious history.

The English revolution was not fully nationalistic in the modern sense because the necessary idea of a common culture did not yet exist. Nationalism today is not just political, based on civil liberties and rights; it is about one's cultural identity. For the nationalist, the self-identity of the people as a single whole should be embodied in the state. Whereas for earlier theorists politics was the sum of civility, for modern nationalists culture is the driving force of politics. The era of nationalism was born together with the idea of cultures and peoples.

These particularistic notions took hold slowly against the prevailing ideal of universal governance left over from older times. The ancient city-states had not evolved into the modern nation-state, but they had given way to the ideal of world rule based on the model of the Roman Empire. The idea of civilization was similarly universalistic, although universalisms sometimes competed: in the West, civilization meant Christianity; in the Middle East, it meant Islam. The alternative conception of civilization and culture as particular to each people was not available in Locke's time. The source of social cohesion and order remained political, and the new concept of the people would emerge fully only in the eighteenth century.

Reaction to French Universalism

In the history of ideas, the dominant movement of the seventeenth and eighteenth centuries was the rationalism of the French Enlightenment. The Age of Reason saw universal truths in secular terms, but the belief in a single system of truth remained. The era was marked by the belief that all genuine problems were solvable by the proper application of reason, that the solutions were universal and could not conflict with each other. Like the truths of mathematics, the answers to social problems must fit together into a single pattern, discoverable by rational thought. The goal of enlightened thinkers was to find this universal answer, or system of answers, to the problem of how to live well. By discovering the way things really worked, social problems could all be solved. One must follow the lead of the mathematicians and scientists who had taken the first crucial steps. Their early successes seemed to justify the Enlightenment's optimistic belief that solutions to all problems – philosophical, moral, social, and political – were soon to be had.

The dominance of rationalism in thought was matched by the social and political supremacy of France during this period. But while the arts and letters flowered in France and other European nations, the disunited German-speaking regions seemed to lag behind. While some Germans of this era began to emulate the French, others reacted against them, coming to define themselves as other-than-French. The sense of 'otherness' was a great stimulus to the concept of cultural identity. The earlier proto-nationalism in England, for example, had its roots in the collective rejection of Rome, and the Puritan Revolution was sparked by the perceived return of Roman Catholic rule. But the anti-French, anti-rationalism of the eighteenth century had a special importance. In the new secular age, the resistance was not sought in an alternative religious universalism. The Enlightenment could not be escaped by changing churches; instead, the reaction against French ideas meant the rejection of universalism itself.

As described by Isaiah Berlin, some German thinkers began to search for a new source that made Germans unique: 'The inner life, the life of the spirit, concerned with the relation of man to man, to himself, to God – that alone was of supreme importance; the empty materialistic French wiseacres had no sense of true values – of what alone men lived by ... Gradually this German self-image grew in intensity, fed by what might be called a kind of nationalist resentment.'[17] According to Berlin, Johann Gottfried von Herder was the first promoter of the idea of culture as a form of shared consciousness. Elsewhere, Berlin traced related ideas to Vico and Machiavelli,[18] but in Herder's search for the organic sources of German cultural uniqueness, the modern concept of culture – and thus the idea of a society in the holistic sense of 'a people' – first emerged. Cultural differences were not just superficial variations of behaviour overlaid upon universal principles of social organization. For Herder, culture was the defining spirit of each person and each people. Our culture makes us what we are. According to Berlin: 'This was a novel doctrine ... What, for him, makes Germans German is the fact that the way in which they eat or drink, dispense justice, write poetry, worship, dispose of property, get up and sit down, obtain their food, wear their clothes, sing, fight wars, order political life, all have a certain common character, a qualitative property, a pattern which is solely German, in which they differ from the corresponding activities of the Chinese or the Portuguese.'[19]

Thus the Germans make up a culture, or society, in the modern sense, and the Chinese make up another, and the Portuguese yet another. And it is in recognizing these particularities that the modern idea of a society as a cohesive cultural whole was born. This was the source of the modern idea of culture as defined by Edward Tylor in 1871: 'that complex whole which includes knowledge, belief, art, morals, law, customs, and any other capabilities and habits acquired by man as a member of society.'[20] With this idea in place, cultural unity rather than political association could come to be identified as the foundation of society. Each people was a single thing, whose unifying principles were cultural rather than political. Customs and folkways replaced the positive laws of the state as the organizing force and defining characteristic of society.

The new sources of civility were pluralistic rather than universal. Political theorists from Plato and Aristotle through to Hobbes and Locke had seen the principles of the well-ordered polity as everywhere the same. Even Aristotle's empirical approach culminated in universal principles of best governance because the *telos* of human fulfillment did not vary across borders. By contrast, the new social thinkers saw each people as unique. Pluralism did not necessarily lead to relativism – abstract justice could remain universal – but the question of the good life became more complex. Political laws aimed at justice now could be seen as existing alongside another set of organizing principles, and these were unique to each people. The political order could support but no longer constituted the civil order. The new, pluralistic idea of culture offered an alternative explanation for the source of civility. Civil society had become social rather than political, and civilization in the new sense could mean different things among different peoples.

Meanwhile, a second Enlightenment, without the characteristic rationalism of the French movement, was occurring in Scotland. The philosophers of the Scottish Enlightenment had very different approaches to the kinds of problems addressed by the thinkers of the Cartesian rationalist school. With Adam Smith, for example, the great society was not one that was rationally constructed but one that arose naturally through the coordinating principles of what Burke would call 'enlightened self-interest' and what Smith famously called the 'invisible hand.'[21] A well-ordered society had its own rules of organization apart from those imposed by the state. These rules, or organizing principles, meant that society could be seen as a single orderly entity, which the state should serve. Thus Smith described the role of the state in terms of its duties to society.[22] For Smith, as for Burke, the state should be neither the embodiment nor the master of society but its servant.

With Smith's friend and colleague Adam Ferguson, the phrase 'civil society' was presented for the first time in the title of a major work.[23] Ferguson made explicit his debt to Montesquieu,[24] and there are similarities between them. Both men studied Ancient Rome as an exercise in comparative history, both recognized the cultural differences of various nations, and both may be seen as predecessors of the modern cultural sciences. But where Montesquieu was essentially still a rationalist, Ferguson and his Scottish colleagues expressly were not. Where rationalists proceeded by searching for first principles from which a blueprint for society could be drawn, Ferguson denied that society's constitutive rules could be understood in this way: 'The peasant, or the child, can reason, and judge, and speak his language, with a discernment, a consistency, and a regard to analogy, which perplex the logician, the moralist, and the grammarian, when they would find the principle upon which the proceeding is founded, or when they would bring to general rules, what is so familiar, and so well sustained in particular cases. The felicity of our conduct is more owing to the talent we possess for detail, and to the suggestion of particular occasions, than it is to any direction we can find in theory and general speculations.'[25]

Ferguson rejected the rationalists' goal of guiding social behaviours by the dictates of abstract theory. Thus he complained about his era: 'It is peculiar to modern Europe, to rest so much of the human character on what may be learned ... from the information of books ... We endeavour to derive from imagination and thought, what is in reality a matter of experience and sentiment: and we endeavour ... to arrive at the beauties of thought and elocution, which sprang from the animated spirit of society.'[26] This 'animated spirit of society' was an idea closer to Herder than to Montesquieu. Where the latter still wanted to derive from social diversity a single set of principles, Ferguson, like Herder, was more consistently a pluralist. 'Nations ... like private men, have their favourite ends, and their principal pursuits, which diversify their manners, as well as their establishments.'[27] Ferguson celebrated the diversity of cultures and saw that competition among them was inevitable. In fact, he thought conflict was beneficial to the development of their distinctive virtues. 'Athens was necessary to Sparta, in the exercise of her virtue, as steel is to flint in the production of fire.'[28]

Civil society, for Ferguson, did not arise from conscious or purposive decision but, rather, emerged slowly from historical circumstances. Indeed, Ferguson did not define the term and actually used it infrequently (in the 430 pages of the original text, it appeared perhaps twenty times). Instead, Ferguson described the gradual historical development of Western nations. Where he did come close to a definition, it revolved around the character and virtues of a free people. 'During the existence of any free constitution, and whilst every individual possessed his rank and his privilege, or had his apprehension of personal rights, the members of every community were to one another objects of consideration and of respect; every point to be carried in civil society, required the exercise of talents, of wisdom, persuasion, and vigour, as well as of power.'[29] The essential accomplishment of Ferguson's book was to describe civil society in terms of *the people;* that is, as arising through the gradual evolution of a way of life, which we have come to call a culture.

The Scottish thinkers influenced Edmund Burke, whose rejection of French rationalism was concurrent with Herder's. Beginning with his earliest published writings, Burke was critical of the reliance on abstract reasoning to provide guiding principles for politics.[30] Against the French Revolution his critique reached its height. Unlike Irish and American secessionists, whom he saw as defenders of their traditional rights, Burke viewed the French revolutionaries – the 'sophistick tyrants of Paris'[31] – as ideological zealots bent on destroying the existing social order so they could rebuild society according to a rationalistic blueprint that was based on nothing but 'the nakedness and solitude of metaphysical abstraction.'[32] Burke argued that politics should be guided by acknowledged traditions rather than by pure speculation, and in doing this he did for England what Herder had done for Germany: he idealized the existing practices, mores, and values of the English, arguing in effect that these constituted their cultural identity. Thus Burke wrote of 'our national character'[33] and the 'fabric of ... society.'[34] For him, it was 'British Tradition *versus* French Enlightenment.'[35] That tradition, he argued, constituted a set of normative rules that political leaders should follow rather than create anew. Thus, for Burke, the state should be the servant of civil society – now understood as a set of evolved cultural practices and beliefs – rather than its master or its embodiment.

Two Conceptions of the People

Although both were anti-rationalistic, emphasizing the particularities of each people, the German and Anglo-Scottish visions of society and culture differed in their emphasis. From the beginning, the German idea was centred on spontaneity and growth. Herder saw poetry, folk songs, and myths as the central carriers of the developing German essence. The more free a people, the more spontaneous these expressions of its cultural essence. This spontaneous freedom sometimes might approach a kind of lawlessness, even savagery. In German, *Kultur* means both culture and civilization. But civilization in the expressive, romantic tradition was less about civility than about free creativity. This is the ideal that Kant would try to tame, Hegel would attempt to universalize, and Marx would make materially productive. The creative will of the people as a single whole – governed by rationality for Kant, emergent in history for Hegel, coming to consciousness as a productive class for Marx – was the essence of culture in the tradition centred in Germany. These German writers sought, in their different ways, to universalize the pluralistic force that romantics like Herder had unleashed.

In doing this, they led the way to the re-identification of civil and political society. Kant identified civil society with the juridical state; Hegel saw the distinction between state and civil society as merely transitory; Marx was forthrightly hostile, seeing civil society as the realm of egoism and money-grubbing.[36] They resisted the pluralization of ideas about the best way to live, in favour of their own universalistic principles. Nevertheless, the conception of the people as a discrete entity, so that each society was unique, had become established. Each society had come to be seen as an organized whole. Democracy meant that the state should serve society, whether as a Rousseauvian embodiment of the social will or, in a more instrumental sense, as a means to attain the greater social good. In either case, civil society and political state were no longer presumed to be synonymous. Kant, Hegel, and Marx had to work to reunite the political and the civil because they had become distinct.

A similar understanding of the people as a single entity had emerged on the British Isles. But for these writers, the pre-political basis of society was less about its creative essence and more about a common morality and evolved traditions. Here the emphasis was not on the free development of the people but, rather, on the emergence over time of structured rules and orderly virtues. In this account, there was little of Herder's veneration of folk songs and myth making as the essence of culture. The arts did not constitute culture; it was the other way round. In its Anglo-Scottish meaning, to be civil was to be well mannered and decorous. Ferguson's ideal included appreciation for the arts and sciences, but the focus was more on acquisition of the proper rules of social behaviour. It was only in the orderly, civilized society that the arts and sciences could prosper – not because they were the essence of civility but because the ordered society provided freedom from destructive barbarity. The veneer of civilization in this view was thin and could be destroyed by an excess of the spontaneous freedom celebrated by the Continental romantics. In this tradition, democracy was the best form of government for a civilized people, as long as its excesses did not become a threat to the evolved virtues that made it possible.

If democracy is a contested notion, then this is, in part, because the idea of the people means different things in different traditions. Democrats on either side agree that the people should rule – the people should be free, and the state should serve the people – but they differ in their respective conceptions of the organizational basis of a free people. Is the people a spontaneously flourishing entity centred on culture as expressive freedom or does a society consist of an evolved set of mores, customs, and rules? Is progressiveness or social order the defining essence of civil society? This remains a divisive question, despite the agreement that democracy is a good thing.

Meanwhile, a third school of thought has arisen with modernity. In this school, the good of the individual is rarely subordinated to the good of society, however defined. Here society does not exist as a good in itself – a good that may sometimes come before the good of the individual. In the modern age, the idea that the good of society should generally trump individual rights is deemed offensive. It seems illiberal, potentially coercive, perhaps even fascist to think about social wholes as good in themselves. The issue of how the state should serve society has been submerged under the weight of the question of the relationship between the state and the individual. Individual rights, either as protection against the state or as demands upon the state, seem to have taken over our political language. One of the difficulties in describing the contentious meaning of democracy as collective freedom is that its competing meanings have been devalued by the individualizing movement of modernity.

Yet they have not disappeared. Democracy remains an approbative political concept. Almost everyone believes that it is better to live in a democracy than in a non-democracy. The idea also seems to retain a sense of holistic, communal goodness. Democracy is not just a means to individual ends; it is how society rules itself. But the question remains: What is a society and a culture? One of the reasons we have difficulty in describing the communal good is that we have not recognized the variety of our conceptions of the people. Talk of individualistic rights dominates the field of political discourse, while the opposing camp, which sees the good as located in society as a whole, is divided.

A democratic people is a free people. Underlying the tension between conceptions of the people is a related conflict between versions of liberty. These underlying values, we will see, arose within the two traditions surveyed here. To understand it, we must trace the history of two great ideas of liberty.

3
From Ancient Virtues to Modern Values: Positive Liberty and the Creative Will

Today, when we describe the reasons for our actions, we are more likely to talk about values than virtues. The older language of virtues sounds restrictive, allowing little room for free individuals to live according to their own beliefs. Value-language is about the autonomy and dignity of the individual, while virtue-language is about established social roles and traditional ways of life.[1] Where the idea of virtue remains current today, it takes the political form of civic virtue as inspired by Rousseau, whose ideas, as we shall see, were prototypically modern.[2]

The transformation in moral language is important to the idea of democracy because it occurred together with the emergence of one of the major modern conceptions of liberty. People are free, in one of the meanings of the word, if they are able to create, or at least to choose, their own values. Nothing like this kind of freedom was conceivable using the language of virtue. While the new conception sometimes takes trivial, relativistic forms, as in the claim that it is wrong to 'make value judgments' about others, its roots go very deep. At its best, it is the ideal that each person has inherent worth.

The fundamental question of morality is simply, 'What is good?' One way to answer this question is by asking, 'Where does the good come from? What is the source of goodness?' The belief in the inherent worth of each person is based on the idea, to use the modern moral language, that each person is a source of value. We believe that something good can come from each person, that everyone has the power to generate goodness, to create value. The power to create value is centred in the human will, therefore value comes from the will of each person. As Immanuel Kant put it, nothing is unconditionally good but a good will. While he saw the good will as something other than earthly, Kant's argument was about each person as the source of goodness. One of the modern answers, then, to the fundamental moral question, 'What is good? Where does it come from?' is that goodness is willed by each person.

To define one's own values is the ultimate act of self-creativity. The freedom to produce one's own values and, thereby, to create oneself is the essence of positive liberty. In politics, positive liberty – the freedom of self-determination, connoting self-rule and self-creativity together – is among the most important of the competing themes of modern democracy. If positive liberty means that each person is a source of value, then what was the source of the modern value we call positive liberty? It emerged from an endless controversy about the meaning of the good.

The Good in Antiquity

In the Homeric epics of the eighth century BC, virtue was understood only in the context of specific social roles. In Homer's time, the concept of a good human being did not exist. Goodness was an attribute not of persons, as such, but of particular social functions. To be good was to be a good soldier, a good leader, a good husband, or a good wife. Virtue was defined as excellence in the fulfillment of one's function. Whether one was honourable or shameful depended on how one performed in one's role, and the most important role was that of the military leader. According to Arthur Adkins, 'The most powerful words to commend an individual in Homeric Greek are the adjectives *agathos* and *esthlos*, with the abstract noun *arete* ... *Agathos* and *esthlos* in Homer denote and commend men who are effective and successful fighters, whether formally at war or defending the *oikos* in what passes for peace in such a society.'[3] Typically translated, *agathos* means good and *arete* means virtue, although these translations lose the teleological connotation of the originals. Each *oikos* was an extended household, whose survival depended on the *arete* of its leader.

In the competitive, military world of Homer, the social roles from which ideas of the good were derived were ordered and hierarchical. The narrative unity of the epic poets' imaginations led them to see social life as a single whole, but the reality of Homer's era was variety and rivalry among *oikoi*. The idea of a single Greek civilization would not arise until the Persian Wars in the early fifth century BC. It would take this threat from outside to encourage a semblance of unity among Greeks in the emergent idea of Panhellenism. From these wars, *arete* would become associated with the military success of Greece as a whole.

Apart from the Persian Wars, additional forces would transform Greek life between the Homeric and classical eras. Through trade and colonization, the world would begin to open. Greek settlements were established throughout the Mediterranean, from which Greek commerce extended yet further. According to Harold Baldry, 'The natural result is a greatly increased awareness of the diversity of human life ... Those affected ... no longer saw mankind on a single pattern.'[4] If military threats united Greeks, the total effect of the changes in Greek life was to encourage the recognition of human variety.

Group differences were manifested in two ways; first, between Greeks and *barbaroi*, and second, among Greek cities. Both kinds of conflict would contribute to the universalistic reaction that emerged from the classical period. With the opening of the Mediterranean world, the distinction between Greeks and barbarians would encourage the Panhellenism found in writers like Hesiod and Herodotus.[5] Beginning as a doctrine of difference, it led to a search for the superior characteristics that the Greeks best exemplified. But merely by focusing on these attributes in the abstract, the idea could emerge of purely human qualities, which were shared by all but with which the Greeks were best endowed. Most important among these qualities was *logos*, or reason, and this was an attribute derived from language and education rather than from blood. When Greek civilization was subsequently absorbed into the Graeco-Roman world, the old distinction between Greek and barbarian would fall away, as the Romans understandably rejected it. What remained was the idea of a single set of human qualities with reason held as supreme.

But before the Roman conquest, the unifying idea of Panhellenism, conceivable when Greeks thought of themselves in comparison with non-Greeks, was not achieved politically. The Greek city-states remained disunited and competitive. While a few institutions, like the Olympic Games, were held in common, they were exceptions to the rule of variety and rivalry among cities. In the classical period a new school of thinkers, the Sophists, would come to emphasize the differences within Greek civilization. Freed from geographical and social constraints by their profession as itinerant teachers, the Sophists would promote independence of thought. Among their teachings was the idea that as local customs varied so did virtues. Against the universal criteria of goodness holding for all, Protagoras proclaimed that humanity itself is the measure of all things. As people vary, so does the good.

Plato and Aristotle sought to counter this relativistic view with their respective universalistic accounts of goodness. They lived in an era of decline. The Athenian dominance of Greece during the time of Pericles had ended, and Athens lost the Peloponnesian War while Plato was a young man and Aristotle was not yet born. In their different ways, Plato and Aristotle were champions of the life of contemplation, but their society was under threat. Among the apparent symptoms of social degeneration was the disturbing new idea of diversity in visions of the good. Against this diversity they would erect their universalist philosophies.

Like the defenders of Hellenic superiority, Plato's teacher Socrates had emphasized *logos* as the supreme characteristic of the human *psyche*. *Logos*, or reason, was an attribute related to the faculty of speech, which distinguished humans from animals. This had been a common Greek idea, appearing as early as Homer.[6] With Socrates, the hierarchy of virtues would be reset with *logos* at its apex. Later, the idea of the *psyche* would begin to be transformed to emphasize the human will – incipiently in the thought of Augustine, climactically in the eighteenth century with the birth of the modern idea of value. There the will would become that part of us that 'values,' that enables us to create our ends for ourselves. But for Socrates, the *psyche* was the part of us that reasons rather than wills.

Plato would teach that the soul consists of three parts, with reason properly ruling over the spirit and the desires. Reason was the ability to grasp the eternal Forms and, thus, must itself be eternal, living on after the body dies. In this way, he incorporated the doctrine of the immortality of the soul, which had been shared by Socrates and which had belonged to the older Orphic tradition. The highest Form was that of the Good, so reason was the ability to perceive goodness, which was defined as eternal, abstract, and universal. From this model would emerge Plato's ideal republic. They should rule who have the greatest reason, who are best able to perceive goodness in its pure form.

The idea of the supremacy of reason, then, had begun with a search for what makes Greeks unique and superior to foreigners: Greeks had language, *logos*, and reason, while barbarians merely produced sounds – *bar, bar, bar.* With Socrates, the Pythagorean and Orphic belief in the immortal soul was conjoined with reason, which Plato further connected to an eternal, abstract conception of the good. This ideal of goodness was not associated with any particular way of life but was universal. Plato thus solved two problems. First, he defended the superiority of reasoned contemplation while justifying the social order in which such a life was supreme; second, he countered the relativism that had arisen with the Sophists. The good for Plato became universal, abstract, and singular.

However, Plato's account of the singular good was not without rivals, which also drew on and further developed traditional Greek beliefs. Best known is that offered by Aristotle, who universalized the Homeric teleological conception of worthiness. The idea that something was good to the extent that it fulfilled its proper function was taken up by Aristotle, who had, like Plato, accepted the immortality of the soul. For Aristotle, the tripartite soul represented three kinds of telos, or three levels of animation, with reason being superior to spirit and desires. These three levels of telos acted together to form the natural end towards which human life was compelled to move. Thus the soul was a first cause for human life not as an initiating action but as a kind of attractor towards which each life should develop. Thus Aristotle disjoined the human telos from Homeric social roles so that humanness itself became a role or function. The good life could then be judged as that which conformed to the proper human telos, the proper balance among reason, spirit, and desire.

Reason for Aristotle should rule by guiding one to the good life, but his justification was very different from Plato's. Where his teacher saw the Form of the Good as existing independently, prior to all apparent phenomena, Aristotle believed that the good consisted in the fulfillment of the true human telos. But whatever their differences, the arguments of Plato and Aristotle continued to employ the Homeric language of the virtues – even as they imposed their own priorities so that the philosopher now ruled over the soldier. As MacIntyre summarized, 'Aristotle's belief in the unity of the virtues is one of the few parts of his moral philosophy which he inherits directly from Plato. As with Plato, the belief is one aspect of a hostility to and denial of conflict either within the life of the individual good man or in that of the good city. Both Plato and Aristotle treat conflict as an evil ... For Aristotle, as for Plato, the good life for man is itself single and unitary, compounded of a hierarchy of goods.'[7] This unity, however, must be judged, within the context of the beliefs of their day, as an invention rather than as a discovery. The world within which Plato and Aristotle lived was one of diversity and dissensus concerning the good.

Two lessons may be drawn from the story of the good in antiquity. First, while the ancient Greeks had commonalities of belief, such as ideas of the immortal soul and of the supremacy of reason, as well as a common language of virtue, these could be combined in different ways to produce conflicting accounts of the good. Second, the desire for a universal account of the good did not produce a single answer. Instead of universalism, the Greeks of the classical period produced competing universalisms.

Unity under Rome

Universalism would come to reign but not because a philosopher had found the single truth. It would be imposed rather than discovered, not through philosophy but through military prowess. The Macedonian, Alexander, had been Aristotle's student, but it was by his might rather than his learning that he would succeed in promoting unity. His military conquests would succeed in giving rise to a new universalism. Under Alexander, the world familiar to the Greeks had expanded again. At home, inter-city competition was renewed after his death and continued until the Roman intervention two centuries later, but Alexander's expedition had taken Greek civilization forward into the world.

The Hellenistic era following Alexander was a period of transition from Greek to Roman dominance, and it was marked by the search for a new understanding of the good. A new universalistic philosophy arose with Stoicism, which emphasized the uniformity of nature and morality. Their *polis* was the world, a cosmopolis, in which every person was a citizen. The Stoics comprised an international school whose leading members were not Greek, and who could disjoin Greek ideas from their supremacist roots. With the Stoics, *logos* would become natural law or universal order. The reasoned life became personalized, and the virtues became the personal or internal attributes of intelligence, bravery, justice, and self-control. Each was defined as the search for a kind of knowledge. The source of all knowledge, in turn, was God, who gave order and motion to the passive matter of the universe. Thus reason was the search for natural order, and goodness was conformity to the natural order found through wisdom.

The Stoic school bridged the classical Greek and Graeco-Roman periods. The late Stoics were Roman and included the ex-slave Epictetus and the emperor Marcus Aurelius. The distance in social circumstances of these two men shows the nascent egalitarianism and pan-humanism of Stoic teaching. While Aurelius viewed Christianity as a hostile competitor to established ideas of natural order, late Stoicism, with its emphasis on a benevolent God, would ease the way for the new religion.

Stoic beliefs were combined with Plato's idea of the good by the Neoplatonists, following Plotinus and his disciple Porphyry in the third century AD. Through them, God became identified with the Form of the Good, the ultimate reality from which everything else acquired secondary, or derivative, existence. Worldly substance was an emanation from the One. Just as light, by its nature, fills a void, so the real and the good both flowed from God. Evil was understood in the negative, as the absence of good, so God was the source of good but not evil. The Neoplatonist idea of God as the origin of all things would eventually become official Christian doctrine, although the emanationist ontology would be revised. Rather than seeing earthly existence as an overflowing from the nature of the One, the Church, after Augustine, would teach that reality and goodness were created *ex nihilo* by the will of God. Morality would become a matter of divine command, and goodness would become a creation of will.

But before Christianity could come to dominate moral thought in the West, it first had to struggle to survive. Roman emperors, from Nero in the first century AD to Diocletian in the early fourth, had ordered the execution of Christian leaders, who were seen as a threat to the Roman way of life. For the later emperors especially, the goal was to strengthen the Roman worldview by suppressing a competing set of beliefs. The perceived danger to their way of life, as it had been in classical Greece, was the twin threat of invasions from outside and of growing diversity from within. But the policy of hostility towards Christianity would end when Constantine the Great became a convert to the new religion in 312. With this action, Christian doctrines would be united with political power, and its teachings would flourish. With the Council of Arles in 316, Rome was recognized as the

centre of Christianity, and the teachings of the Roman Church would become the dominant universalistic doctrine in Europe for a millennium.

As its name proclaims, the Catholic Church is intrinsically universalistic.
In the words of St. Cyril of Jerusalem, who was born around the time of
Constantine's conversion, 'It (the one, holy, Catholic church) is called Catholic because it extends over all the world, from one end of the earth to the
other, and because it teaches universally and completely all the doctrines
which ought to come to men's knowledge.'[8] The Church was infallible, and
the pope was God's living representative on earth: his authority was divine
and beyond question.

However, Catholic authority, even conjoined to political power, was not
enough to put an end to differences over doctrine. An early example was
the Arian controversy over the unity of God and the direct divinity of Jesus.
Arius believed that Jesus belonged among the creatures of God, created by
the divine will, and thus was not part of God. This conflict, which led to the
banishment of Arius and his followers by Constantine, would presage later
disagreements about the limits of God's creative will. In this and in later
controversies, neither the Church's political power nor its dominance of
the schools of philosophy could contain the evolution of moral ideas, as
competing visions of the good continued to come into conflict.

With the decline of the Roman Empire, the forces of fragmentation would
again be felt, and again a great thinker would come to reassert the universal. The invasion of Rome by the Goths in 410 AD was interpreted by pagan
thinkers as a sign of the disapproval of the ancient gods. Augustine answered with his distinction between the worldly city and the City of God.
Human conflicts belonged to the former, while the divine remained eternal
and universal. For Augustine, as for the Neoplatonists, the permanence and
ontological priority of the divine world was established by conjoining Platonic and Christian ideas so that God was identified with the Form of the
Good and thus was the source of all things. Augustine followed the
Neoplatonist theodicy, defining evil in the negative, as the absence of the
real and the good. Certain angels and early humans had misused their freedom of will, straying from God's truth. But he did not believe that reality
and goodness emanated from God like a light; rather, he believed that creation was a deliberate act. With the replacement of emanation with intention, the idea began to emerge that goodness was a wilful creation.

This marked a critical turning point in the idea of the good. Expressed in
modern language, the new idea was that things have worth to the extent
that God endows them with value. Value, unlike virtue, is a wilfully created
thing. The essential difference can be seen in the fact that value is a verb as
well as a noun. The good was what God actively values through the power
of His will. The idea of an active, wilful God had pre-Christian roots in

Genesis, which describes creation *ex nihilo* as God's deliberate act. In the new Christian religion, this Judaic belief in a creative personal deity was combined with the Neoplatonist search for the source of all truth and goodness. Later, the old Orphic concept of the immortal soul would be interpreted in ways inspired by the Stoic turn inward, with the result that the search for its essential attributes led to the distinction between will and reason. Finally, in the modern era the idea of the will would be secularized, the human will would become the source of value, and the long transition from virtue to value would be complete.

But in medieval times the language of morality remained that of virtue, and the Christian virtues eventually became dominant. Christians inherited the Neoplatonic idea of virtue as the elimination of the earthly desires and dependencies that stood between humans and God. God was the ultimate reality. All temporal things were contingent on God's continuous creative power. God was not just the originating cause but the ongoing source of earthly existence. The influence of the older emanationist view remained, but now it was God's continuous will, rather than His simple presence, that was the source of the real and the good. Hence, God was ruler as well as creator. This persistent contingency of worldly creation is central to the idea of divine omnipotence. Nothing beyond the logical law of non-contradiction limited God's power, not even his previous creative acts. This was the morality of divine command, which flourished a thousand years after Augustine.[9]

Augustine was a critical figure in a second way, in his teachings about the human soul. In both the classical Greek and Stoic accounts, virtue produced happiness or fulfillment because those who act in accordance with virtue found themselves in harmony with truth and goodness. But in the Christian doctrines, rewards and punishment depended not on the effects of one's actions but on whether one's soul became closer to God. This question of virtuous behaviour turned on internal motivations rather than on external results. In this way, the soul came to be seen as the part of our internal being that decides how to act and was no longer seen primarily as the part of us that reasons, as Socrates and his followers had held. With Augustine, the soul became the seat of volition as well as reason. This is not yet the modern view, because for Augustine the focus was on whether one chooses to go with God or towards evil. The good will was judicious rather than creative. The idea that one should go in one's own unique way was far from his conception. Yet his elaboration of the idea of the free soul was a critical step in the modern direction.

Under the political and spiritual influence of the Roman Church, Christian doctrines after Augustine would change little through the middle ages. The permanent power of God, whose earthly representative was the pope, was a great unifying idea. But in the thirteenth century, the platonically inspired universalism of the Church would come up again against the contending universalism of Aristotle. His works had not been entirely forgotten but had been folded into Neoplatonic interpretations. As his writings were reintroduced in less adulterated ways, Aristotle's alternative, more empirical, explanation for the existence of the universe came again into circulation.

Renaissance and Reformation

At the beginning of the eleventh century, very little of Aristotle's writing was available in the Christian West. But his ideas influenced Muslim and Jewish thinkers like Averröes and Maimonides in the twelfth century, and their commentaries were translated into Latin. Meanwhile, James of Venice and others travelled to Constantinople, where they translated Aristotle's works. For the West, the exchange of ideas between religions and across borders led to the rediscovery of an alternative universalistic philosophy.

This presented a problem to the Church because some of Aristotle's ideas contradicted its official teaching. Among the most important of these was Aristotle's cosmology, according to which the existence of the world did not depend on the will of God but was itself eternal. God was the prime mover in the causal order, but not its creator. The new naturalism seemed to threaten the authority of the Church. If God's creative power were denied, then the role of the Church as earthly mediator would be weakened. It reacted with authority. Certain works by Aristotle and Averröes were banned, but this seemed to stimulate interest in their ideas. At the University of Paris, at the very centre of Scholastic thought, a group of heterodox scholars turned towards rationalism and naturalism. The Bishop of Paris responded in 1277 by condemning 219 propositions. A similar condemnation was proclaimed at Oxford, the second great Scholastic centre.

Christian philosophy was thus forced, at just the time when the exchange of ideas had led to new questions about the nature of truth and goodness, back upon strictly theocentric foundations. The good was whatever God decreed, and reality was whatever God created: both depended on the omnipresence of the Creator for their ongoing existence. Thus Augustine's doctrine of a wilful god as the source of goodness was restated and reinforced by Duns Scotus and William of Ockham. According to divine-command morality, whatever was good was good purely because God continuously willed it. This conception of the good was taken up by thinkers from Jean Gerson to John Calvin in France and from Gabriel Biel to Martin Luther in Germany. Typical was Luther's assertion: 'What God wills is not right because He ought, or was bound, so to will; on the contrary, what takes place must be right, because He so wills it. Causes and grounds are laid down for the will of the creature, but not for the will of the Creator – unless you set another Creator over him!'[10]

The idea that God was continuously present in the world would give impetus to renewed spiritualism. The experience of God could be felt directly within each human soul, without the intermediation of the Church. Rather than making the Church more powerful, the will of God was now given such a comprehensive role that no earthly intermediary was needed. Thus the Church, in banning Aristotelian-inspired ideas about natural cosmology, inadvertently gave rise to Luther's rejection of its own authority.

The immediacy of God's presence promoted a new sense of individualism. As described by Alasdair MacIntyre, 'The crucial feature of the new experience is that it is the experience of an individual who is alone before God. When Luther wants to explain what an individual is he does so by pointing out that when you die, it is you who die, and no one else can do that for you. It is as such, stripped of all social attributes, abstracted, as a dying man is abstracted, from all his social relations, that the individual is continually before God.'[11] Yet we should be cautious about identifying Luther too closely with the rise of individualism because he came, in his dispute with the humanist Erasmus, to reject the idea of free will. Humans had limited freedom, Luther argued, because God ultimately controls the human will. The modern, secular idea of the free individual at the heart of liberalism had its more important source in the humanist movement from which Luther departed.

Humanism arose partly in reaction to the authority of the Church and partly in reaction to the Scholastic dominance of education in the late medieval period. The term is taken from the Latin *humanitas*, which in Cicero had meant education following the Greek idea of *paideia*, training in the virtues, which is what distinguished humans from animals. The original educational ideal was thus rooted in the Greek idea of *logos*, or reason. But the humanists would contribute to a modern conception of education as self-making – a product of will as much as of reason. The myth of the original humanists was that the classical period had been the birthplace of the true spirit of freedom, which had been lost in medieval teachings. Thus the humanist practice was to rely on original Greek and Latin texts rather than on Scholastic interpretations. However, the concept of freedom (and, hence, of value) that would emerge with the humanists was very different from any that had been conceived by Greek philosophers, even though it arose from ancient ideas.

The first great humanist of the Renaissance was the fourteenth-century Florentine exile Petrarch, who was an avid reader of Latin. Among Petrarch's favourites were the Stoics, via Cicero, and Augustine. The latter had taught that morality implied freedom of the will because in order to be considered morally responsible, one must be understood as free to do ill or to do good. But for Augustine, freedom consisted only of the choice between good and evil. This conception of freedom could be reconciled with the classical idea of the soul as the seat of reason: to choose to be good was to be rational. But, as the free will might also choose evil, rationality and freedom were distinct attributes of the soul. The question that arose among the Scholastics was, which was more important, reason or will? Petrarch believed it was will. This idea would lead in time to a very different conception of freedom than either Augustine or the Greeks had imagined – a will that could act creatively as well as morally and rationally.

Another Northern Italian, Pico della Mirandola, was educated into the humanist tradition in the fifteenth century. His best known work celebrated the dignity of humanity, a theme of humanists like Marsilio Ficino, the founder of the Florentine Academy. Ficino had made the human soul the centre of the universal order, but Pico added that humanity was free to choose its place in the hierarchy between heaven and earth. In Pico's 'Oration,' God tells Adam,

> We have given you, Oh Adam, no visage proper to yourself, nor any endowment properly your own, in order that whatever place, whatever form, whatever gifts you may, with premeditation, select, these same you may have and possess through your own judgment and decision. The nature of all other creatures is defined and restricted within laws which We have laid down; you, by contrast, impeded by no such restrictions, may, by your own free will, to whose custody We have assigned you, trace for yourself the lineaments of your own nature. I have placed you at the very center of the world, so that from that vantage point you may with greater ease glance round about you on all that the world contains. We have made you a creature neither of heaven nor of earth, neither mortal nor immortal, in order that you may, as the free and proud shaper of your own being, fashion yourself in the form you may prefer. It will be in your power to descend to the lower, brutish forms of life; you will be able, through your own decision, to rise again to the superior orders whose life is divine.[12]

Pico was nothing if not precocious, offering, at age twenty-four, to debate the Scholastic teachers publicly on 900 propositions and then to resolve all questions within his own philosophical system. However, we should resist reading these words as thoroughly modern. Pico was not suggesting that through creative wilfulness humanity could shape its own nature in an original or unique way; rather, he believed that humanity could choose to emulate either the heavenly spirits or the earthly beasts. This freedom was exercised in imitation rather than creativity. Pico's was an eloquent restatement of the Augustinian conception of the free will as given to humans to enable moral choice. Goodness was determined by God and was not yet centred in the free human will, as moderns like Kant would later claim. For Pico and the Renaissance humanists, it was still God, not humanity, who created value. The dignity of humanity was in having a choice between the high road and the low one, but it was not yet seen as able to create its own way for itself, as the creator of its own ends.

Thomas More translated the life of Pico into English. More too was influenced by Augustine, who had located the source of wickedness in the city of man as distinct from the City of God. While More would not teach rebellion against earthly authorities, he combined the evolving humanist ideas about freedom with Augustine's attention to the problems of human society. The result was that More would see social institutions, to which he contrasted his Utopia, as the source of human unhappiness. His contribution was in imagining how earthly problems could be attenuated by human actions, a theme that later would reappear with Rousseau.

The best-known humanist was More's Dutch friend, Erasmus. His version of the New Testament emphasized the work of Saint Paul and the Greek Fathers as early reformers of the Church, and he rejected Scholastic doctrines in favour of a simpler, earlier Christianity. But he was not a revolutionary and eventually sought to distance himself from Luther's growing stridency. Against the latter's rejection of the idea of the free human will, Erasmus answered with scepticism, suggesting that human reason and biblical teachings were inadequate to decide the issue. While his caution did not allow him to judge between the relative power of will versus reason, his scepticism suggested the deficiency of the latter.

Luther was more radical. He thought that neither the will nor reason was the most important quality of the soul; rather, God's creative power was present in every human soul because He had created in each soul the attribute of faith. By 'personalizing' religion in this way, Luther contributed to the idea of humanity as the locus of goodness even as he rejected the emerging humanist idea of freedom. In effect, Luther took up the idea of God's permanent creative presence on earth but gave it an individualistic twist. The dominant quality of the soul was faith, through which each person could know God directly. The true church, for Luther, was a priesthood of all believers in their unmediated relationship with their creator.

Luther's inward turn was continued by John Calvin, who thought the presence of God was evident to everyone through a kind of divine sense. One does not know God so much as experience Him, the way one experiences thunder without 'knowing' its essence. Every soul was imprinted with the image of God, despite the fallen nature of humanity. With Calvin, human freedom had a greater role than it did for Luther, but it was as a source of sin more than as a source of goodness. Those who perversely turned away from God were driven by pride or self-love, but their rejection of God's truth was nonetheless free and wilful. Faith came from one's openness to knowledge of God, while evil came from the soul's wilful freedom. Thus, although Calvin saw reason and will as attributes of the soul, he did so in a way that could not be reconciled with Luther's idea of faith. Furthermore, Calvin differed from Luther about the possibility of rehabilitating human society. While Luther tended to see existing institutions as irredeemable, Calvin attempted to institute social reform. Under his leadership, Geneva would become a moralistic republic. A century and a half after Calvin, a Genevan watchmaker named Rousseau would teach his son, Jean-Jacques, that their home was the equal of Sparta or Rome at their height.

In summary, the response of the medieval Church to Aristotle's rediscovered cosmology contributed to two larger reactions. One was the Reformation, as thinkers like Luther and Calvin rebelled against the Church's power, stressing instead the direct power of God over humankind. The second was the intellectual movement known as humanism, which arose against the dominant but ossified Scholastic teachings. Among the results of these clashing ideas was a continued transformation of the conception of the good. The theme emerged in the West that the source of good was the creative, wilful power of God. The good became that which God actively valued. Although the older language of virtue continued to be used, the way was coming clear for value, as a verb as well as a noun, to overtake the vocabulary of morality.

The greatest single contribution of Renaissance humanism concerned the conception of art. In the Latin, from which they took the term, *ars* meant skill or method, a more particular form of general knowledge, or *scientia*. For the humanists, art meant mastery of a higher skill, without denoting any particular area of specialization. A master like Leonardo was at once a great scientist, craftsman, and painter. The Renaissance gave to modernity the conception of art as mastery, which secondarily meant creativity but mainly concerned power. With the romantic movement, which arose in reaction to the Enlightenment, this power would become associated with the creative will. The final step would come with the secularization of divine-command morality, and the good would come to be seen as that which humans actively, wilfully valued.

From General Will to Will to Power

If the humanist movement influenced Luther and Calvin, it also affected Catholicism. In the early seventeenth century, a Catholic reformer named Cornelius Jansen avoided Scholastic dogmatism by returning to the earliest Church writings. His study of Augustine, who had argued, against Pelagius, that salvation came not from good deeds but entirely from God's grace, led Jansen to emphasize God's wilfulness as the sole source of redemption. Nothing a human being could do could save his or her soul; God's will was unaffected by human actions. But the doctrine of predestination seemed to conflict with Saint Paul's declaration that God 'will have all men to be saved' (1 Tim. 2:4). This controversy led to the view among Jansenists, like Arnauld and Pascal, that God had a *volonté générale* for the salvation of all human-kind before the Fall but a *volonté particulière* to save only certain souls there-after. This distinction was turned by the Cartesian rationalist, Malebranche, into the assertion that the particular will of God ruled in specific cases, but His general will was towards order and regularity in the universe. God's general will was the source of law, in both the moral and scientific senses, while his particular will was miraculous; that is, local and arbitrary. From this religious lineage, the general will became a well-known and widely debated concept in France long before Rousseau.[13]

The general will was the source of justice and lawfulness, while the par-ticular will was concerned only with the interests of one person or group. The condemnation of selfish *amour-propre* began as a criticism of the desire that God should be partial to oneself. With steps from Bayle to Montesquieu, the superiority of the general over the particular became secularized as a criterion of good governance. Finally, the connection to divine will was bro-ken completely by Diderot, whose 1755 *Encyclopédie* article on 'Natural Rights' depicted the general will as the universal morality of the human species. By reason alone, one may learn that one's individual interests are in harmony with the good of the species. For the atheist Diderot, the general will was the secular source of morality, as every enlightened individual must discover.

Rousseau's own contribution to the *Encyclopédie*, his *Discourse on Political Economy*, also referred to the general will. But Rousseau famously rejected the Enlightenment optimism about modern humanity. In an early version of the *Social Contract*, today commonly called the *Geneva Manuscript*, he included a chapter aimed directly at Diderot's argument. In the civilized – which for Rousseau meant fallen – state every person's interest was demon-strably at variance with the common good. Even in the happier natural state, each person's interest was his or her own. Furthermore, no one can know of the universal good other than as a generalization from the concep-tion of good within one's own society. We must become citizens of a repub-lic, wrote Rousseau, rather than members of universal society. The cosmopolitan ideal is hollow and misleading because it excuses us from our true local obligations.

The French Enlightenment was largely a movement of well-bred men of letters, and France was the leading European power of its age. For the Genevan Rousseau, Diderot's universalism was foreign. Rousseau turned the ideal of general will towards the republican ideal of citizenship and then merged it with the humanist emphasis on education and personal improvement. On one hand, the great republic creates its own citizens; on the other, the general will is the source of political legitimacy. Rousseau's importance was in putting these two together: if the general will rules, and if great rulers shape the people's will, then it follows that the general will is self-creating.

Rousseau was not an atheist, but his conception of goodness operated at the secular, political level. The general will, as the source of goodness on earth, was self-sufficient: it was its own source. Just as the God of divine-command morality was not dependent on an external source for His existence – God had no creator outside of Himself – so the general will was self-created. With this intellectual step, freedom came to be seen as self-creativity. For Rousseau, a people is free only when it wills its own goodness, when it is the self-sustaining source of its own morality. In this collectivist form, positive liberty as the freedom of self-creativity was born. The human will became the fountain and foundation of goodness.

Positive liberty is sometimes described as autonomy or self-rule, and sometimes as self-determination, but its deeper meaning is self-creativity. I am freest when I decide not just what to *do* but what to *be*. To create myself is not to invent myself as a thing but as a person; that is, as a motivated, active being. I must decide for myself not just how to achieve my given ends but what those ends will be. Thus it is not just my abilities or attributes but my own moral ends that I create as a free person. I define myself by creating my own values – by inventing, or discovering, or choosing, or at least endorsing, my own animating ideals. I am the self-sufficient source of my own goodness.

Such was the power of Rousseau's central idea, although he saw it as a collective political attribute. With him, the creative will as the source of goodness could for the first time be located firmly in the secular realm. Like the will of God, the general will was not to be held to a pre-existing standard of goodness. He wrote of the general will as the divine-command moralists had written about the will of God: 'Merely by virtue of its special nature, the sovereign is always everything that it should be ... It follows from what has gone before that the general will is always in the right.'[14] Divine-command morality could begin to be replaced by the command of the secular will.

The next individualizing step can be seen in Kant, even as he tried to show that each person's free will should remain on a common path. Kant took from Rousseau the idea that to be free is to rule oneself, but he did not accept the earthly existence of the general will. Generality was not an attribute of the common will but was the regulating ideal of each individual will. For Kant, as for Diderot, generality again became universality. The good will, like the will of God in divine command, was constrained only to rule without self-contradiction. Thus, his categorical imperative held that we act rationally when the law we wilfully give to ourselves can be made universal. But the will that Kant held central belonged not to the republic but to the individual person.

The free person was not just the follower of given ends. Each was the creator of his or her own ends because the ultimate end was the free will itself. Unlike things, the actions of free persons were self-caused. The will was the self-sufficient cause of human action, with no cause outside of itself. The same principle, the self-sufficiency of the will, held in morality: the will of each person was not a means to achieve given ends but was an end in itself. Each will had its source of goodness within itself. This was the meaning of Kant's best known words: 'Nothing in the world – indeed nothing, even beyond the world – can possibly be conceived which could be called good without qualification except a *good will* ... The good will is not good because of what it effects or accomplishes or because of its adequacy to achieve some proposed end; it is good only because of its will, i.e., it is good of itself ... Its full worth [is] in itself.'[15] Kantian autonomy is about self-rule, but his conception of the good was centred in the will itself. Rational rules can never express the substance of goodness but can only be judged by the formal criterion of universality. The true source of value in Kantian morality is the will. In our moral freedom, we belong to the causally self-sufficient realm of God.

The requirement of universalizability of self-given laws followed from the equality of wilful individuals, each of whom was an ultimate source of value. A rational moral law must apply to each free will equally because each is self-sufficiently both active and good. Thus the categorical imperative could be put in a second way: each person must be treated not merely as a means to an end but as an end in him- or herself.

The creative will had become the source of value. Kant's definition of freedom as autonomy, not as rule-following but as value-creating, has been described by Isaiah Berlin. 'If the source of moral or political rules is external to me, I am not free, not capable of rational choice ... This is what Kant means by saying that autonomy is the basis of all morality: to be at the mercy of some outside force, whether blind nature or some transcendent power, God or nature, that orders me as it wills, is heteronomy, a form of dependence on something that I do not control, slavery. I, and I alone, must be the author of my own values.'[16]

Kant thought he had solved the Rousseauvian problem of reconciling individual creative freedom with conformity to the whole while avoiding the problem of whether God's will precluded that of humanity's. In our freedom, we belong to God. But others would come to see this new, value-creating kind of freedom in a secular form. Berlin continues: 'But some of Kant's romantic successors drew out the full consequences of the view that values are commands, and that they are created, not discovered. The old analogy between moral (or political) and scientific or metaphysical or theological knowledge is broken. Morality – and politics so far as it is social morality – is a creative process: the new romantic model is that of art.'[17]

The romantic movement would flower in the eighteenth century in tandem with the French Enlightenment. Romanticism in Germany was given impetus by the dominance of French arts and letters at the time, with the result that German thinkers like Johann Gottfried von Herder, one of Kant's students, were driven to seek the source of uniqueness of the German *Volk*,[18] just as the ancient Greeks had searched for the source of their superiority over barbarians. The collective creative will of the German people could be seen in its songs, poetry, language, and folkways. The idea of 'cultural values' here could begin to emerge, the source of which was human rather than divine. God's laws were universal and formed a single whole, but the values of human cultures were particular and many. What we now call cultural pluralism, which in the last chapter was shown to be a prerequisite to the emergence of civil society as a modern idea, emerged from the process of the secularization of the source of goodness. The historical fact of pluralism in conceptions of the good acted as a kind of engine of conceptual history, as competing ideals continually came up against each other. This led eventually to the idea of cultural pluralism. The modern ideal of multiculturalism is an effect of this process rather than its cause.

While Kant had sought to end the argument over whether reason or will was the dominant attribute of the soul, others would reject his solution. A hundred years after Kant's *Metaphysics of Morals*, Friedrich Nietzsche would publish *Beyond Good and Evil*, in which he mocked the 'tartuffery of old Kant as he lures us along the dialectical bypaths which lead, more correctly, mislead, to his "categorical imperative."' Kant's arguments were no more than 'the subtle tricks of old moralists and moral-preachers.'[19]

Nietzsche believed that true creativity in values required that one overturn morality rather than find foundations for it, as Kant had sought to do. He thought that Kant's critical philosophy was a series of tricks in veiled support of false Christian virtues ('tartuffery' alludes to Molière's comedy about religious hypocrisy). Christian morality was precisely what Nietzsche wanted to overthrow – but not because he wanted to return to an older system of virtues or to find a new one, as is sometimes supposed. He was not interested in finding a better morality; rather, he saw wilfulness as the overthrowing of morality again and again in an ongoing process of creativity. Above all else he was the champion of the value-creating will for its own sake, which he would call the will to power. Like Rousseau and Kant, Nietzsche made the free will the source of all value, only he did so in a purer form, without what he thought were crypto-Christian worries about moral harmony. While his progenitors still wanted to replace divine morality with something humanistic, Nietzsche was happy to reject it altogether in favour of the free will itself.

While he thought the ancient virtues were more noble – that is, more powerful – than the 'slave morality' of Christianity, it was the will itself whose value-creating power he exalted. 'The noble type of man feels *himself* to be the determiner of values, he does not need to be approved of ... he knows himself to be that which in general first accords honour to things, he *creates value.*'[20]

The idea of the wilful creative hero of the romantic movement thus finds its most powerful statement in Nietzsche. More than others, Nietzsche saw that to create oneself one must destroy all conventions. Thus pure creativity also must be destructive. 'And whoever must be a creator in good and evil, verily, he must first be an annihilator and break values. Thus, the highest evil belongs to the highest goodness: but this is creative.'[21] The creative genius, whom Nietzsche called the *Übermensch*, must be the enemy of traditional morality. 'Behold the good and the just! Whom do they hate most? The man who breaks their tables of values, the breaker, the lawbreaker; yet he is the creator.'[22]

Similarly, Nietzsche rejected the fruits of reason as the best of human accomplishments. Mere scholars, content to discover facts, know nothing of true creativity. 'In comparison with a genius, that is to say with a being which either *begets* or *bears* ... the scholar, the average man of science, always has something of the old maid about him: for, like her, he has no acquaintanceship with the two most valuable functions of mankind.'[23] The genius knows how to create – or to procreate, following Nietzsche's jest – to inseminate and give birth to the good. The true philosopher, like Zarathustra, is a genius in the literal sense of the word – a creator who is the true source of value.

Where the divine-command moralists believed in the omnipresent will of God as the ongoing source of goodness and reality, Nietzsche believed in the idea of eternal recurrence. As pointed out by Hallowell and Porter, 'The doctrine of the eternal recurrence instantiates the continual act of willing against the world's valuelessness ... The doctrine reflects the modern position that mastery and freedom are linked. Such an idea is found in theology where the two are linked in God, who created reality *ex nihilo* ... The eternal recurrence doctrine supposedly shows that humans, too, can do the same by continually asserting their wills each returning moment over a meaningless reality, which by definition means that there are no limits (the equivalent of *ex nihilo*) on our assertion of meaning.'[24]

Thus, the transition from the language of virtue to that of value became complete. God's declaration of self-sufficiency, 'I AM THAT I AM' (Exodus 3:14), had been understood by divine-command moralists as, 'I will that I will,' after Augustine replaced emanationism with intentionality as the divine source of creation. With modernity, it became the foundational assertion of self-sufficient individuals. Only in the nineteenth century did the study of values, referred to as axiology, begin, with Nietzsche himself often counted among its originators.[25] Before that time, values in the modern sense did not exist, because the human will was not understood as the source of value.

The relationship between positive liberty and value creation is in the be-lief that one is most free when one creates one's own ends. This ideal may be called autonomy or self-determination, but a more precise term is autotely.[26] Each of us is the source of, or contains, our own telos. I am free when I make my own goals, when I create my own character by choosing the defining ends of my life. This concept of freedom as self-sufficiency is a core value (to name it in its own language) of modernity.

But in an important sense Nietzsche was wrong. The value we call posi-tive liberty did not emerge from the will of a creative genius. As did every great thinker in this story, Nietzsche worked with the conceptual materials of his tradition. He did not transvalue anything; he only expressed a flour-ishing value that had grown from old roots. The irony of positive liberty is that it is not its own source.

Positive Liberty in Modern Politics

The central political problem that arose with the new ideal of wilfulness is political, as Rousseau and Kant already knew: How should free individuals live together? Negative liberty is about the limits of power, but positive liberty is about empowerment itself. With the latter ideal, the problem of political coexistence becomes especially acute. Four kinds of answers are familiar in modern political thought.

First is Nietzsche's own answer, that creative freedom belongs only to the few. The masses were made to follow, with genius belonging to the *Übermensch* alone. Only these special men (as they were for Nietzsche) were able to face the terrible reality of their freedom. In our own day, something like this answer has been taken up by the followers of Leo Strauss, leading them to distinguish between esoteric and exoteric meanings – truths for the few who lead and truths for the many who follow.

Second is the romantic withdrawal from politics itself.[27] To turn away from political action is inevitable for those who want to assert the power of the creative will in its pure form but who are unwilling to follow Nietzsche to his anti-egalitarian conclusion. Modern romanticism fancies itself as postmodern, but it is of a traditional lineage. Today, the postmodern move-ment has turned towards ironical self-absorption by disengaging itself from effective political action, and it exists most securely in the creative haven of departments of English.[28] Postmodernists, despite their desire to transcend all categories and boundaries, have merely avoided the difficult choices of politics.

The third choice is to seek a way, as did Kant and Rousseau, to reconcile this concept of freedom with social equality. To follow this path is to try to synthesize each creative will into a harmonious whole. In this view, politics is about overcoming conflict. The questions that actually divide modern democracies, such as differences about the proper distribution of wealth, are seen by these theorists as illegitimate; only when social equality has been established can democracy truly begin. For those who see politics this way, the highest ideal will be some version of solidarity or fraternity, defined as creative power-in-unity and idealized as the progressive self-direction of society as a whole. As described in Chapter 7, this is the ideal of socialists, participatory democrats, and civic virtue theorists today. It is the ideal of writers as different as Charles Taylor and Jürgen Habermas, and it explains the lingering attraction of Marx.

Finally, the idea of freedom as wilful creativity may be joined to a second conception of freedom, that of negative liberty.[29] The latter freedom may be described as security against the will of others. It is the obverse of tolerance; tolerated persons can be said to enjoy the security of negative liberty. Taken together, positive and negative liberty are the defining poles of liberal individualism, as described in Chapter 5. The two most famous statements of this political view, belonging to the nineteenth and twentieth centuries, respectively, each allude to both concepts of freedom – wilful action and security against the will of others:

> That principle is, that the sole end for which mankind are warranted, individually and collectively, in interfering with the liberty of action of any of their number, is self-protection.[30]

> Each person is to have an equal right to the most extensive basic liberty compatible with a similar liberty for others.[31]

The coexistence of socialism and liberalism (among other ideologies of the modern era) is an example of the ongoing conflict between conceptions of the good. Pluralism of this kind was a fact of ancient times, as it is of modern life. The contest of goods led, without any of the major historical actors being aware of the process, to the development of a new language of morality. This new language of values makes it easier to recognize the fact of pluralism itself. We have moved, unevenly but unceasingly, from pluralism in conceptions of the good to value pluralism.

4
The Teleology of Modern Time: Negative Liberty and Human Nature

Sometimes in clashes between groups, sometimes in contests between religions, and sometimes in competing philosophical doctrines, the fact of pluralism led to changes in moral language. From this long process emerged the idea of the value-creating human will. To be free in this sense is not just to act but to be self-ruled, to create one's telos for oneself. Animals act but are not self-directed. Unlike animals, humans are the authors of their own rules. We are free when we write our own story, choose our own role, define our own character. At the heart of the positive conception of liberty is wilful self-creation.

But the long contest over the good also led to a second modern notion of freedom. Liberty in the second sense means security against the will of others. Again, the initial modernizing event was the rediscovery of Aristotle in the twelfth century, which led to a new naturalistic understanding of the world. The eventual result would be the modern scientific notion of causality and new ideas about human freedom. Initially, liberty in the negative sense was seen as freedom from outside causation, freedom from external force or hindrance. The seed, if not the fruit, of the new idea of negative liberty was the Cartesian belief that human beings were unique because they were outside of the mechanical world of causation. The idea of natural causation was next adopted by empiricists who would 'internalize' it. On one hand, causal forces from within came to be understood as natural and legitimate; on the other, external causation was seen as an infringement of freedom. The idea of negative liberty emerged as the absence of coercion or obstruction in the pursuit of our natural, God-given ends. With ongoing secularization, negative liberty became the belief that human ends must be respected as given.

The empiricists of the seventeenth century did not see freedom as Kantian autonomy, the power to give law to oneself; rather, to be free was to be unfettered in the pursuit of happiness, and happiness was defined in naturalistic terms as the process of fulfilling our given propensities. Negative liberty in this tradition was teleological, following from the belief that the ends of life were given by nature. Where Kant had talked of the dutiful will as the locus of goodness, the empiricists believed morality could be found in the process of human nature.

Teleological moral theories, like those of Aristotle and Aquinas, are distinctive in that they do not disunite the notions of right and good. By contrast, modern 'neutralist' theories hold that rights are justifiable without appeal to a general conception of the good. While the father of rights-based liberalism is sometimes thought to be John Locke, he belonged to an alternative tradition in which the good was natural and God-given. His natural law theory was teleological: right and good were united in the pursuit of happiness. Individuals had the right to life, liberty, and property, as given by human nature. Rights were natural, and the natural was good.

Unlike positive, or wilful, liberty, which began with divine-command morality after the rejection of Aristotle's naturalistic cosmology, the alternative conception of freedom began with the acceptance of Aristotle, most importantly by Thomas Aquinas. He attended the University of Naples in the thirteenth century, when Aristotle's original works were being reintroduced to the West. Aquinas took up the Aristotelian idea of an overall telos towards which human life was properly directed, but he gave it Christian content. The summum bonum, the highest good towards which one should aim, was in the heavenly afterlife. Aquinas also understood the Stoic idea of natural order in a teleological way. God was the prime mover of nature – the ever-present cause of all existence. However, the Church's condemnations of 1277 in Paris and Oxford included some of Aquinas's propositions during the controversy over Aristotelianism. Aquinas had died three years earlier, but his followers continued his teaching. In the following decade, Thomism became the official doctrine of the Dominicans, rivalling the Franciscan adherence to Duns Scotus and Ockham. In 1323, Aquinas was canonized, and his Aristotelian view of nature eventually became official Church doctrine. In the seventeenth century the Thomist revolution, in turn, became oppressive, as Galileo was arrested for his alternative naturalism.

In his own time, Aquinas's reputation suffered because he rejected divine-command morality and the contingency of earthly existence. He taught that each person is drawn towards the knowledge of God, which can be achieved perfectly only in heaven. In the present life, people could achieve only a second-rate form of fulfillment, yet here too they must follow natural law and the right order of things. As the unmoved mover, God ruled on earth. Cosmology, theology, and morality were in unison in Aquinas's naturalistic system. This led to an emphasis on reason over revelation and faith. Following Aristotle's method of dialectical reasoning, Aquinas thought that God's law could be known on earth.

This logico-verbal method was attacked by other Aristotelians of the era, including Roger Bacon. He was a student of Robert Grosseteste, the first chancellor of the University of Oxford, who had been a leader in the Aristotelian renaissance. Grosseteste was an early practitioner of experimental science, of which Bacon became a promoter. They provided an important corrective to Aristotle's axiomatic method, which did not allow for amendments by experiment and observation. With this emendation, Aristotle's influence at Oxford in the thirteenth century led to the birth of English empiricism. Three centuries later, Francis Bacon would point out the importance of falsification to the experimental method. Support for a theory can only be gained by the gradual accretion of experience, but disproof could come in a single dramatic experiment. However, Bacon's empiricism was not yet a worldview because it lacked an essential feature – an appreciation of the importance of time.

Bacon's amanuensis for a brief period was the youthful Thomas Hobbes, who later became acquainted with Descartes and Galileo. From the latter came an understanding of inertial motion, which had been missing from Bacon's new science. With this discovery, a new worldview was born. With Hobbes, empiricism began its evolution into a theory of how people should live together. In this tradition, nature was both the starting point for knowledge and the source of right and good. Human nature was a causal process, which provided the telos of life. Far from a value-neutral scientific conception, the empiricist understanding was thoroughly normative. To be normal was to follow a natural moral teleology.

The teleology of human nature was summarized as the pursuit of happiness. We do good by seeking our given ends, by refusing to be diverted from our natural course. Perversion and depravity come when human nature is defied or defiled. In this view, human nature is not an obstacle to free, creative, spontaneous goodness (to use, for positive libertarians, redundant terms) but an approbative notion conveying a sense of rightness. When we do right, we become happy – not in the hedonistic sense of achieving pleasure but in the Aristotelian sense of achieving our proper fulfillment. In this view, human goodness is about achieving our given telos.

The new conception of human nature developed from the discovery by Galileo of inertia, which was absorbed into Aristotelian teleology. Aristotelian physics had held that the earth was the centre of the universe, surrounded by spheres of water, air, and fire. Earthly objects fell, and smoke lifted skyward, because they were naturally pulled towards their given place. But, against Aristotle, Copernicus showed that the movements of the stars and planets could be explained much more simply if the sun, not the earth, was the centre of motion. If the sun was the centre, then the earth must be in constant movement.

The question then arose as to why the force that produced this motion was not felt by humans on earth. Did not an object move only because force was constantly applied to it? Why do we not feel the force upon us that keeps us moving around the sun? Galileo, using the experimental method, disproved the Aristotelian assumption that things would naturally stop moving unless a force was applied to them. He found that when he rolled a ball down a curved slope it would continue upward on a facing slope, stopping only when it reached its starting height. Reducing the angle of the second slope did not alter the outcome; the ball would roll further but would come to rest only when its initial height was reached. If the second incline was reduced to zero, he reasoned, then the ball would continue to roll on forever. Therefore, motion does not require a constant application of force. Only *changes* in motion are felt as force. No one has a sense of motion on earth as it moves because no force is being applied to us. The explanation of curvilinear orbits awaited Newton's discovery of gravity, but Galileo had discovered inertia. Movement, not rest, was the natural state of things.

What has all this to do with human freedom? From the point of view of positive liberty, nothing. A thinker in this tradition will argue that, while freedom requires the absence of external force, this is only a condition, not the essence, of true freedom. Negative liberty is necessary in order for positive liberty to be effective, but it is not our highest freedom. The internal impetus of free action must come spontaneously from the will. This was the teaching of Kant, and it is the foundational belief of positive liberty. In this view, real freedom is the wilful overcoming of natural effect, but empiricists saw things differently.

Underlying the empiricist alternative is the belief that freedom is about belonging to the natural flow of things. The will is not without effect in this tradition, but its role is in judiciousness rather than creativity. The telos of human nature is corruptible through excess or misdirection, and the will is free to do good or ill. But it does not *create* good. The good is in the teleological process of the natural causal forces within us. The *pursuit* of happiness – not the achievement but the pursuit – is the purpose, or telos, of life. This was the theme of the most important empiricist of the early modern era, John Locke. While it has no champions among Kantian moralists, it is a philosophy that many people follow in their daily lives. Just as positive liberty is sometimes manifested in a cheap relativism in which all values are subjective, negative liberty sometimes takes the form of crass economic materialism. But in either case, the underlying ideal is old and deep. People value liberty of both types in superficial as well as in serious ways.

While Locke is best known to us as a political theorist, his magnum opus was a work of naturalistic psychology. In *An Essay Concerning Human Understanding* (1700), Locke provided the conceptual foundations for the understanding of freedom that would come to dominate Anglo-American political thought. Hobbes knew and was influenced by Descartes, but he had objected to the latter's dualism. In rejecting Descartes's twofold materialism, Hobbes eliminated what Descartes had sought to provide – a theory of the mind. But Hobbes had nothing with which to replace it. Locke amended Hobbesian mechanicism, in which human life was seen as a natural causal process, by adding what Hobbes crucially had lacked. Locke accepted that the mind and soul were separate from the body, but he bridged the Cartesian divide with an empiricist theory of knowledge. By synthesizing Hobbesian and Cartesian ideas, Locke laid the foundation for his political theory. To understand the development of his ideas, therefore, we must go back to his two predecessors.

Descartes and the Freedom of the Soul

With his distinction between mind and body, Descartes was a critical figure in the story of freedom as liberty from outside causation. He rejected the logico-verbal methods of Scholastic Aristotelianism in favour of empiricist techniques. Although he would later look for greater certainty than sense data could provide, he adopted the observational way of study that Aristotle himself had used. To use modern career categories, he began as a scientist rather than as a philosopher. Cartesian dualism originated only later as a corrective to the deterministic implications of his scientific worldview.

While we know him best for his distinction between mind and matter, Descartes's first achievement was in physics. Inspired by a religious-like vision at age twenty-three, Descartes had come to believe that the universe could be interpreted entirely in terms of mathematics. His cosmology, in which objects were connected by vortices of motion, would be given wide respect until rivalled by Newton. But with the condemnation of Galileo in 1633, Descartes suppressed his own theory. *Le Monde,* written in the same year, would be published only after his death. His cosmology, based on the eternal logic of mathematics rather than on the omnipresence of divine will, seemed to describe a godless universe and a soulless man. In a mathematically driven universe, what freedom did the human soul have to follow God? Drawing on religious exemplars, Descartes's answer was to add to his cosmology an entire second order of reality. The dualism of mind and body, or thinking substance and extended substance, had its source in Descartes's desire to save a special place for God and the human soul outside of the mathematically determined world of matter.

As Descartes tells the story of the genesis of his dualism, he had been able to devise a system of physics that could explain the entire material universe, including the unconscious actions of the body (now called autonomic functions). However, his physics could not account for the operations of the mind. He recounted: 'Examining the functions that might result in such a body, what I found were precisely those that may occur in us unconsciously ... the very operations in which irrational animals resemble us; but I could find none of the operations that depend on consciousness and are alone proper to us as men; whereas I could find a place for these on the further supposition that God created a rational soul, and joined it to the body.'[1] In this way, Descartes would redraw the ancient line between body and soul. He did not initiate the distinction but, rather, understood it in a new way. The physical realm was causally determined, but the mind and soul were free. Bodily actions were caused by external stimuli, which created movement along the nerves and vibrations in the pineal gland (as the only non-double gland in the brain, the probable nexus of mind and body). The resulting passions, in turn, produced bodily movements. While the mind could have some effect in reconditioning the passions, most bodily actions were externally caused. But in thought, the mind was free.

With Descartes, the mind and soul became the same. By identifying the two, he found a new, more egalitarian foundation for the Platonic elevation of reason over the lower attributes of the soul. Following Aquinas, the Scholastics had adopted an Aristotelian conception of the relationship of the soul to the body. Official church doctrine held that the body was resurrected, so the Scholastics rejected Plato's teaching that reason alone was immortal in favour of Aristotle's idea that the soul is a 'form,' or animating telos, of the body. In *On the Soul*, Aristotle had discarded the idea that the soul is a separate entity residing within the body, arguing instead that the soul is the end or function for which the body exists: as eyesight is to the eye, so the soul is to the body. Soul-as-form and body-as-matter were two aspects of the same substance.

For his part, Descartes went back to Plato. Body and soul were not aspects of a single thing but were distinct substances belonging to different orders of reality. As he summarized it: 'I recognise only two *summa genera* of realities: intellectual or mental ... realities, i.e. such as belong to a mind or conscious ... substance; and material realities, i.e. such as belong to an extended substance, a body ... And even if we supposed that God had conjoined some corporeal substance to such a conscious substance so closely that they could not be more closely joined, and had thus compounded a unity out of the two, yet even so they remain really distinct.'[2]

In the 'Discourse,' he had nodded towards the ancient divisions among the 'rational ... vegetative [and] sensitive' aspects of the soul,[3] but Descartes would go on to argue that only reason properly belonged to the soul. In the *Meditations* he sought to demonstrate that the vegetative and sensitive functions were purely physical, which left only the rational to be identified with the soul. In this way he could reassert Plato's idea that reason was the immortal aspect of the soul. 'The mind (or soul of man, between which I find no distinction) is immortal by its very nature.'[4] But reason was not just the ability to discern higher Platonic realities such as the Form of the Good. Descartes's novelty was to identify reason with ordinary thinking, thus making the mind, rather than philosophical contemplation alone, the seat of all consciousness. Reason belonged equally to everyone, and the reality of the soul was obvious to each of us by the evidence of our own thought.

The essence of the mind was thought, just as the essence of matter was three-way extension in length, breadth, and depth. The idea of extension was fundamental to Descartes's mathematical universe, and we will see how it was taken up by Locke. For Descartes, the absence of extension was what made the soul immortal. The body could whither and disintegrate into primordial bits because it was mere extended substance, but the existence of the soul was not contingent in this way. Precisely because it was not extended, the soul could live on. This crucial Cartesian distinction between extended and unextended substances would be challenged by Hobbes, while the idea of extension would be revolutionized by Locke.

The soul, for Descartes as for the classical philosophers, was not just distinct from the body but was superior to it. It was the mind, now identified with the soul, whose existence could be verified by the direct evidence of its own thoughts. Therefore, its existence could be known more perfectly than that of the body. And since knowledge of perfect existence was conceivable only through the idea of God – God was perfect existence – the mind or soul was closer to God than was the body. The soul, for Descartes, remained a religious notion. Its ideas were innate and divinely created. The body existed in the causally determined world, but the mind was free before God. Descartes thus would associate freedom with indetermination. He argued that 'we are so conscious of the freedom and indetermination that occurs in us, that there is nothing we comprehend more evidently or more perfectly.' While this knowledge conflicted with the belief in God's preordination, Descartes asserted that we must merely let this dilemma stand, since God's power 'must from its very nature be incomprehensible to us.'[5] Freedom as indeterminacy was for Descartes something of which we could have certain knowledge.

But, for Descartes, freedom did not include the belief that human ends must be respected as such. He did not envision a natural teleology of human life because nature was external to the soul. Ideas were innate but human ends were not. By cleaving resolutely to the belief in freedom as indeterminacy, his dualism had alienated humanity from any natural ends. Freedom, for Descartes, was to be detached from any directive force outside of the solitary human mind. Just as Luther found faith to be a divinely created attribute of the soul, so Descartes looked for the source of all knowledge in innate ideas and solitary reason. His project from the beginning had been to replace received knowledge with a system devised by the unaided mind. By consigning the laws of nature to the external physical realm, Descartes denied any knowledge of the given ends of life.

Hobbes and Mechanistic Deism

Mechanicism is typically considered the antithesis of a teleological theory. The former envisions the universe as a purposeless machine, while the latter endows in it an ultimate purpose. Hobbes presented a synthetic view, in which the purpose of nature was in the causal process of the human passions. Where religious thinkers would follow the new scientific ideas to seek God in nature, leading to the 'natural religion' of Deism, Hobbes originally applied this conception to the study of human nature and politics. Humanity had a telos, but one that was evident as a natural process of ordinary life rather than as a higher purpose.

Like Descartes, Hobbes would find a way to reconcile freedom with a world infused with natural causation while still maintaining (or appearing to maintain) a role for God. While Descartes exempted the mind and soul from causation, Hobbes described mental processes in naturalistic terms. By seeing causality as active within the soul or mind, Hobbes took a step towards redescribing Aristotle's teleological view of human striving in the causal language of modern science. After discovering Euclidean geometry, Hobbes sought to apply scientific thinking to political philosophy. But more important than Euclid was the influence on Hobbes of Galileo, whom he had visited in 1636.

Galileo's discovery of inertia was critically important in the history of ideas because it reformed a number of core beliefs. Galileo's revolution was more upsetting than Darwin's because, unlike the latter's, it came in an age when godlessness was virtually inconceivable. For this reason, it took much longer for its implications to be developed. In the Scholastic era God was integral to scientific explanation, and no alternative worldview was available. The Stoics had taught that God gave order and motion to the world, and the Scholastics adopted the Neoplatonic idea that God was omnipresent. Meanwhile, Aristotelian physics supposed that rest, not motion, was the unaffected state of things. Combining these beliefs, official Church doctrine in the late medieval period held that the continuous motive force of nature was God. Natural processes occurred only because, at every moment, God willed them onward.

Galileo's discovery allowed early empiricists such as Hobbes to modify the Aristotelian idea of a first cause, or unmoved mover, which Aquinas had identified with the Christian God. In Aristotle's physics and Aquinas's theology the unmoved mover was required to be continuously present because otherwise all motion would stop. This understanding was threatened by Galileo's discovery. God could now be described as active at the beginning of creation but not necessarily thereafter. Direct interventions, or miracles, were still conceivable but were now thought to be outside the realm of science. Their reality would become controversial. The supernatural was now understood as that which is not scientific. The 'natural religion' of Deism could now develop, together with a renewed teleological theory of the good. This was the theory of human nature, which located the Aristotelian doctrine of purposiveness in the natural passions. This new naturalism brought Aristotle's teleology to common life: Our telos is in our nature.

Hobbes described the new vision succinctly: 'For he that, from any effect hee seeth come to passe, should reason to the next and immediate cause thereof, and from thence to the cause of that cause, and plunge himselfe profoundly in the pursuit of causes; shall at last come to this, that there must be (as even the Heathen Philosophers confessed) one First Mover; that is, a First, and an Eternall cause of all things; which is that which men mean by the name of God.'[6] Whether or not Hobbes accepted the divinity of the causal process, he clearly believed it was the source of meaning and purpose in human life.

The new science was centrally about force and motion. It was not about inert physicality – not materialism but mechanics. Its core idea was a new understanding of the forces that move physical bodies. The idea of energy, which the seventeenth century called the *vis viva*, or living force, was its central discovery. Hobbes would apply this new idea of causation and momentum to psychology and political philosophy. Nature, as Hobbes understood it, was mechanical. His theory is more aptly described as mechanistic than materialistic. This distinction allows us to see that Hobbes, whatever his religious beliefs, could argue that he had retained a place for God in his philosophy, if not the omnipresent one of the Neoplatonic tradition.

According to Hobbes, God had created the natural causal order. If nature were a line of dominoes, it was God that had set them up and then tipped the first one over. In the opening line of the *Leviathan*, Hobbes defined nature as 'the Art whereby God hath made and governes the World,' but thereby wrote him largely out of the story.[7] His was the 'absentee God' of later Deists, and, like them, Hobbes would be suspected of crypto-atheism. But whatever private beliefs he held, his naturalism shifted the focus from God to humanity. Humanity imitates God and nature by creating Leviathan in his own image. Thus in order to understand the Commonwealth we must first understand humanity. Hobbes followed the Protestant turn inward: Where Luther had seen faith, created in humanity by God, as the most important attribute of the soul, Hobbes saw the essential components of human nature in scientific, causal terms.

In the *Leviathan*, Hobbes described Galilean inertia: 'When a Body is once in motion, it moveth (unless something els hinder it) eternally.'[8] From this followed the empiricist theory of knowledge: 'Sense in all cases, is nothing els but originall fancy, caused (as I have said) by the pressure, that is, by the motion, of externall things on our Eyes, Eares, and other organs thereunto ordained ... All Fancies are Motions within us, reliques of those made in the Sense.'[9] We are what we are because the forces of nature move through us in certain ways.

These natural propensities were what the empiricists called the passions, and they were about reaction rather than originative action. They defined the ways individuals were acted upon by the world. The older meaning of passion is shown by its kinship to 'passive.' For example, the Passion of Christ refers to submissive suffering. What Hobbes meant by the passions was the natural propensity of a person to react in given ways to the causal stimuli of the world. Thus, he described human nature in terms of our given inclinations as part of the natural causal order.

For Hobbes, then, the ends toward which we are drawn were given by nature rather than wilfully created. Natural freedom was the momentum within us that defines our essence and purpose. The will was only one step in the process of this internal action. The idea of free will, he claimed, was a semantic confusion and was as meaningless as a round rectangle.[10] Deliberation was the process of weighing the benefits and consequences of fulfilling one's competing appetites, and only after deliberation did the will come into play. The will was the last act of deliberation, upon which voluntary actions directly depended. Since this process was one of continuous causation, it made no sense to say that the will was free. Hobbes even denied that will was unique to humans because animals, too, were driven by competing appetites and needed to deliberate before acting.

With the passions that drive human actions taken as given, freedom became the absence of constraints on voluntary action. Causal forces initiated by God or by nature are the essence of life, and the things towards which we move are given in our nature. From Galileo's laws of motion, Hobbes concluded that human ends are natural. Liberty consists of this natural movement, of which God is the first cause. The two essential components of the idea of negative liberty follow from this. First, our ends are given by our nature and are beyond question. Second, anything that hinders our movement thereby limits our freedom. In short, Hobbes's natural teleology revised the Aristotelian teleology of human nature in a way that implied the negative concept of liberty.

The human telos was not the completion of humanity's highest end, as in the contemplative life that was the summum bonum for Aristotle; rather, the human telos was to be found in the ordinary nature of the passions, whose fulfillment is a continuous process rather than a final end. Hobbes wrote, 'For there is no such *Finis ultimus*, (utmost ayme,) nor *Summum Bonum*, (Greatest Good,) as is spoken of in the Books of the old Morall Philosophers. Nor can any man live, whose Desires are at an end, than he, whose Senses and Imagination are at a stand. Felicity is a continuall progresse of the desire, from one object to another.'[11] This new teleology of inborn human nature was less exalted but more egalitarian than the old one, as it belonged, by nature, to everyone. If we know our own passions, then we know those of all others in similar circumstances; from this knowledge, a theory of proper governance could be formed.[12]

True freedom, then, was the absence of impediments to one's natural ends. The natural process within each person took its elementary form in the basic life function of self-preservation, which Hobbes saw as the fundamental natural right. His naturalistic teleology thus implied both negative liberty and natural rights, as in the famous passage, 'THE RIGHT OF NATURE, which Writers commonly call *Jus Naturale*, is the Liberty each man hath, to use his own power, as he will himselfe, for the preservation of his own Nature; that is to say, of his own Life ... By LIBERTY, it is understood, according to the proper signification of the word, the absence of externall Impediments.'[13]

Hobbes seemed to foresee the alternative accounts that would later identify freedom with wilful power, but he warned against them. 'But when the impediment of motion, is in the constitution of the thing it selfe, we use not to say, it wants the Liberty; but the Power to move, as when a stone lyeth still, or a man is fastened to his bed by sicknesse.'[14] This distinction between liberty and power marked a critical departure from the ancient idea of freedom. The ancient Greek idea of *eleutheria* had had two related meanings, involving, on the one hand, the ability of people of excellence to rule over others, and, on the other, the right not to be ruled over themselves. The freest person was the successful tyrant who had the greatest *agathon* and was highest in *arete*.[15] Nowhere in the ancient concept was there room for the freedom of ordinary people. By distinguishing between power and liberty, Hobbes, though not a political liberal, put in place a concept of freedom that would allow Anglo-American liberalism to develop. With Hobbes, liberty from the coercion of others became something that belonged, by nature, to each person.

However, Hobbes's theory had left no room for the mind or soul as a real entity. He had rejected the Scholastic dualism of 'BODY, and SPIRIT, which in the language in the Schools are termed, *Substances, Corporeall*, and *Incorporeall*,' arguing that this was another confusion of terms. '*Substance incorporeall* are words, which when they are joined together, destroy one another, as if a man should say, an *Incorporeall Body*.'[16] This marked a point of departure for subsequent empiricists.

Locke's Synthesis: The Temporal Theory of Mind
Locke returned to Descartes by accepting the ancient distinction between body and soul, but then he mended the rift between the two realms. He did so by reconciling this vision with the Hobbesian internalization of natural

causality, which he understood in terms of a kind of spatial extension. Locke would argue that causality was a temporal phenomenon. His political theory of rights to life, liberty, and property, and his conception of self-ownership as an aspect of personal identity, followed from his synthesis of Hobbes and Descartes. With this synthesis he gave to empiricism a theory of the mind.

Locke followed Hobbes in believing that the ends of human life were given by nature, that each person had a propensity to act in certain ways in response to the causal stimuli of the world. Human life was a natural process, of which God was the designer and first cause. This teleology of ordinary life may appear bourgeois or otherwise insufficient to many readers when compared to the higher fulfillment sought by Aristotle or Saint Thomas or by the historical telos of Hegel or Marx. But in the views of its adherents, the natural teleology of the new science was, nonetheless, a moral ideal. Central to this ideal is the notion of a causal sequence of action and consequence. Time, understood in a modern way as related to spatial dimensions, is the central theme of Locke's understanding of the mind.

Locke was deeply interested in Cartesian ideas, to which the *Essay Concerning Human Understanding* was largely a response.[17] He would provide the empiricist tradition with a theory of knowledge by reconciling Cartesian dualism with the causal view of human nature pioneered by Hobbes. Locke rejected the Cartesian doctrine of innate ideas, but he did not believe human nature was changeable. The mind was analogous to a blank page – but a blank page of a specific kind. Human nature was steady and fixed, consisting in the natural capacities that everyone shared. Locke wrote, 'Nature, I confess, has put into Man a desire of Happiness, and an aversion to Misery ... These may be oberv'd in all Persons and all Ages, steady and universal.' In disputing the existence of innate ideas, he continued, 'I deny not, that there are natural tendencies imprinted on the Minds of Men.'[18] The tabula rasa was not such that it could become anything at all. It was predisposed to absorb certain marks and not others, and to react in certain ways.

Locke was not a Cartesian, but his theory of the mind originated in the attempt to reconcile empiricism with the dualist model. As all knowledge was based on sense experiences, mind and body were initially connected causally. But as physical events caused the mind to have ideas, the mind subsequently used this knowledge to control the motions of the body. Locke accepted Hobbes's internalization of natural causation while retaining for the mind and soul a special place in the natural order. Following Hobbes, he understood the passions in causal terms: 'A Body ... when it is set in motion it self, that Motion is rather a Passion, than an Action in it. For when the Ball obeys the stroke of a Billiard-stick, it is not any action of the Ball, but bare passion.'[19] Causal forces act upon inanimate objects to produce motion, but they act upon sensitive creatures to produce ideas: 'The *efficacy* whereby the new Substance or *Idea* is produced ... is called *Passion:*

which efficacy ... in intellectual agents, to be nothing else but modes of thinking and willing; in corporeal agents, nothing else but modifications of motion.'[20]

Locke was concerned with distinguishing unreasoned passionate behaviour from true moral action, and so he developed a conception of moral agency that Hobbes had lacked. For Locke, personhood was a moral concept. Like Hobbes, he began from the belief that human nature is such that good produces pleasure and evil produces pain: '*Pleasure* and *Pain*, and that which causes them, Good and Evil, are the hinges on which our *Passions* turn.'[21] But he also sought to open a space in the causal chain of human experience for moral deliberation. Descartes provided a model for doing so by seeing the mind as a separate space, free from material causation. Locke tried to reconcile this moral freedom with the new empiricist teleology.

For Locke, the continuity of consciousness was enough to establish the identity of the person: 'For since consciousness always accompanies thinking, and 'tis that, that makes every one to be, what he calls *self*; and thereby distinguishes himself from all other thinking things, in this alone consists *personal Identity*, *i.e.* the sameness of a rational Being: And as far as this consciousness can be extended backwards to any past Action or Thought, so far reaches the Identity of that *Person*; it is the same *self* now it was then; and 'tis by the same *self* with this present one that now reflects on it, that that Action was done.'[22] The key to Locke's theory of mind, as this passage begins to show, is extension in time.

Again, the central difference between materialism and mechanicism is that the latter is dynamic; that is, it includes the temporal dimension. This constitutes a central difference between the traditions of positive and negative liberty. Time was not an important concept in the story of positive liberty. Like the God of divine command, the human self-creator is not limited by the past. Every self-creator is a source of good, and every renewal always begins *now*. Each spontaneous act has its source in the present moment. Status, not process, is important here. By contrast, the tradition of negative liberty was centrally concerned with the natural process of time.

A mechanical understanding of the universe brings to materialism the additional element of time. To understand Locke's amendment to Descartes properly, we must recognize that causality is a temporal concept describing the way one thing follows naturally from another. Cartesian dualism, by contrast, might be called twofold materialism, including two separate orders of substance. However, materialism itself is static. Descartes was keenly aware of Galileo's discovery of inertia, but his famous distinction between mind and body severed the dynamic, or causal, connection between the two. In this way, he thought he had liberated the mind. His theory of perception and action, in which vibrations in the pineal gland were caused by sensations and gave cause to bodily reactions, belonged to the causal realm.

The mind had a special status apart from the physical world, but status is never dynamic. The empiricist tradition gave to Locke a conceptual advantage because it led him to emphasize time and memory in his theory of mind. If consciousness for Descartes was the present state of having thoughts, for Locke it was the continuous action of awareness in time. One's identity consisted not of one's current thoughts but of the related powers of long-term memory and short-term contemplation.

To understand Locke's temporal theory of mind, we may return to the geometrical ideas that he, like Descartes, employed. The basic concept of geometry is extension. If we take a single point, geometrically described as having zero dimension, and stretch it out in a single direction (i.e., if we extend it infinitely), then we get a one-dimensional line. If the line is extended in a perpendicular direction, then we get a two-dimensional plane of infinite length and width. When we extend the plane in the direction of depth, the result is infinite three-dimensional space. Three-way extension gives us the three-dimensional world of width, height, and depth. To have three-way extension is to have bodily existence, as Descartes knew. At any particular instant in time, we can describe every material object using these three spatial dimensions. We can also describe its position relative to every other object.

The Cartesian liberation of the mind from causal determinacy was based on the severance of the extended world of matter from subjective world of consciousness: 'Extension in length, breadth, and depth is what constitutes the very nature of corporeal substance; consciousness is what constitutes the very nature of a conscious substance ... We thus readily get two clear and distinct notions or ideas: one of created conscious substance, the other of corporeal substance; provided that we carefully distinguish all attributes of consciousness from attributes of extension.'[23] This distinction was precisely what Locke ignored. The elusive substance of the mind, he suggested, consists in the extension of space into time through the power of memory.

In addition to extension in three dimensions, a second criterion of material existence is continuity in time: a physical object exists if it has extension and duration together. Locke knew that three-way extension is sufficient to describe the static material world,[24] but his breakthrough was to see time as the fourth order of extension: 'Duration is fleeting Extension.'[25] Thus he anticipated the modern understanding of time in terms of the fourth dimension. As Locke put it, 'There is another sort of Distance, or Length, the *Idea* whereof we get not from the permanent parts of Space, but from the fleeting and perpetually perishing parts of Succession. This we call *Duration*.'[26] To understand the material universe, then, we must consider space (which Locke called 'expansion') and time (or duration) together. Long before modern physicists like Minkowski and Einstein, Locke discerned the integrity of time and space: 'Expansion and Duration do mutually imbrace, and comprehend each other; every part of Space, being in every part of Duration; and every part of Duration, in every part of Expansion.'[27] As we now say, space-time is a continuum with four dimensions.

Instead of contrasting the material world of extension to that of conscious subjectivity, Locke's genius was to see the mind in terms of the fourth order of extension. He joined the dualistic but static materialism of Descartes with the dynamic mechanism of Hobbes and, thereby, bridged the Cartesian divide. While Locke struggled to articulate his insight into the nature of space-time and its implications for human experience, it is, nonetheless, a temporal theory of mind that is contained in his *Essay*. For example, what we call time, he called duration, reserving the former term for measured periods (like hours or years) of temporal extension. Updating his terminology with the modern language of physics, we can bring Locke's duration into our time. Space-time (or expansion-duration) is a single continuum, and consciousness is a temporal phenomenon.

Since we are unable to envision four dimensions, we must rely on analogy to describe space-time. Suppose we were to collapse three-dimensional space back into a single point. This point, we imagine, contains the three ordinary spatial dimensions. By relating time to the fourth dimension we extend three-dimensional space into an additional dimension, as our imaginary single point comes to be gradually drawn out – extended – into a line. In this sense, the passage of time is the gradual extension of three-dimensional space into a fourth dimension. The key to Locke's theory of mind is to see human experience as the movement – or, more precisely, the extension – of each of our lives along this time-line. Through the power of memory, we have continuous existence across time. We exist not just in three dimensions but, through consciousness, in four dimensions. This was Locke's concept of human existence and personal identity, which includes duration as well as physical extension. We have a continuous identity because the time-line of our lives is extended.

Another way to envision time as extension is to think about its relation to motion. If time were to stop, then the only observable effect would be that nothing would move. Motion can occur only with the passage of time. In order to visualize time as a process of extension, think about reality as depicted in two dimensions, as a series of pictures. In a single two-dimensional picture everything is motionless. The appearance of motion occurs only when we have a sequence of pictures. If we imagine this sequence not as a movie but as a growing stack of pictures, like a flip-stack of animated cartoons, then we can more readily envision time as extension. Every time something changes another picture is added to the stack; every action in this two-dimensional world requires the addition of another slice of time. Motion occurs only as the stack of two-dimensional pictures gradually grows thicker; that is, as it becomes extended into the third dimension of depth.

As you watch the stack of pictures grow, you are envisioning the process of extension from two dimensions into three. In a two-dimensional world, you are watching the extension of time. The world is 'thickening' with every motion. The same thing is happening with our three-dimensional world. Things change position relative to each other – motion occurs – only because another slice of time has been added. As this stack of three-dimensional pictures grows, our universe becomes extended in the direction of the fourth dimension. Time is this process of extension.

Notice that time is not the fourth dimension; rather, it is the process of extension into an additional dimension. For two-dimensional creatures (like our flip-stack cartoon characters), time would be the process of extension into the third dimension. A fully extended four-dimensional creature would experience time as extension into the fifth, and so on. For us, with our fully extended world of width, height, and depth, time is the process of extension in the direction of the fourth dimension. But it is the process of extension, not the dimension itself.

Nor is time a kind of movement; rather, it is the characteristic of our universe that makes it possible for three-dimensional objects to change position relative to each other (aka motion). Only by the process of extra-dimensional extension (aka time) is motion possible. Time, motion, force, causation, and energy – the *vis viva* of the seventeenth century – are aspects of the same process of extension. Objects move continually because time proceeds naturally. Putting the same thing another way, objects in motion tend to stay in motion because the process of time draws them onward. Because the process of time is ongoing, Aristotle was wrong to say that objects naturally come to rest. The law of entropy seems to suggest that eventually they will come to rest or, at least, that the only remaining motion will be the diffused vibration of background radiation. (Would time then enter a cycle, with a few 'slices' repeated endlessly? Or would extension continue in new directions and time carry on?) For our lives, however, entropy is beyond the horizon of meaningful events, which occur because the process of time is ongoing.

Rather than a big bang, the source of the causal flow of nature for the early empiricists was God. This was the core idea of the natural religion of Deism. It implied a natural teleology, and this part of the empiricist tradition remains at the centre of one of our common values – the negative conception of liberty. The intuitive sense that 'natural' means 'right' has very deep roots in our culture. According to the empiricist teleology, time / motion / force / energy / causation – in a word, nature – provide the telos of human life. Humans are unique in the causal, energetic process of time not because we are apart from it but because we experience it as it happens. So intimate is this experience that we may properly be said to be willing participants in the natural flow of events. Nature is in us, of us, and by us. We belong to the process of natural causation because, unlike unconscious objects that exist only in a series of three-dimensional instants, we exist for a moment in the fourth dimension. We are participants in our own extension. In this sense we each deserve our future and are responsible for our own past.

The insight underlying Locke's theory came from Galileo. An object in motion tends to stay in motion, unless another object imparts its own motion onto it. Causality is another aspect of, or name for, the process of time. Inertia (or momentum) flows with time and causality as the process of extension continues. By the natural forces of causation, one event leads to another. Momentum is that which bridges static instants. Following the empiricist worldview, Locke applied the idea of momentum to psychology to try to answer the riddle of Cartesian dualism. From Hobbes, Locke took the idea that causality, in the form of sensual perception, is the basis of the vital unity of mind and body, distinct but conjoined. Locke described one's conscious mind and physical body as united by one's sensations: 'All whose Particles, whilst vitally united to this same thinking conscious self, so that we feel when they are touch'd, and are affected by, and conscious of good or harm that happens to them, are a part of our *selves*: *i.e.* our thinking conscious *self*. Thus the Limbs of his Body is to every one a part of *himself*.'[28] The material world causes sensation. This temporal process occurs within the mind, so consciousness is the awareness by the mind of causal forces as they occur within it. 'Consciousness is the perception of what passes in a Man's own mind.'[29] Consciousness is a stretch of time in which past, present, and future, for a moment, exist at once. The momentum of stimulus-sensation-reflection-reaction unifies one's mind and body. Consciousness is a causal wave of experience of which one is self-aware.

Our minds are not separate from the physical causal order; instead, a conscious mind is defined by the awareness of the causal forces within it as they occur. These include perception, reflection, and decision. Human beings differ from inanimate objects by being aware of causality as an internal experience. Our thoughts are the causal forces of nature within us, and they begin with sensation. The kinetic energy of the world gives rise to sensations and these become thoughts. They may be understood as mental energy, which returns to the world as kinetic energy with our bodily motions. The *vis viva*, or living force of the world, is what constitutes human life. By being aware of this process for the moment while it happens, the mind becomes conscious of itself. Because we each occupy a small moment of time, of short but tangible duration, we are able to reflect on our own mental activity and to participate in the flow of events that define us. This flow is the empiricist teleology, which Locke summarized as the pursuit of happiness.

For Locke, personhood is continuity in time, made possible by the power of memory. One's personal identity is not based on continuous thought, as

Descartes's theory had suggested; instead, we know who we are because we are able to unite our past and present thoughts in the present moment. Memory provides us with this temporal capability. But besides long-term memory, each of us is aware of time *as it happens*. Unlike mere physical objects, we are aware of ourselves as having momentary presence, or fleeting extension, long enough to experience the extension of time as it occurs. We are able to hold on to a few instants until they become a moment. In Lockean terms, consciousness may be defined as the process of memory by which we inhabit more than a single point in time. Today, we distinguish between short- and long-term memory. A kind of very short memory enables what Locke called the faculty of contemplation, by which the mind is able to perceive its own ideas 'by keeping the *Idea*, which is brought into it, for some time actually in view.'[30] Consciousness is made possible by the power of the mind, related to memory, to hold on to an idea for more than an instant of time.

An instant differs from a moment: the former has no duration while the latter has a short but real one. In the analogy of an extended time-line, an instant is a zero-dimensional point, but a moment is a short line-segment. The duration of a moment is its fleeting extension. The conscious moment has duration, or extension, in time. Locke's idea was that consciousness is the awareness that we occupy a moment in time, during which we are able to reflect on our own mental processes. Thus he wrote of the 'consciousness whereby I am my *self* to my *self* ... This every intelligent Being, sensible of Happiness or Misery, must grant, that there is something that is *himself* ... that this *self* has existed in a continued Duration more than one instant, and ... may be the same *self*, by the same consciousness, continued for the future. And thus, by this consciousness, he finds himself to the be *same self.*'[31]

Described in modern psychological language, then, consciousness is based on the shortest of short-term memory – call it present memory – by which an instant becomes stretched into a moment. According to Locke, 'Such a small part in Duration, may be called a *Moment*, and is the time of one *Idea* in our minds, in the train of their ordinary Succession there.'[32] This moment is what we call the present. It is of short but non-zero duration. Our consciousness is a short line-segment along the time-line of our lives or (to switch analogies) a number of time-slices in our four-dimensional 'stack,' which are united by our present memory. During the present moment, we exist – in the strict philosophical sense of having extension – in the fourth dimension of time. Consciousness is the present awareness of time as it happens. Inanimate objects exist only in three dimensions at a time, but humans are self-aware because our consciousness is extended in time. It is only because we have this ability that we can reflect on our own thoughts and experience.

'Reflect' here is used in the metaphorical sense of bouncing back and forth within the temporal space of our minds, but this reflection happens so quickly and continuously that back-and-forth are united into a moment. The power of reflection provides us with the means of introspective consciousness. Thus, Locke called reflection 'that notice which the Mind takes of its own Operations.'[33] By the temporary extension of present memory, we are conscious, or present to ourselves. We know we exist because, unlike insensible objects, time for us is stretched into a conscious moment. A being without the power of present memory would be unable to reflect upon its own mental processes and, therefore, would not be self-conscious. Reflection is made possible by the power of present memory. When this mental power fails, the mind falls unconscious. Present memory, in effect, opens a space in the fourth dimension of time, allowing us to perceive our own thoughts as they occur. This was Locke's concept of mind as reflective and self-perceptive. The mechanism that enables this wonderful human ability remains little understood, but a modern psychologist inspired by Locke might look for the seat of consciousness in the physical process of memory.

The proper metaphor for the empiricist theory of the mind, then, is not an internal movie screen upon which our experiences play. If we return to the image of a flip-stack of pictures, we can see that the screen metaphor must be amended by adding the dimension of thickness, or time. Rather than a two-dimensional movie screen, the mind is like a thickness of glass, through which the light of our experiences takes time to pass. The glass has its own internal reflections and refraction, and these are present to us for the time that the light of experience remains with us. It is during this time that conscious thinking takes place. Deep in thought, we have a greater number of internal reflections. The light of the moment becomes more energetic, and the present moment is further extended. The glass of human minds may vary somewhat in thickness and reflective power.

Thoughts and experiences are patterns in the beam of light, and these patterns may be differentiated according to their complexity. Our extended mental energy, as it passes through our neurological system, forms into patterns of meaning. The information is in the extended pattern rather than in the raw data of sensation. To enlarge upon Locke's categories, we might say that an idea is a regular or recurring pattern of thought, a theory is a pattern of ideas, and an understanding is a pattern of theories.

As a subjective conscious entity, I do not have thoughts and experiences; I am a flow of thought and experience, which begins with sensations. Hume was clearer on this point than Locke.[34] Our sensations are received and interpreted in the context of our ideas, theories, and understanding. Once having done this, finally, we act. As an objective physical entity, I am a body with nerves and a brain that has extended patterns of neurological activity. This neurological energy is caused by the world and is returned to the world when I act. As a subjective mental entity, I am an extended flow of experience. Selfhood is a temporal process made possible by a sensory-cognitive-motor apparatus. This is the empiricist theory of the mind: Time is the process of extension into the fourth dimension, and we are partially extended four-dimensional creatures. I ammmmm, therefore I think.

The minimum duration, or time-extension, of the present moment could be compared to the time it takes to read a simple sentence. We do not understand words sequentially but put them together in extended unit-phrases. To make meaning, these must coexist in time as one. To understand Locke's theory of the mind in a direct way, try to feel the temporal moment it takes to comprehend a simple phrase: 'The cat brought the bird from the yard to the kitchen.' The cat and the bird, the yard and the kitchen, do not arise in turn and disappear in succession but exist together for a moment. The words hold together long enough for us to make meaning of them together. A simple sentence fills a conscious moment, and its meaning is a pattern in time. You are conscious because you are able to hold on to a few words for a moment. Without the ability to hold the components of a basic sentence in the mind at once, we could neither understand speech nor read. Nor could we think, because thinking takes time.

The evolution of consciousness, Locke's theory could be taken to suggest, may have arisen together with language, which further may have emerged from the ability to associate one event causally with another. Perhaps animals began to understand cause and effect when they became capable of associating events (such as a fire) with their effect (such as a burn). This association, like that between subject and predicate, requires that both be held in the mind at once. Once an animal becomes able to hold on to this moment long enough, not just to react (avoid the fire) but to form an idea (fire is hot), it can begin to communicate in ideas.

The longer one's present-memory, if we follow Locke, the higher one's consciousness. As he pointed out, a being that was aware of time in its completeness would be all-knowing: 'God's infinite Duration being accompanied with infinite Knowledge, and infinite Power, he sees all things past and to come; and they are no more distant from his Knowledge, no farther removed from his sight, than the present: They all lie under the same view.'[35] We may speculate, following this suggestion, that the higher the consciousness of a being, the longer the duration of its self-aware moment in time. For example, contemplative religious practices, like meditation, might be interpreted as an attempt to lengthen one's present moment. Prayer, to give this idea a religious interpretation, may be a form of meditation that brings the devotee closer to God.

In summary, Locke reconciled Hobbes and Descartes by understanding mental activity as fundamentally temporal. Thoughts are presently remembered experiences, which begin with sensation and end with chosen action. This theory of mind bridges the familiar materialism-dualism dichotomy. It might be called time-extended materialism. It is dualistic in that it is a double-aspect theory. Mentally, consciousness is subjectively felt as an extended flow of experience over which we have some control. Physically, it is a four-dimensional pattern of self-controlled neurological activity. The difference is not in the substance of mind and body but in the point of view from which one describes it. From the shore, the stream of thought looks like a four-dimensional pattern of energy; from within the stream, it feels like the flow of experience.

The Empiricist Want of Will

If there is anything to these last few speculations, Locke's theory may have untilled fertility in various fields of enquiry. However, the resistance to his ideas is not difficult to understand. The broad run of moral philosophy since Kant has been towards the alternative tradition, which accorded more importance to the will as the self-sufficient source of good human actions. (The empiricist teleology seems to have entered the culture of modern life more easily than the culture of progressive moral theorists. If the theory described here seems new, it is only because an old idea has more often been practised than theorized.) For Kant, the will was the only thing on earth that could be unconditionally good because its choices were not determined by empirical conditions or by natural inclinations. In his view, the world of systemic causality is irrelevant to human goodness. In the post-Kantian tradition, 'systemic' has become a signifier for victimization and oppression rather than good order. We must liberate ourselves by political will from systemic forces. For those who see the world in this way, Locke's theory of the self must be retrogressive, if properly understood, because it limits the creative role of the will. For those who follow Kant, the human will should be apart from, and ride above, the human animal, like a perfect rider upon a broken horse. For Locke, the will was not free in the same way. It could bridle but not spur.

According to Locke, because we are able to hold on to the causal forces within us for a moment, we are able to deliberate and choose. We are not just passive reactors. The power to hold on to a moment gives us the ability to judge among possible outcomes. Our inclinations and passions are many, but not all pleasures lead to a happy life. Consciousness gives us the power *not to act* upon every desire within us but only upon those that lead to our best overall ends, those that fit within the pattern of our lives as a whole. Fulfillment, or happiness, is in the extended pattern of our lives, in the chase as much as in the catching. The pursuit of happiness is a temporal process but one over which we have an important degree of control. We are moral beings because we have the power to block some inclinations, thereby allowing others to proceed in their natural course. The power that makes this possible is not creative wilfulness but judgment.

During the conscious moment, we participate in our experiences by constraining or redirecting impulses within the context of our patterns of thought. Because we exist in time, we can think ahead to anticipate the consequences of following the competing impulses of our nature. The moment of conscious thought allows us, as it were, to reach forward in time to envision consequences before performing our chosen action. For the conscious moment, before and after exist at once. Within that moment, we are free. Once the moment passes, our freedom ends. Are we free while we are choosing? Yes, because the moment has not yet passed. Freedom happens *now*. The question of whether we can change the future is meaningless because we only live through the moment. In the interim between past and future, in the present moment, we live with conscious freedom and moral responsibility for the thoughts and choices that lead to action.

The human will, however, is not the originative cause of our actions; rather, we belong to a causal flow of activity, within which we have limited options. Moral responsibility arises through the freedom of thought, as our impulses and perceptions compete for attention within the extended overall pattern of our ideas. By attending to them, or not, we rechannel our energies towards actions of our conscious choice. The impulses within us are many, and the experience of sorting through them is what we experience as wilful action. If I decide to hold up my hand, the event is not without antecedents. Something must occur to make me want to hold up my hand – some suggestion, urge, or chain of thought. My will comes into play when I channel the antecedent forces within me towards the action or when I refuse to do so. To have the subjective experience of willing is to be conscious of this process.

In physical terms, thought is a self-controlled four-dimensional pattern of neurological activity. It is self-controlled in that the pattern changes through an ongoing process of feedback, or reflection. However, the feedback mechanism is not something external to the process – it is not exogenous information added to the system after mental actions are completed – but is part of the four-dimensional pattern itself. The mind does not *have* a feedback mechanism; it *is* a feedback mechanism. The idea here is tricky because of its self-referential quality, but consciousness consists of self-monitoring. This ongoing feedback process allows the pattern to change in a self-controlled way so that certain possibilities of neurological activity, or neural pathways, are suppressed or blocked, while others are reinforced or opened, depending on how it feels to do so at the moment – on whether a new thought seems right in the context of our understanding, whether a potential action suits our overall purposes. We choose what to do next from the possibilities currently open to us, and we judge according to the on-going, or extended, pattern of our ideas. Ideas, then, are consciously re-shaped sensations, like a scattering of light transformed into patterns as it passes through a self-controlled prism. We make sense of sense data by shaping them into intelligible patterns, upon which we act.

This is the story that Locke attempted to tell, using the ideas of his time. He argued, as had Hobbes, that we are wrong to believe that we cause our own actions by the power of will. The will is not the free cause of any action but is merely the ability to suppress, and thereby rechannel, inclinations through the power of reflection. The cause of our actions is the natural flow of events within us, over which the will has only a negative power. However, this power is sufficient to establish our moral responsibility for our actions. According to Locke,

> The power to suspend the prosecution of any desire makes way for consideration ... For the mind having in most cases, as is evident in Experience, a power to *suspend* the execution and satisfaction of any of its desires; and so all, one after another; is at liberty to consider the objects of them; examine them on all sides, and weigh them with others ... This seems to me the source of all liberty; in this seems to consist that, which is (as I think improperly) call'd *Free will*. For during this *suspension* of any desire, before the *will* be determined to action, and the action (which follows that determination) done, we have opportunity to examine, view, and judge of the good or evil of what we are going to do; and when, upon due *Examination*, we have judg'd, we have done our duty, all that we can, or ought to do, in pursuit of our happiness; and 'tis not a fault, but a perfection of our nature, to desire, will, and act according to the last result of a fair *Examination*.[36]

Through the power of self-control, we are both free to act and responsible for our actions. The ability to control our passions by rechannelling our internal forces – that is, by refusing certain inclinations in favour of others – is what separates moral humans from amoral animals. We can reflect and need not give in to every urge. Gratification for us can be delayed or denied if we judge a pleasurable action to be contrary to our greater good. Human nature is not transcendable, but its potentialities may be achieved to a greater or lesser degree. Unlike the nature of animals and inanimate objects, human nature is our own responsibility. Because we can control ourselves, we rightfully suffer the consequences and reap the benefits of our actions over the long term. In this view, the ability to be active in time, to plan and to make temporary sacrifices, is what makes humans morally responsible. Unlike post-Kantian ethics, in which every act of self-rule is a new creative beginning, the morality of the empiricists is centrally temporal, involving rewards and penalties as the consequence of one's behaviour. From the point of view of the alternative tradition, the empiricist morality is punitive. The self-creativity of positive liberty is not temporal, not limited by past actions, because it is about transcending the existing human condition. Each free act is a new beginning because freedom is about causal self-sufficiency.

Locke's theory suggests a compatibilist answer to the problem of determinism, the difficulty of reconciling natural causality with moral responsibility. Does his answer mean that we can change the course of history? Or is the future perfectly predictable? If a super computer were programmed with the velocity and decay rate of each particle in the universe, then it should be able to predict the future. If this is so, then how can we say we are responsible for our fate? The future will be what it will be, and we have no ability to change it. Critiques of predictability based on chaos theory or quantum mechanics are not helpful because randomness leads just as surely to fatalism. An adequate solution would require not indeterminism but a theory of personal control, a justification for the belief that each of us has a conscious and deliberate influence over our own actions. Did Locke provide such an answer? We can supplement his theory by speculating about infinite branches towards alternative futures, by 'bending the time-line' of history into the fifth (or higher) dimension. For Locke, such possibilities might belong to God but not to man. He denied the spontaneous freedom of the will and sought instead an intuitively satisfying account of our place within the order of nature. We are free in the sense that we experience the flow of nature within us and participate actively in it. We change the future not by our positive creativity but negatively, by ruling out certain actions. Nature exogenously causes me to act in given ways, but, within the limits of my nature, I have certain powers of reflection and refusal. Because I am a conscious participant in the causal process within me in these ways, I am responsible for my actions. I deserve my future and own my past, whether for good or for ill.

Had Locke lived in modern times, he might have explained his theory of mind in the terms used here. For him, the vocabulary of the space-time continuum was not available. Nonetheless, the temporal model of the mind, in which consciousness is momentary extension into the fourth dimension, is clearly what his theory entailed. For Locke, it solved several problems together. What is the will? It is participation in the causal process within us. We do not just ride a wave of causation, we are the wave. What is a mind? A mind is the causal process of experience of which we are momentarily aware, through which we are self-aware. What is the substance of which the mind consists? It is our partial (because it is only momentary) extension into the fourth dimension through the power of present memory. What is consciousness? It is extended, patterned mental energy. Our consciousness is higher than that of animals, but it is not the highest that can be imagined. A fully extended four-dimensional mind would have all of its experiences present at once, but we have only a moment. As the moment passes, our present slides into long-term memory as our wave of experience rolls on. What is moral responsibility? It is a form of self-ownership, in which one's actions are part of oneself.

If the creative will is central to positive liberty, then, in the tradition of negative liberty, the will is about judiciousness. The power of will in this view is the ability to distinguish happy ends from unhappy ones and to judge properly the best way to pursue happiness. Furthermore, the temporal theory of the person suggests that, since continuity is the essence of identity, delayed gratification is sometimes in our best interests. The pursuit of happiness is a process more than a result, and it is in the overall continuity and pattern of our lives that our best interests must be judged. Judging is not entirely rationalistic but, rather, counts very much on learning and experience. It is a process of living more than a logical intellectual function, and its proof is in the outcome rather than in the criteria of choice. Where the positive concept of liberty sees the will in terms of spontaneity and self-creativity, the negative concept understands it as judgmental, including the ability to forego pleasure in the interests of happiness.

If I become impoverished by my own lethargy, I am responsible for my fate. If accident impoverishes me, I am more to be pitied than scorned. But, either way, it is my fate that I own, and it is my responsibility to bear it. The ownership of one's experiences and actions is at the core of this moral vision. The conceptual roots of self-ownership are very old. The modern mind-body distinction began, with Descartes, as a doctrine akin to the Augustinian division between the divine and earthly realms, and it was further grounded in ancient Orphic beliefs about the eternal soul. With a twist on the Platonic elevation of reason, the mind, or soul, came to be seen as superior to the physical realm, not just for philosophers but for everyone. This would lead to the 'possessive' quality of the developing idea of the individual: the mind or soul was that which inhabited or took possession of the body. If Hobbes and Locke endorsed this idea, they did not merely read 'market relations' into the conception of the person in order to justify an inequitable social order.[37] Like thinkers of any age, their view of human nature was influenced by the world they knew, but the ideal of self-ownership is deeper, historically and conceptually, than an economistic theory can describe.

From his idea of continuity of identity, Locke concluded that each conscious being has responsibility for its prior actions. Our prior actions are part of our identity. If identity is temporal extension, then the memory of our actions establishes them as part of ourselves. Our actions remain our own – we continue through memory to own our experiences – and so we remain responsible for our actions. This conception of self-ownership was more than metaphorical for Locke, for whom self-memory – long-term, short-term, and momentary – was the essence of personhood.

The idea that we must suffer the consequences of our actions is implicit in ownership as the sense of mastery, in that one has responsibility only for what one can control. This derivation of ownership from responsibility was borrowed from Hobbes, who, in turn, had claimed ancient sources: 'A PERSON, *is he whose words or actions are considered ... as his own ...* And then the Person is the *Actor*, and he that owneth his words and actions is the AUTHOR, in which case the Actor acteth by Authority. For that which in speaking of goods and possessions is called an *Owner*, and in Latin *Dominus*, in Greek *kurios*; speaking of Actions, is called Author. And as the Right of possession, is called Dominion; so the Right of doing any Action, is called AUTHORITY.'[38]

Both senses of ownership – mastery and responsibility – were equally present in Locke. For example, in the *Essay:*

> *Self* is that conscious thinking thing, (whatever Substance, made up of whether Spiritual, or Material, Simple, or Compounded, it matters not) which is sensible, or conscious of Pleasure and Pain, capable of Happiness or Misery, and so is concerned for it *self*, as far as that consciousness extends ... That with which the *consciousness* of this present thinking thing can join it self, makes the same *Person*, and is one *self* with it, and with nothing else; and so attributes to it *self*, and owns all the Actions of that thing, as its own, as far as that consciousness reaches, and no farther ... In this *personal Identity* is founded all the Right and Justice of Reward and Punishment.[39]

Locke's was an essentially moral notion: one has responsibility only for the things that are joined to one's continuous consciousness by self-awareness or upon recall by memory. If I do things while 'out of my mind,' I will not be properly conscious of doing them and therefore will not remember them. Those actions do not belong to me because they are not capable of being joined to my consciousness. They are not my responsibility. I do not own them, in both senses of the word, connoting responsibility as well as mastery.

Actions that are joined to a continuous person in that sense belong to him or her, and ownership of those actions connotes moral accountability. This was Locke's moral theory of the person, which he called a forensic, or legal, notion, establishing both rights and responsibilities in law. Self-ownership was based on the morality of responsible agency: '*Person*, as I take it, is the name for this self ... It is a Forensick Term appropriating Actions and their Merit; and so belongs only to intelligent Agents capable of a Law, and Happiness, and Misery. This personality extends it *self* beyond present Existence to what is past, only by consciousness, whereby it becomes concerned and accountable; owns and imputes to it *self* past Actions, just upon the same ground and for the same reason as it does the present.'[40]

With this idea of the person as a moral and legal notion, Locke established the concept of self-ownership. His better-known argument in the second *Treatise of Government* is an extension of the twin ideas of responsibility and mastery based on the continuity of consciousness. We own those things that we consciously, voluntarily act upon. By doing so, we join them to ourselves. Self-ownership was the foundation of the right to private property.[41] God had given the earth to humans to enjoy, but many kinds of enjoyment are inherently private, occurring when the fruits of the earth are joined to the person. Each person has a right of private property in edible things like acorns and apples, which are joined to the self by the actions of collecting and eating. Furthermore, Locke reasoned, there must be a right of property over the soil to which one joins one's labour in order to grow those things. His theory of property was thus an extension to the physical world of his theory of the person. We own all those things that in various ways become joined to our person by our voluntary acts, as we cause changes to occur in the world for which we are responsible. Causality, in the form of labour, was integral to both Locke's moral theory of the person and to his theory of property.

Whether this extension of ownership as joining-to-consciousness through voluntary action can justify all the steps in Locke's argument is of course open to question. His proviso that there must be 'enough and as good left in common for others' suggests that the ownership of non-bodily property is at most a derivative, or secondary, notion to that of the absolute right of bodily self-ownership.[42] Self-ownership was self-evident, but, for Locke, non-bodily ownership was supported by the additional belief that the fruits of the earth were given to us by God, while the supposed right of private accumulation further depended on money as an invention against spoilage. The further Locke moved from his argument based on one's responsibility for and mastery over one's own actions, the more numerous the additional arguments he required. But whatever the merits of his further suppositions, his basic theory of self-ownership must be seen as a development of the ancient idea of the soul's relationship to the body.

Liberty and self-ownership together were derived by Locke from the conception of nature as a causal process. Although originating in a naturalistic philosophy, Locke easily moved to the normative conception of the free, moral person. His teleological account of human nature, enriched by the understanding that allowed him to see life as a process rather than as a status, provided the foundation for the tradition of liberalism that would grow beyond his own place and time. Adjectives like 'unnatural' and 'abnormal' have moral content in this view, which they do not in the tradition of spontaneous liberty.

Critics of private property may resist the idea of self-ownership, but its historical effects were not all harmful. For example, before Hobbes and Locke, the reigning theory of property was based on family continuity rather than on individual right, as Tocqueville described.[43] The latter's aristocratic reservations notwithstanding, the new theory was compatible with the end of primogeniture and a more egalitarian distribution of property. A further effect of the new concept of the proprietary right to one's own body was the understanding that slavery is an offence against common humanity.

Before this principle became established, it could be thought reasonable that some humans were, by nature, slaves. While the full story of the end of slavery is beyond the scope of this discussion, the suggestion here is that Locke's contribution was essential to it. With Locke, slavery became something that had to be rationalized. He suggested weakly that slaves had lost their God-given right to self-ownership by forfeiting their lives in war.[44] The significance of this short chapter in the *Treatise* is not the quality of its argument but the fact that Locke felt that an argument had to be made. He had derived the essential principle that would lead eventually to the end of Anglo-American slavery, and even though he did not reach that conclusion himself, he saw that his own principle required a new justification of slavery, which he tried ineffectually to supply. Self-ownership is the antithesis of slavery, and so it now had to be defended. Eventually, the argument for equal self-ownership would triumph over the various rationalizations, and the practice whereby one person could own another would be finally discredited.

Positive versus Negative Liberty

The common theme of the early theorists of negative liberty was that the ends of individuals and groups must be respected as given. Obstruction of the pursuit of those ends may sometimes be necessary in political society, but in every case where this occurs, someone's liberty has been diminished. The great contribution of the empiricists, especially Locke, was in understanding the importance of time as a defining dimension of human life. This allowed a return to a teleological view of the good life, in which happiness was defined in temporal terms as a process rather than as a result. In his introductory note to the readers of the *Essay*, Locke compared the mind to a hunter: 'Its searches after truth are a sort of hawking and hunting, wherein the very pursuit makes a great part of the pleasure.' Happiness came in the active pursuit of true human ends as much as in their achievement.

Because Locke's theory of mind is tied to his moralism, philosophers of positive liberty have missed the richness of the former in their hurry to reject the latter. His ideal is more than mere Puritanism in philosophical disguise, and it is not just a superstructural manifestation of an unjust economic foundation. The empiricism of Hobbes and Locke, and the moral ideal of self-ownership, have deep and honourable roots in Western philosophy. If some of our fellow citizens live out the pursuit of Lockean happiness, then perhaps we should accept this as an example of ongoing diversity with regard to conceptions of the good. It is not the morality of self-creativity, but it is an understandable account of what it means to live a good life.

The essential difference between positive and negative liberty is that the former is about self-determination, by which our ends or values are to be created for ourselves. The latter is about the absence of external coercion and obstruction in the pursuit of our ends, which are given and therefore inviolable. To give precise terms to these concepts, positive liberty is about *autotelic power* (freedom to give our ends to ourselves), while negative liberty is about *telic security* (freedom from the power of others as we pursue our given ends).

Both concepts have their roots in ancient ideas about what it means to live a good life. Competing conceptions re-emerge in new ways in different eras, but the lines of continuity remain. While modernity must be understood as unique in certain ways, and while our differences with the past should not be ignored, neither can we understand ourselves without knowing the conceptual history of our values. If the roots of both concepts of liberty reach to our earliest recorded ideas, then it seems probable that they both will remain with us.

In more recent times, the two ideals would come together in the belief that human dignity requires that each person be seen as both powerful and inviolate, as having autotelic power and telic security at the same time. This was the ideal of liberal individualism that would emerge in the nineteenth century.

5
Splitting the Individual:
The Subatomic Values of Liberalism

With the concept of freedom as the absence of obstruction in the pursuit of our given ends, the way was made clear for the political theory of individualism to emerge. Named by Alexis de Tocqueville in the nineteenth century, who saw it as a kind of insularity, its ancestry was in the marriage of the two new theories of freedom. The free individual possesses both of the modern concepts of liberty: self-directing power and freedom from the power of others. Unlike the proto-individualism of earlier eras (like that of Descartes or Hobbes), individualism could now become not just a theory of the person but a vision of how free people should live together. In this view, society was an aggregate of individuals who were self-ruled but tolerated the self-rule of others. This is the central ideal of liberalism, in which the individual is the locus of value. Liberals differ on whether this value is given or is self-created, but they agree that the highest good belongs to the individual.

Both of the modern concepts of liberty developed from ancient sources. Positive liberty grew from the secularization of divine-command morality, as the creator of goodness *ex nihilo* came to be understood as the human will. In the eighteenth century, among certain Continental thinkers the human will became the source of value. While it began as a collective notion in writers like Rousseau, it was individualized by writers like Kant. In this view, we are free when we determine our ends for ourselves.

A parallel process, centred in England, occurred with negative liberty. This idea began in the late medieval era with a step away from the Neoplatonic omnipresent God of divine command towards the more naturalized Deism of the First Mover. By God's design, human beings had a range of natural desires and passions. To be free was to pursue one's given ends without obstruction. Liberty in this tradition became the pursuit of happiness.

This view was not an endorsement of simple hedonism but was akin to Aristotelian *eudaimonia*, or fulfillment, although it took a less exalted, more egalitarian form. Happiness, as Locke construed it came in the process of pursuing the ordinary ends of human life. For Locke, these ends were given by God as human nature, but with John Stuart Mill they became purely secular and individualistic. In his maturity, Mill came to see the causal process of human nature as leavened with self-creativity. Combining English empiricism, which accepted the inviolability of given human ends, with the emergent Continental idea of the creative human will, Mill was among the final progenitors of individualism as a political idea.

In the Hobbesian and Lockean tradition, the individual was not exalted as the ultimate source of value. While Locke sometimes hinted at the Rousseauvian idea of the collective will, for example in alluding to the 'the public will of the society,' his conception of liberty was essentially different.[1] The human will for him was not the source of value, as it would be for the followers of Rousseau. Liberty for the early empiricists had nothing to do with the creation of human-centred value.

However, the ideas of Hobbes and Locke would lead to the English utilitarians' belief that good and evil were synonymous with pleasure and pain. The identification of goodness with pleasure followed from the empiricist notion of the person, for whom all ideas began with sensation. Hedonistic utilitarianism was presaged in Hobbes and Locke, although with them the secularizing trend was incomplete. Some sensations were pleasurable and others painful, and from these sense data the ideas of good and evil were constructed. For Hobbes, '*Pleasure* therefore, (or *Delight*,) is the apparence, or sense of Good; and *Molestation* or *Displeasure*, the apparence, or sense of Evil.'[2] Since all sensations were a species of motion, set into action by God, our desires and appetites were God-given, and so Hobbes could argue (whether or not he believed it) that the source of morality remained divine. However, the step towards secularism was clear.

Locke similarly claimed, 'The infinite Wise Author of our being ... has been pleased to join to several Thoughts, and several Sensations, a *perception* of *Delight* ... It has therefore pleased our Wise Creator, to annex to several Objects ... a concomitant pleasure.'[3] From this it followed that morality was based on pleasure and pain, as consistent with God's design of human nature. 'Good and Evil, as hath been shewn ... are nothing but Pleasure or Pain ... *Morally Good and Evil*, then, is only the Conformity or Disagreement of our voluntary Actions to some Law, whereby Good or Evil is drawn on us, from the Will and Power of the Law-maker; which Good and Evil, Pleasure or Pain, attending to our observance, or breach of the Law, by the Decree of the Law-maker, is that we call *Reward* and *Punishment*.'[4]

Locke was not a hedonist, advocating pleasure either for its own sake or as a secular source of goodness. The pleasantness of certain activities was derived from the fact that God approved of them (although in the extreme, as with an excess of heat or light, the same activities might become a source of pain). Thus, God could be seen to approve of moderate enjoyment of some activities, while disapproving entirely of others. Morality for Locke

remained religious rather than secular and hedonistic. The source of morality was a neo-Aristotelian First Mover, the 'absentee God' of Deism, who
was the designer of human nature.

Locke distinguished immediate pleasure, which he admitted everyone
seeks, from true long-term happiness. The latter required judgment and the
suspension of short-term desires. Happiness was a constant pursuit. 'For all
that we desire is only to be Happy. But, though this general *Desire* of Happiness operates constantly and invariably, yet the satisfaction of any particular *desire* can be suspended ... till we have maturely examin'd, whether the
particular apparent good, which we then desire, makes a part of our real
Happiness.'[5] The pursuit of happiness was the long, active process of following the ends of human nature in accordance with one's best judgment.
In the continuous flow of human nature, the free person was responsible
for his or her life's course.

Utilitarianism and the Secularization of Negative Liberty

By the mid-eighteenth century, however, Lockean psychology had crossed
the English Channel, and its moral content had become transformed. With
French writers like the encyclopaedist Claude-Adrien Helvétius, the temporal notion of experience was turned into a static doctrine of sensation. Time,
the vital concept of empiricism, was no longer a factor. Memory for Helvétius
was merely a weakened form of sensation, and the passions, which for empiricists were the given propensities of one's nature, were only varieties of
pleasure and pain. The goal of Helvétius was not to explain human nature
as given but to demonstrate the malleability of each person. In the Continental tradition of liberty after Rousseau, to whose generation Helvétius
belonged, freedom was the spontaneous overcoming of nature. Spontaneity and self-creativity required that one free oneself from the temporal, causal
process. One's past, which for Locke had been the key to identity and moral
responsibility, was precisely what a spontaneous self-creator must surmount.
(John Stuart Mill noted, 'The disrespect in which history was held by the
philosophes is notorious; one of the soberest of them, D'Alembert we believe, was the author of the wish that all record whatever of past events
could be blotted out.')[6] Locke's psychology, with its rejection of innate ideas,
was, with thinkers like Helvétius, on the way to becoming a theory of infinite creative growth.

Among the followers of Helvétius was Jeremy Bentham. Although an En-
glishman, he belonged to the rationalism of the Enlightenment in France,
where his ideas were acclaimed. A precocious student, at an early age he left
the English tradition behind, joining the French revolution in ideas. For
the empiricists, the new causality had been a worldview, which included
not just an explanation of events as they were but an ethic of how things
should be. For the rationalists of Bentham's era, however, the source of

morality was secular and human. For them, science was just a tool for performing the emancipatory task of social creativity. Using the new scientific thinking, they hoped to build a better, more rational society. Science was just a means; their end was social progress.

Bentham's life-long goal was to reform the legal system in a rational, scientific way. His method was to treat happiness not as a process but as a quantum. Happiness was not a teleological pursuit, not the telos of a moral subject, but an objective status that could be measured and aggregated. If pleasure and pain were quanta that each person contained, then the good could be quantified by measuring and tallying the happiness of each person. The result was a static consequentialist theory, in which the end to be achieved was the highest overall state of happiness. Thus, while the idea of pleasure as goodness had its source in empiricism, Bentham departed from Locke's dynamic, temporal teleology by treating happiness as a state. Bentham's theory of human nature owed more to Epicurean hedonism than to Aristotelian fulfillment; among his goals was the rehabilitation of the Epicurean label.[7] He returned, in a sense, to the earlier empiricist, Hobbes, who had been influenced by an Epicurean friend, Pierre Gassendi. However, Hobbes had followed the temporal understanding of causality after Galileo's discovery of inertia. Bentham was a rationalist who sought a timeless theory of the good. The temporal flow of causation – from perception to thought, and from reflection to action – was not of interest to him. This simplification had a conceptual benefit: the advantage of pleasure as a status, as compared to happiness as a teleological process, was that the former seemed objective and measurable. By quantifying pleasure and pain, the greater good could be calculated. The Enlightenment ideal of a rational society could be achieved.

Bentham's *Introduction to the Principles of Morals and Legislation* (1789) was the foundational treatise of utilitarianism. As its title suggests, his theory was explicitly political, a conception of how free persons should live together. His understanding of society was individualistic in the modern, liberal sense. Bentham denied that a community was a real entity. 'The community is a fictitious body, composed of the individual persons who are considered as constituting as it were its members. The interest of the community then is, what? – the sum of the interests of the several members who compose it.'[8] In politics as in morality, the individual is the fundamental reality, to which all other considerations should be reduced. Society was an aggregate of self-interested, self-contained individuals rather than a Rousseauvian association or a Burkean contract of past, present, and future.

In the more nuanced political thinking of John Stuart Mill, the criterion of good governance was not just the happiness of the social aggregate but their moral and intellectual improvement.[9] He was less categorical than Bentham in denying the reality of the community as a real entity, especially earlier in his career. In his discussion of nationality in his *Westminster Review* essay on Coleridge (1840), for example, he pointed to the importance of social cohesion, in the form of common nationality, as one of the three pillars of civil society. (The other two were self-restraint and loyalty.)[10] By the time of the *Considerations on Representative Government* (1861), however, nationality was a problem to be accommodated or, where possible, attenuated by assimilation.[11] His best-remembered work, *On Liberty* (1853), appeared in the interim; there, Mill revitalized the idea of the individual as the locus of goodness. The endurance of Mill's individualism is due to his more developed conception of the person. With the Mill of *On Liberty*, the two concepts of freedom were joined.

Mill's Synthesis: Empiricism with Positive Liberty

If Bentham's genius was the rationalistic simplicity of his moral system, it was also his failing. The currents of thought that were coming together in the eighteenth century were richer than could be described by the reduction of goodness to pleasure. His critics included the thinker who tried to enrich utilitarianism by reconciling it with the empiricist telos. John Stuart Mill was a man caught between traditions. As Isaiah Berlin described it, his work 'was an attempt to fuse rationalism and romanticism: the aim of Goethe and Wilhelm von Humboldt; a rich, spontaneous, many-sided, fearless, free, and yet rational, self-directed character.'[12] Mill was born into the empiricist tradition. His father, James Mill, produced his own work of empiricist psychology based on a theory of association between concurrent and consecutive sensations as the source of all knowledge. According to the elder Mill, our conceptions of particular objects are made up of clusters of associated sensations. The task of education was to ensure that students learned to form the associations that would lead to happiness. As his son would put it, James Mill's 'fundamental doctrine was the formation of all human character by circumstances, through the universal Principle of Association, and the consequent unlimited possibility of improving the moral and intellectual condition of mankind by education.'[13] Locke's tabula rasa was transformed into a doctrine of human perfectibility through psychological conditioning.

James Mill had lost his religious faith over the problem of theodicy, the difficulty of reconciling the fact of evil with the belief in an omnipotent God. John Stuart Mill, who became the object of James's educational ideas, would grow up indifferent to religion. In his teens, he read Locke's *Essay*, as well as Hartley and Hume, and then his father's psychological treatise (as it was being written). From these sources, the younger Mill took up the empiricist psychology but followed his father in rejecting the belief in God as the designer of nature. Happiness was the good in a purely secular sense, as a matter of psychological fact rather than of divine intention.

However, in his young adult years, the ideas Mill had inherited – perfectionism through psychological conditioning and morality based on pleasurable sensations – came to seem hollow. Empiricism without the animating force of a meaningful first cause had lost its teleological power. Life for Mill came to seem empty. This led to what he described as his 'mental crisis,' a five-year period of depression and ennui. In his *Autobiography* he described the turn in his thinking: 'My course of study had led me to believe, that all mental and moral feelings and qualities, whether of a good or of a bad kind, were the results of association ... But there must always be something artificial and casual in associations thus produced. The pains and pleasures thus forcibly associated with things are not connected with them by any natural tie ... I was thus, as I said to myself, left stranded at the commencement of my voyage, with a well-equipped ship and a rudder, but no sail.'[14]

Mill's crisis was spiritual as much as mental. He had lost faith in the meaning of life. Without a religious justification, utilitarian morality and empiricist psychology had come up empty. Nevertheless, Mill did not return to religious traditions to recover from his depression; rather, he slowly came to find a new secular vitality in romanticism and Continental liberalism. He would synthesize these ideas (following the lead of Wilhelm von Humboldt) with the English tradition of negative liberty. The result was the argument of his most important book.

Mill tells us that he emerged from his depression with two new ideas. First, happiness is not the direct end of life but comes as a side effect or by-product of seeking one's own ends: 'Ask yourself whether you are happy, and you cease to be so. The only chance is to treat, not happiness, but some end external to it, as the purpose of life.' The understanding of happiness as foundational, as itself the end of life, was not a belief by which one could live, at least not 'the great majority of mankind.'[15] Most people's happiness came in the pursuit of the ordinary ends of everyday life. For deeper thinkers, however, human happiness should be considered more broadly, as he elsewhere put it, in 'utility in the largest sense, grounded on the permanent interests of man as a progressive being.'[16] Mill's utilitarianism remained consequentialist, but its end was not pleasure or happiness directly. Nor did happiness come through the pursuit of happiness in the Lockean sense, following the ordinary inclinations of human nature; rather, it could be found in the gradual process of an individual's creative growth. Locke's teleological view of happiness as a process rather than as a result was taken up by Mill, but he turned it towards a progressive individualistic end.

The new end provided the second major change in Mill's thinking: 'I, for the first time, gave its proper place, among the prime necessities of well-being, to the internal culture of the individual.'[17] This theme would lead Mill to renew his ideas about character formation. Rather than finding a new systematic philosophy, he turned instead to romanticism. On one hand, his new focus led him to the theory of historical progress of Comte and the Saint-Simonians; on the other, he returned to the problem of causality, determinism, and the freedom of the will. Earlier empiricists had suggested that liberty consisted in the absence of impediments to natural causality; that is, to the pursuit of one's God-given ends. Mill remained a political reformer, retaining above all else the belief in the improvability of human beings. His abiding project was not to justify accepted ideas about the ends of life but to work towards better ideals. To reconcile empiricism with a more progressive conception of freedom, he turned to a self-determinist theory of character formation through the active power of the will:

> During the later returns of my dejection, the doctrine of what is called Philosophical Necessity weighed on my existence like an incubus. I felt as if I was scientifically proved to be the helpless slave of antecedent circumstances; as if my character and that of others had been formed for us by agencies beyond our control, and was wholly out of our own power ... I pondered painfully on the subject, till gradually ... I saw that though our character is formed by circumstances, our own desires can do much to shape those circumstances; and that what is really inspiriting and ennobling in the doctrine of free-will, is the conviction that we have real power over the formation of our own character; that our will, by influencing some of our circumstances, can modify our future habits or capabilities of willing.[18]

Thus Mill found his renewal by embracing the belief in self-creation, although in a way that retained the empiricist idea of causality. He had come to accept, in other words, the concept of positive liberty not as pure creative freedom of the will but as a more limited power of self-development. Crucially, Mill did not become a romantic egoist. He continued to believe that freedom must include the absence of outside interference and that human nature could be explained in terms of causality. However, among the causes of human action was self-determination, not directly in pure wilfulness, but indirectly in the way we are able to influence our own internal growth. One's behaviour is determined by one's character, but among the influences upon one's character is the desire for self-improvement. In the *System of Logic*, Mill argued against those who believed that external forces were entirely responsible for character formation:

> In [their] words ... [a man's] character is formed *for* him, and not *by* him; therefore his wishing that it had been formed differently is of no use; he has no power to alter it. But this is a grand error. He has, to a certain extent, a power to alter his character. Its being, in the ultimate resort, formed for him, is not inconsistent with its being, in part, formed *by* him as one of the

intermediate agents. His character is formed by his circumstances ... but his own desire to mould it in a particular way is one of those circumstances, and by no means one of the least influential ... We are exactly as capable of making our own character, *if we will*, as others are of making it for us.[19]

Where Locke had written of identity, Mill wrote of character. He was able to retain the Lockean idea of responsibility for one's behaviour because one's character was, in part, self-created. But Lockean identity and Millian character were not precisely the same. The most important difference was Mill's addition of an attenuated version of positive liberty. While Locke had believed in responsibility for the play of causal forces within the mind because, through reflection and judgment, one participated in that process, Mill thought one had a degree of self-creative power. He returned to the familiar theme of life as a process and to the morality of personal responsibility. Mill took a step beyond his tradition but did not entirely abandon the empiricist psychology and its moral teleology; instead, he synthesized this ideal with a new one.

With Mill, human freedom became a dualistic notion, including both positive and negative liberty. Self-creation was joined to the natural process of human nature but not in a way so as to dominate it. Mill remained a liberal, not a Nietzschean romantic. Since each person was a being with given ends, everyone was equally deserving of negative liberty. Mill's individualism retained respect for the inviolability of others. Yet each person's defining ends were transformable in part through self-effort, so the good became personalized for each individual. Positive and negative liberty came together in his axiom: 'The only freedom which deserves the name, is that of pursuing our own good in our own way, so long as we do not attempt to deprive others of theirs, or impede their efforts to obtain it.'[20]

However, Mill's accomplishment was not entirely original. He credited another thinker who had achieved the same synthesis – as it were, from the other side. Wilhelm von Humboldt, working from within the German romantic tradition of positive liberty, had amended his own inherited system of thought by adding the Lockean idea of negative liberty. The result was the dualistic conception of freedom upon which Mill had founded his liberalism. The new idea belonged to no single tradition alone but was an international creation. Mill introduced positive liberty to empiricism, while Humboldt brought negative liberty to romanticism. The result was the same – a new political theory of individualism.

Humboldt's Synthesis: Romanticism with Negative Liberty
Individualism is a compound notion, combining constitutive elements nurtured in different traditions but belonging exclusively to none. Stephen Lukes

has pointed out that, historically, individualism had distinct connotations in different geographical regions: 'Nineteenth century in origin, it exhibited different meanings in different countries, though by now these have merged ... Its French meaning has always tended to be pejorative, signifying ... social dissolution ... Its German usage has tended to stress the Romantic idea of individuality, the notion of individual uniqueness, originality, and self-realization, applied initially to the cult of individual genius, notably the artist ... In England ... it came to signify the minimum of state intervention, as opposed to socialism or collectivism ... [while in] the United States, it early became a catchword for free enterprise, limited government and personal freedom.'[21]

Humboldt's *Limits of State Action* was written in 1791 but was not published until 1854, five years before Mill's *On Liberty*. Humboldt belonged to the German romantic movement that emerged in the eighteenth century. Rather than for a single rationalistic system of thought, their search was for sources of diversity and uniqueness. While some among these writers sought to establish the distinctiveness of Germans as a people, others emphasized each person's originality. The motto of the latter romantics was individuality rather than individualism. The romantic ideal of individuality would provide the title of the central chapter of Mill's *Liberty*. The key to individuality was self-creativity, with which state and society should not interfere. With the latter qualification by writers like Mill and Humboldt, individuality became liberal individualism, a political theory of how autonomous people should live together.

Humboldt's best known contribution is the idea of *Bildung*, fulfillment through the self-development of the individual's unique powers and capabilities. This was the idea that would appear so attractive to the mature Mill. Humboldt had written, 'The true end of Man ... is the highest and most harmonious development of his power to a complete and consistent whole ... This individual vigour, then, and manifold diversity combine themselves in originality; and hence, that on which the whole greatness of mankind ultimately depends – towards which every human being must ceaselessly direct his efforts, and of which especially those who wish to influence their fellow-men must never lose sight: individuality of energy and self-development.'[22]

The idea of freedom as the process of creating a unique self, which Humboldt summarized as *Bildung*, was common to German romantics,[23] but Humboldt was unusual among his fellows in combining it with a Lockean political vision. In the first place, he recognized the empiricist idea of the passions as vital to experience. 'The impressions, inclinations, and passions which have their immediate source in the sense are those which first and most violently show themselves in human nature ... They constitute the original source of all spontaneous activity, and all living warmth in the soul.' But Humboldt immediately added that 'the refining influences of culture [give] a new direction to the soul's energies.'[24] Furthermore, he would find a way to reconcile empiricist naturalism, in which desires and passions were forces of nature, with a different kind of naturalism, which saw nature in terms of growth and spontaneity:

> Even inanimate nature, which, proceeding according to unchangeable laws, advances by regular steps, appears more individual to the man who has been developed in his individuality. He transports himself, as it were, into nature itself; and it is in the highest sense true that each man perceives the beauty and abundance of the outer world, in the same degree as he is conscious of them in his own soul. How much closer must this correspondence become between effect and cause – this reaction between internal feeling and outward perception – when man is not only passively open to external sensations and impressions, but is himself also an agent?[25]

This was the same solution Mill reported reaching to the problem of freedom in the face of causal determinism. The soul was not just a passive recipient of sensational forces but had its own power of agency, including the ability to influence its own internal nature. The key was in the Kantian idea of moral agency as autonomy, or self-rule. Humans were ruled by causal law, but, to some extent, its forces were under the control of each person. We are self-ruled, even while being ruled by nature, because we each have a degree of control over the impact, or shaping effect, that sensations have upon us. In this way, Humboldt (and later Mill) sought to transcend rather than overturn Lockean empiricism. In Humboldt, the Kantian and Lockean ideas of freedom became joined.

Locke's influence on Humboldt was also evident in his conception of the state. Its role was to protect life and property: 'To counteract the evil which arises from the tendency man has to transgress his proper limits, and the discord produced by such encroachment on the rights of others, is the essential object of the creation of the State.' From this it followed that the 'security of citizens in a society depends chiefly on transferring to the State all private pursuit of redress ... hence of judging disputed cases and of protecting the successful litigant in his rights.'[26] Thus the only end of the state was to ensure the security, or the negative liberty, of the people. This argument culminated in the famous conception of the state as a security guard and no more: 'The state must prohibit or restrict such actions ... as imply ... the infringement of others' rights, or encroach on their freedom or property without their consent or against their will ... Beyond this, every limitation of personal freedom lies outside the limits of State action.'[27]

With Humboldt, in his marriage of English and German conceptions of freedom, the two constituent values of individualism were clear. His book is about the reconciliation of two concepts of liberty, which he named as power and security. He saw power as developmental in his idea of *Bildung*. But Humboldt was also explicit in naming security as essential to liberty, because it was the foundation of political, or legal, freedom: 'I call the citizens of a State secure when, living together in the full enjoyment of their due rights of person and property, they are out of the reach of any external disturbance from the encroachments of others; and hence I would call security ... the assurance of legal freedom.'[28] Power and security, positive and negative liberty, became the two defining poles of liberal individualism.

The Political Theory of Individualism

These are the foundations of the political idea of individualism: the power to find our ends for ourselves and the security to engage in their unhindered pursuit. Both power and security are essential to the freedom of the individual, but where the first is about the internal generation of those ends, the second concerns their protection from external disruption. While critics of liberalism may worry about its tendency to produce anti-social atomism, the ideal of the individual is not just about selfishness or private acquisition; rather, it brings together the two great concepts of liberty. Since both kinds of freedom are teleological in that they concern the ends of the free individual, the 'subatomic' values of individualism may be defined, building upon Humboldt, as autotelic power and telic security.

The same core values animated Mill's work, although his discussion of these themes was typically more cautious and less abstract than was that of Humboldt. As with the German writer, the ideal of individual self-development was at the core of Mill's mature thinking. For example, his *Considerations on Representative Government* sought to balance the goal of personal improvement through modified participatory citizenship against the danger to individuality posed by majoritarian tyranny. In *On Liberty* his argument against traditionalism anticipated at times the darker romance of Nietzsche, as in his description of Christian morality as weak and defensive compared to the 'Nobleness' of paganism, or in his admiration for the purer power of individuals in earlier eras. But, unlike Nietzsche, Mill retained a respect for the dignity of ordinary people, whose gradual self-development he wished to assist. The difference was that Mill continued to see each person as inviolable, in the tradition of Hobbes and Locke. As he put it, 'Over himself, over his own body and mind, the individual is sovereign.'[29]

Once the two ideas of freedom were fixed together, the political concept of the free individual could emerge in the nineteenth century. Individualism is the belief that the individual's ends are (1) self-determined and (2) worthy of respect as given. The tension between power and security – between creative renewal and the givenness of ends – would be resolved in the 'black box' of the individual's soul, into whose darkness no others need peer. The tensions of living – whether to accept the ends of life given by one's religion or culture, whether to choose among a range of options, or whether to create one's own original way – belonged only to the private person.

Despite the genius of this solution, liberalism has had its critics. They point out that the cost of this resolution is atomism, the privateness of individualistic decision making. However, the critic who would seek to attenuate this atomism must face the conflict between the givenness and the creation of ends. The opposite of atomism is some form of social cohesion under common ends, but this requires that the question of givenness versus creativity – the decision that liberalism grants to the individual – be reopened. To overcome atomism, therefore, is to return to the tension between positive and negative liberty.

Attenuating the atomism of liberal individualism would require two steps. First, the contest of priority between autotelic power and telic security would have to be decided one way or the other. Second, the dominant value – either the creative renewal of progressive ends or the orderly sanctity of given ends – must be resituated in society as a whole rather than granted as private to each person. If individualism is to be overcome, then freedom must be understood as a communal attribute – the value of freedom must be shared by all of us together. In short, the choice, if one rejects liberalism, is between socialism and conservatism. The former sees progressive freedom as the highest ideal of society; the latter sees the sanctity of evolved social institutions as inviolable. Each is a communal vision of freedom, but each defines freedom in its own way.

There is one alternative scenario, whereby the collective is defined as having a corporate soul whose growth must be nourished and protected. However, since the growth of a collective requires different kinds of resources than does that of an individual, the concept of the developing group-soul may lead to doctrines of nationalistic expansion. The embodiment of positive and negative liberty together in the corporate 'individual' may be an idea that tends towards aggressiveness and territorial expansion. The exemplar, of course, is fascism. The ideal of the self-developing collective soul gives rise to troubling connotations unless it can be reconciled with an internationalist theory about the equal right of all nations to grow. Just as individualism as a political theory is about people living together through respecting each other's limits, a collectivist version must include similar provisions about *Lebensraum* for all. In practice, it would require a supra-national police force or super-power to adjudicate conflicts, which sometimes would be called on to suppress the growth impulses of expansionist nations. In short, it would require a security guard to watch over states.

Meanwhile, within democratic nations, arguments over freedom continue. The modern condition in politics, whose roots are deeply entrenched in the culture of modern democracy, is that we have no final answer to the question of the priority of positive and negative liberty. When the conflict between ultimate values comes onto the public agenda, citizens inevitably differ in their politics – not in their values but in their priorities regarding conflicting values. If Isaiah Berlin was right in saying that our shared values conflict irredeemably with each other,[30] then, at its best, democratic politics will reflect the tensions among legitimate but contradictory ideals of the good society. Thinkers throughout history have differed in their conceptions of the good. In the moral language of the modern era, this contest of goods is expressed as value pluralism. In politics, it takes the form of ideological diversity.

Note that pluralism is not identical to relativism in beliefs and values. Relativism is the idea that each person or culture is the source of unique values and ideals. Pluralism is the idea that our culture provides all of us with conflicting values and competing ideals. *We* share values, but *they* conflict with each other. Relativism means each of us is unique and separate; pluralism means each of us is similarly torn. Relativism is a hollowed version of the ideal of positive liberty in which all values are subjective; pluralism is the recognition that other ideals besides positive liberty also belong to our culture.

This is the theory of democracy towards which we are moving: Democratic politics, in its highest form, is about the permanent conflict among shared but conflicting values. Political disagreements often have illegitimate sources as well, but democracy will always be discordant because there is no final answer to the inherent conflict among our common values. Politics is about value conflict. The attempt by political thinkers to truncate the range of legitimate disagreement is part of the political game, a strategic move in the perpetual argument of democracy. Not equality, not liberty, not community, but pluralism in values is the defining characteristic of democracy.

Liberal individualism is one solution to the conflict between freedoms, but not everyone is a liberal. To some, society has its own independent value, which sometimes conflicts with that of individuals. Most people would agree that on certain occasions this is so. For example, if the survival of the community is directly threatened, as in war or national disaster, most people would agree that individual liberties may rightly be curtailed. The great political question is what the precise balance of values should be. Particular theorists have their own priorities among the great values, but these various orderings are not universally shared. The conflict between positive and negative liberty, and the tension between society and the individual, have given rise to the permanent ideological divisions that characterize modern democratic societies.

Modern Liberalism

Liberalism was born a twin. On one side were Continental liberals (to use labels of convenience) who favoured the romantic freedom of individuality – spontaneity, self-expression, and the wilful breaking of traditional normative bonds. Self-creativity required the removal of constraints, whether those of society or of one's given nature. For these romantic liberals, uniqueness was the highest achievement. The everyday economic pursuits of unliberated individuals, and the social system that rewarded them, were, at best, a hindrance to true freedom and, at worst, a source of moral degradation.

On the other side were Anglo-American liberals, for whom freedom remained closer to the negative notion of independence from outside interference. These classical liberals, or negative libertarians, saw the ordinary pursuits of individuals as legitimate and even exemplary. Material acquisition and success in one's work were signs of a life well lived. Inequalities of outcome were corollaries of personal achievement, while competition was what enabled this ordinary mode of excellence. The proper ends of life were neither mysterious nor distant but could be found in the pursuit of ordinary wants and needs. The success of the 'self-made man' was economic rather than artistic because his desires were understood as natural and commonplace.

Today the rough geographical distinction between liberals, between the European Continent and English-speaking nations, has diminished. The ideas and values of democracy are international, but the division between left-liberals and right-liberals remains. Both sides retain the ideal of the self-directed individual, but they disagree about whether one's ends are given or are self-created. While individualism remains a synthetic ideal combining positive and negative freedom, the priority of liberties is contentious. Neither side denies the value of either kind of freedom, but each defines them in ways that accord with its own priorities. Right-liberals believe in a form of self-creation but see its apotheosis in entrepreneurial success and economic competition. Left-liberals believe that external constraints are a threat to freedom but see human nature and the social system as the first obstacles to be overcome.

The central idea of modern liberalism is individualism, the freedom of each of us to live the life we wish within the boundaries necessary to ensure the equal freedom of our fellows. Self-creative power, the essence of positive liberty, is sometimes mistaken for individualism,[31] but this is a partial truth at best. As a political theory, individualism must also show that one person's power should not interfere with another's. In the words of a prominent negative libertarian, it must also include 'side-constraints.'[32] Liberalism, with its individualistic core, is a mixture of positive and negative liberty, power and security together. Focusing on the former alone, as romantics might do, is not individualism but egoism. The latter might be turned into a political theory, such as that of Max Stirner or Nietzsche, but not a liberal one.[33]

Modern liberalism is a theory of personal power, limited only by respect for one's neighbour's inviolability. Therein lies the appeal of Rawls's first principle: 'Each person is to have an equal right to the most extensive total system of equal basic liberties compatible with a similar system of liberty for all.'[34] Rawls's originality was in returning to the old contractarian tradition, but with the newer secular idea of the person outlined by Humboldt and Mill. The difference may be seen in Rawls's conception of liberty as compared to Locke's.

For Locke, our ends were given by our nature; for Rawls, they were indeterminate. Thus Rawls would have his contractors come to the original position without knowledge of the substance of their own ends. In Rawls's terms, the contractors in the original position would know they had a conception of the good but would not know what that conception was. The original contractors would seek only to create a framework for the free pursuit of their ends, whatever they turned out to be. In this sense, the right to pursue one's ends came before knowledge of one's ends, so the right should be prior to the good. Where Hobbes's and Locke's contractarianism was justified by the content of God-given ends, Rawls's was founded on the free pursuit of whatever ends a person might have.

Rawls accepted the Kantian idea of autonomy, which he properly attributed to Rousseau: 'Kant's main aim is to deepen and justify Rousseau's idea that liberty is acting in accordance to a law that we give to ourselves.'[35] However, Rawls was not concerned with the content of the particular ends that each person chose; rather, he wanted to correct a deficiency in Kant, identified by Henry Sidgwick, that the universalizability of self-given laws is insufficient to found morality, since a thoroughly bad person may also be consistent. Bad laws can be universalized, or made categorical, without logical contradiction, as in the imperative, 'Kill the sick.' The contractarian argument answered this problem, according to Rawls, not by determining the proper ends of life but by providing a regulatory framework for whatever ends humans chose. In this way, he sought to turn autonomy, or self-rule, away from the self-interested egoism of romanticism and towards the orderly society of liberal individualism. As Rawls put it, borrowing Kant's terminology, 'Liberty in adopting a conception of the good is limited only by principles that are deduced from a doctrine which imposes no prior constraints on these conceptions ... The parties qua noumenal selves have complete freedom to choose whatever principles they wish; but they also have a desire to express their nature as rational and equal members of the intelligible realm with precisely this liberty to choose.'[36] Positive liberty, the freedom to determine one's own ends, was to be limited by the equal liberty of one's fellows.

Rawls was explicit that freedom involved both negative and positive liberty centred in the individual: 'Liberty can always be explained by reference to three items: the agents who are free, the restrictions or limitations which they are free from, and what it is that they are free to do or not to do.'[37] In this view, the statement 'Lincoln freed the slaves' is inadequate because the early emancipators did not also provide for the positive liberty of ex-slaves. Much of the modern Civil Rights Movement is an attempt by left-liberals to correct Lincoln's deficiency.

If liberalism is an attempt to balance both kinds of freedom, then particular liberals often lean towards one side or the other. As noted, Robert Nozick stressed the negative liberty of side-constraints. Similarly, he favoured a temporal view of distributive justice, comparing historical theories to 'current time-slice principles' – process versus status.[38] By contrast, Ronald Dworkin emphasized the romantic side. His liberalism is about individual power. He lamented that liberals had lost sight of the central principle which should be to 'improve the power of citizens, judged one by one, to lead the lives each thinks best for himself or herself.' Instead of the side-constraints of negative liberty, for Dworkin, the power of each individual was constrained by equality of resources, which he made the second principle of liberalism.[39] Egalitarian redistribution of resources does the work for Dworkin that side-constraints did for Nozick: it ensures that empowered individuals can live together. Dworkin, as a liberal individualist, retained a version of negative liberty in his prohibition against external preferences – 'preferences about what others should do or have' – but only as instrumental to the goal of equality.[40] With this emphasis, his liberalism became economistic, concentrating on monetary redistribution requiring a powerful state. Thus, he often sounds like a socialist in liberal clothing. This is not accidental. His egalitarianism-of-power, we will see, is essentially socialistic, yet his individualism is purely liberal. Dworkin is a liberal leaning against a shared fence, chatting with his socialist neighbours about the power of self-rule. They agree amiably about the romantic goal of autotelic power, but they differ about the form it should take, whether it should be vested in the individual or in the group.

Meanwhile Nozick, on the other side of the liberals' common ground, is leaning against a shared fence and chatting with his conservative neighbours about negative liberty. Nozick retained something of the positive notion of liberty, as in his parable of the 'experience machine,' and in his suggestions about the meaningfulness of life.[41] So he, too, is a liberal and an individualist. Nevertheless, in his best-known book, Nozick's emphasis was libertarian rather than romantic. And so he seemed comfortable chatting with conservatives about the value of telic security, even while disagreeing about its proper location; that is, whether our natural (or traditional or God-given) ends are properly embodied in the individual or in evolved social institutions.

Liberalism, then, can be understood as the synthesis of two great ideals: power and security. Liberals move from these essential freedoms to the idealization of rights, again both positive and negative. Implied in their ideal is the rejection of the holistic ideal of community, at least as an entity whose value may sometimes legitimately conflict with those of individuals. This focus has not changed much since Bentham. For example, according to Will Kymlicka: 'Groups have no moral claim to well-being independently of their members – groups just aren't the right sort of beings to have moral status.'[42] Kymlicka's version of belonging is instrumental, valuable not for its own sake but as a means to one's own ends. For him, if we were to recognize the value of community, 'The primary good being recognized is the cultural community as a context of choice, not the character of the community or its traditional ways of life, which people are free to endorse or reject.'[43] At the same time, one's community is supposed to provide 'a constitutive part of who [a] person is. Cultural membership affects our very sense of personal identity and capacity.'[44] But by thinning out the inherent value of community, as liberals like Kymlicka are given to do, the power of community to confer value on its members must proportionately be lessened. From a thing of little value can little value come. If the ultimate source of value is the individual, then it must be the members who confer value upon the community, not the other way around. The value of belonging cannot be derived from the choice to belong. For liberals, the source of value is the individual not the community. Attempts to have it both ways must fail.

Similarly, liberalism cannot include collective rights, properly understood not as rights some individuals have by virtue of their ascriptive characteristics but as the right of the group to make demands on its individual members, or on other groups and individuals, for the good of the group. The coercion of individuals is anathema to liberals. Individuals always come first.

That the ideal of belonging legitimately might limit individual freedom, and justify some level of coercion, is simply beyond the liberal ken. If to belong in a strong sense – that is, in more than a voluntaristic or conditional way – is to limit one's personal autonomy, then liberals must regard belonging with suspicion. Better to deny the authenticity of the ideal than to concede the authority that belonging entails. For liberals, alienation and atomism are better than coercion. This priority does not mean that liberalism is a false ideal. If liberalism is alienating, it nonetheless remains among the true ideologies of our day, and its legitimacy is something that every modern citizen can appreciate. If liberalism is not the perfect answer to our political problems, it is because our values are more complex than any single synthesis can accommodate.

The priority that liberalism gives to the individual is not arbitrary, and its conflict with the ideal of community is not a simple omission; rather, its deficiencies follow from the fact of value pluralism. Still, liberalism is the dominant ideology of our age, and its appeal is immediate and forceful. Competing ideologies, by contrast, struggle for acceptance. More interesting than whether liberalism is legitimate is the question: Might we not have good historical reasons for our liberal bias, even with its corollaries of atomism and alienation? Pluralism tells us that other ideologies may have their own legitimate bases, but might it not still be true that historical events have given us good reasons for the dominance of liberalism?

Still, the advantage that liberalism has in the modern age does not mean that it can be stretched beyond its proper meaning. Liberals are a coalition, and if some among them search for new directions, then the risk is that others will defect. For example, the synthesis of autotelic power and telic security may be summarized in the belief that humans individually own their own powers and capacities. It may tempt some modern liberals, in their search for equality among free individuals, to deny the core idea of the self-ownership of one's own powers. They may claim that we do not deserve the fruits of our own talents. By recognizing the self-ownership of one's autotelic power as central to liberalism, we can see why disclaiming the benefits from our own talents seems so counter-intuitive. (Are there many left-liberal academics who have refused all merit increases or all the extra royalties from a successful book?) Our talents, according to the liberal view of the person, are essential to who we are, to our dignity as self-animated modern beings. To deny this is to offend against both cardinal values of liberalism, undermining both the power and the security of the person. For some liberals, ownership is a moral notion, implying responsibility as well as benefit. If we do not deserve one, then we do not deserve the other. Since we are responsible for the effect of our talents, we also deserve their benefit. If the pull of political discourse has led a few liberals to search for a more substantive egalitarianism, at some point they will leave the majority of liberals behind.

In whatever direction the winds of modern politics blow, liberalism will remain with us. The meaning of political thought is in the pattern of climate, not in the occasional tempest. The modern idea of the free person has ancient sources, including beliefs about the good, about the immortality of the soul, and about reason as that which distinguishes humans from animals.

These ideas, and others throughout history, continuously came up against each other in different combinations and varying interpretations. The process of contestation will continue, but every new idea has its antecedents. No thinker works alone, and each generation of thought begins with the materials it is given. Today, the values of liberalism are among our oldest ideals and have permanent roots in the culture of democracy.

If democracy is about the rule of the people, and if the people see themselves as individuals first, then liberalism has a central place in democracy. Those who desire a greater sense of community in politics, including theorists of democracy who see it as solidarity, will resist this conclusion. The theory of democracy to be offered here, based on the permanence of value conflict, will try to show the place of individualists and communalists as being that of contestants in a permanent, irresolvable argument. This will not be an answer that solidarity democrats will like. For them, the goal of evaluative unity must be conceptually real, even if it is impossible to reach in practice. Without some form of evaluative consensus, solidarity is value-empty. Solidarity democrats must resist deep pluralism just as they resist liberalism. For them, individualism is a theory about the boundaries among people, as is the conflictual theory of democracy.

However, the conflictual theory of democracy, whatever its faults from the point of view of solidarity, is not a theory of individualism; rather, it is about the tendency of citizens throughout history and across cultures to disagree about the nature of the good society. Liberalism is only one vision of how we should live together. Two others, conservatism and socialism, will be surveyed in the next pair of chapters. Each has a place within modern democracy, and each has its adherents and opponents. Modern democracy is about the irresolvable conflicts among them.

6
Conservatism and the Temporal Order

From the point of view of those who see alienation and atomism as the hallmarks of modernity, the dominance of liberalism is a problem. Their goal is to find a more meaningful foundation for the value of social belonging. Freedom of choice is insufficient for this purpose: it is either self-extinguishing, if choice implies real commitment, or it trivializes the value of the thing chosen, if choices can be rescinded on a whim. If one's community is to become a source of value, and if belonging is to provide a sense of identity, then the individual must make some degree of commitment to the authority of the group. The value of community, the sense of belonging to something greater than oneself, can be conveyed only upon those who give up some portion of their autonomy to it. For individuals who want to remain free in the positive sense, who are their own source of value, belonging does not fulfill this role. The values of community and individual autonomy vary inversely: to the extent that the commitment to belong can be revoked at will, to the same extent does belonging become diminished as a source of value. The decision to leave your cultural group is difficult if that group has given you value. The decision to leave a mail-order book club can be made with perfect freedom because your value is not derived from it. Whichever one decides is more important, individual autonomy or communal belonging, they are values that conflict with each other. (We may agree that the right of exit, the freedom to leave one's community, is necessary as a 'safety valve' against tyranny, but the threshold at which it should be opened will depend on one's priorities among competing values.) For many people, personal autonomy is always more important than the value of belonging; for others, liberalism is unsatisfactory.

One of the manifestations of the unhappiness of non-liberals is the desire of some political theorists to reassert the definition of democracy as a collective, progressive ideal. The next chapter will trace the history of that idea, but this one will focus on another form of the politics of belonging. Conservatives see the evolved social order as the basis of the good society.

For progressives, the conservative ideal is beyond the pale, an atavism at best, an outright social evil at worst. Positive liberty is an ascendant value in the community of intellectuals, whose self-creative talents favour this form of liberation. In the academic community, for example, whose institutional mission is to foster self-development, a belief in positive liberty is practically a prerequisite. Conservatives deny the priority of positive liberty, and so they often stand against the modern current of scholarship. Socialists swim across the flow, but their views may be tolerated as merely wrong. The dislike of conservatives goes deeper.

Yet, with each generation, some political thinkers and many citizens adhere to the values of conservatism. For them, the sense of belonging comes with the recognition of supra-individualistic rules and roles. To derive a sense of identity from the social order is to reject the belief that one creates one's own ends. One's identity is given, not self-created. Freedom of the latter kind, to conservatives, is anti-social, destructive of the social order that gives life its meaning. The institutions of society have their own settled purpose, as given by nature, by tradition, or by God. These institutions may evolve by their own momentum, but 'social engineering,' the reform of society by political will, is viewed by conservatives with suspicion. For them, social institutions, like the rules and roles that define our lives, must be respected as given.

If liberalism took the values of self-ownership and negative liberty, and merged them with Continental ideas about individuality and uniqueness, another tradition took negative liberty in the opposite direction, towards a theory of human similarity and social cohesion. These were the thinkers of the Scottish Enlightenment, for whom morality was based on human sympathy. Human nature, they argued, is such that each person has similar ends, defined by the passions, so that we are all capable of vicariously feeling the passions of our fellows. The assumption that human ends are given by human nature, and are thus essentially similar in each person, led to a theory of social unity and order. These themes, in turn, led to the ideas of the best known of the originators of modern conservatism, Edmund Burke. In his view, society was a temporal unity, just as personal identity was a temporal unity for Locke. The source of belonging and self-understanding was one's role in the social and temporal order. Cultural self-understandings were kept alive over time through the memories and habits passed between generations. The focus on learning and communication in this tradition was the contribution of Scottish thinkers like David Hume, who turned empiricism towards an understanding of cultural knowledge.

Hobbes and Locke had provided a natural teleology of ordinary life. The telos of human nature was in the process of pursuing a succession of ordinary ends – the pursuit of happiness. A teleological theory of the good is distinctive in its union of the normative and the descriptive. The severing of 'ought' from 'is' occurred within another tradition – one in which the source of goodness, the human will, was seen as separate from the natural order. In the latter theory, the good is exogenously created: it is something added to, and thus distinct from, the existing world. By contrast, the natural teleologists of empiricism saw goodness as already existing in the process of life. It could be perverted through immoderation or confusion about one's best interests, but its source was in our nature. Today, among philosophers in the tradition after Kant, the moral content of empiricism has not been widely recognized; for the theory's originators, the good was in the fact of human nature. The contribution of conservatives was to point out that morality was a social idea that developed over time to meet the given needs of human nature. Human nature is given, but moral behaviour is learned.

The empiricist tradition, from Hobbes to Locke to Hume, saw the play of nature upon the passions as the motive force of life. The ends of life were given by human nature, and freedom was participation in the flow of life's events. In Hobbes and Locke, reason had a moderating, or regulative, effect on the passions, allowing us to reflect and choose among competing ends. It also provided knowledge of the world that was necessary for their successful achievement. Hume made the instrumental role of reason explicit, arguing famously: 'Reason is, and ought only to be the slave of the passions, and can never pretend to any other office than to serve and obey them ... 'Tis not contrary to reason to prefer the destruction of the whole world to the scratching of my finger.'[1] He was being provocative here, but his argument followed from the empiricist understanding of human nature.

However, the empiricist acceptance of human nature as given seemed to imply licentiousness rather than moral liberty. This was the trend in English thought that Burke would critically summarize: 'The last age had exhausted all its powers in giving a grace and nobleness to our appetites, and in raising them into higher class and order than seemed justly to belong to them.'[2] A tradition that exalted the passions too much had no defence, Burke continued, against the romantic appeal of immoralists like Rousseau. England, he worried, seemed vulnerable to the French export of revolution, in morals as in politics. The corrective to this licentious tendency was to be found in the conventional order that flowed from human nature but that naturally evolved to serve our social ends.

After Hobbes and Locke, empiricism branched in one direction towards utilitarianism and in another towards a theory of common life. The latter was based on sympathy among persons of similar nature, who were given to react in the same way to the same stimuli. Before Smith and Hume, this idea had been developed by empiricists like Francis Hutcheson, who took up the concept of a moral sense, which was the source of our ideas of morality.

This term had originated with Locke's own student, the third earl of Shaftesbury. Like Locke, Shaftesbury argued against Hobbes's conception of the amorality of the state of nature, asserting instead that people were naturally moral. But he also wanted to promote Lockean tolerance against religiously enforced moralism. With regard to the foundation of morality, he wanted to find a middle way between Hobbesian egoism and religious dogma. His answer, following the empiricist doctrine that all knowledge originated as sensation, was that moral knowledge, too, began in this way. The mind, as a tabula rasa, included no innate idea of morality. However, Shaftesbury argued that human nature included an affection for virtue as such, even though human actions were not always virtuous. In his moral psychology, Hobbes had neglected the passions for sociability, fellow-feeling, and the public good. Morality was based neither on self-interest nor on religion but on the sociable passions. Although a Deist, his goal was to show that morality was independent of religious beliefs. He taught that virtue, the pursuit of the common interest, produces a better kind of pleasure than do our more selfish inclinations.

Hutcheson followed Shaftesbury in arguing against self-interest as the basis of morality; rather, disinterested benevolence was the necessary foundation of morals. Morality was based on the pleasure we experience upon becoming aware of virtuous activity. This sensation is analogous to the pleasurable feelings that arise when we perceive an object of beauty. The moral sense is the universal faculty by which we approve of benevolent activity, just as the aesthetic sense is the basis of approval of beauty. Rather than being rooted in self-interest, benevolence aims at the creation of happiness in others. The dictum made famous by Bentham, that morality should be founded on 'the greatest happiness for the greatest number,' was borrowed from Hutcheson's *Inquiry Concerning Moral Good and Evil* (1720). This followed from the way God had made us, so as to be naturally benevolent, concerned with the public interest rather than self-interest alone. Thus Hutcheson, unlike Shaftesbury, appealed in the end to a divine justification for morality.

The utilitarians took the empiricist conflation of goodness with pleasure in the direction of liberal individualism and created a social theory based on the aggregated happiness of all. By contrast, the thinkers of the 'moral sense' school sought a theory of deeper social cohesion. While a liberal might see social unity as a threat to the free development of the individual, as did Mill in *On Liberty*, the philosophers of the Scottish Enlightenment tended to see society as a source of goodness rather than oppression. For them, the problem was not to ensure the development of the individual but to regulate the natural, egoistic passions. The twin beliefs – that a structured society is essential to human well-being and that morality is necessary to regulate the passions – were combined by Hume in the idea of morality as cultural knowledge.

Hume and the Regulation of the Passions

Empiricism had begun with the search for a more naturalistic cosmology. God was the First Cause in the natural process of causality, which thereafter carried on without the necessity of divine intervention. With the secularizing trend of modernity, the empiricist tradition in the eighteenth century cast off even this more distant religious grounding, with the result that a new foundation for morality was needed. This was the role that the moral sense came to fill. However, many of the self-interested passions were stronger than the sociable feelings. Many of the passions were purely selfish, and these were felt with particular force in an uncivilized soul. Natural humanity was not naturally good. How did the simple, natural feelings of sympathy and benevolence become institutionalized into the complex rules and mores of self-governing civil society? The contribution of Hume was to argue that moral behaviour was learned. Justice was conventional, a social institution necessary to protect and promote our given ends. Having grown from natural human interactions, these conventions and institutions themselves came to be recognized as morally good.

With Hume and the Scottish Enlightenment, empiricism became a social science. The central idea of empiricism was in the corollary notions of time, motion, inertia, and causation. For Locke, the causal order was the source of knowledge and goodness together. Hume's move was to redefine causation as custom. Social custom took the place that physical causation had had for original empiricists. Our ideas are not simply caused by sensual forces; rather, we make inferences based on repeated experiences. How do we know, when one billiard ball strikes another, that the second will be caused to move? It is only because we have seen the same sequence before. Every time such a collision occurs, the first ball changes velocity and the second ball begins its motion. Our explanation for these events is based only an induction from repeated observations. According to Hume, 'All inferences from experience, therefore, are effects of custom, not of reasoning.'[3] We have no proof that the future will be like the past – except that it has been, in the past. Since the logic of induction rests on a tautology, our inferences about force and inertia are not self-evidently true; rather, they are learned and passed on. Causation is a customary notion. This did not mean it was false – Hume believed causation was a fact without which we cannot live[4] – but only that its genesis was customary. For Hume, all of our complex ideas are learned over time. If the explanatory stories we tell about the world are able to pass the test of common sense among those who understand them, then they enter the cultural storehouse of our customary knowledge. Hume concluded: 'Custom, then, is the great guide of human life.'[5]

Hume was a member of the school of natural teleology, but he took it in a more social, less atomistic direction. The animating force of life was given in the self-evident passions, and so the original force of morality must be located there as well. While he is famous for a short passage in which he suggests the distinction between 'ought' and 'is,' his was not a dichotomy of facts and values; rather, his distinction was between facts inferred by reason and those that belonged to the passions of human nature. You will be unable to find, he argued, the source of virtue or vice until you consult your own sentiments: 'Take any action alow'd to be vicious: Wilful murder, for instance. In which-ever way you take it, you find only certain passions ... Here is a matter of fact, but 'tis the object of feeling, not reason. It lies in yourself, not in the object.'[6] For Hume, reason could discover objective facts, but to find the force of morality, we must look to the facts of our subjective nature.

However, if the impetus towards morality was in our natural affections, for Hume moral knowledge was learned. Morality is more than simple affection for our fellow creatures (although this feeling is its necessary precondition); rather, it is a complex understanding of how to live together. In short, morality is the knowledge of a culture carried in the habits and mores of society as it slowly develops. Conventional knowledge and evolved institutions, such as the rules of justice that protected property, represented the good order of society as it developed into civility. Civilization, for Hume, was the common knowledge of a society concerning the proper ways for its members to interact. Metaphysical certitude was not available in these matters. All we have are our ideas, which develop gradually in time. These ideas are what allow us to live in society. The source of civility was in the customs and mores by which we learn to attenuate our selfish passions. Hume retained the belief that human nature was given, and he tried to show how social institutions would naturally grow from that basis. His contribution, by which he founded modern conservatism, was to go from the process of human nature to the natural process of society towards civility.

Conservatism is distinctive in its focus on the temporal rootedness of society. Other traditions define the good in their own way. In summary, socialists see the good as created by the political will of society, left-liberals see it as created by each individual, and right-liberals see it in the natural pursuits of individuals. For conservatives, the good is in the movement of society towards civility, as embodied in the inherited institutions that represent a culture's knowledge. The evolved institutions of society are legitimate because they represent, protect, and facilitate the given telos of our social nature. While general principles may be acted upon if they are consistent with the natural order, social institutions, as a rule, should be taken as given. Conservatism is not merely an emotional attachment to the status quo, since by that criterion socialists or welfare-state liberals are sometimes conservative. A suspicion of wilful change is part of conservatism, but it is also a teleology centred in society, a hope for the gradual movement of society towards moral betterment. While progressive thinkers discount this view as an apologia for social inertia, others see the legacy of social order as a source of meaning and goodness. In these contending visions, the contest of democracy goes on.

Hume's morality (based on the natural sociability of individuals) and his conventional theory of knowledge were combined into a vision of social unity in time. Society was united in two ways: laterally among persons and longitudinally across time. First, the similarity of human nature in each person led to a morality of sympathy, which unites individuals into society. Second, the cultural knowledge embedded in social institutions represents the unity of society over time. Hume's vision was nicely summarized by Donald Livingston: 'The moral world is a narrative unity of ancestors, contemporaries, and posterity ... Keep [rationalism] at bay; discover through historical research the deep narrative order of which one is a part; work for the stability and improvement of this order, but be skeptical and diffident about the significance of one's efforts at reform or preservation.'[7]

As an avowed empiricist, Hume claimed that his tradition had produced great improvements in philosophy.[8] Among these thinkers, morality was experiential, but a thoroughgoing empiricist should hesitate to claim a divine source for morality, since God was not directly evident to the senses; instead, the tenets of empiricism suggest we should rely on what we can know, whether or not God made us to have such knowledge. What we self-evidently know about ourselves is that we have certain feelings of desire and aversion. Hume's attempt was to show how these passions, while privately felt and thus inclined to produce self-interestedness, could give rise to the fellow-feeling and impartiality that morality required. His answer was that the passions were similar in all persons, which allowed feelings of sympathy naturally to arise. Social customs may vary across cultures, but human nature was the same everywhere.

The passions in each soul were identical, so the forces that played upon one had the same causal effect on each other. Humans were like similarly tuned musical strings: a note played on one would naturally resonate on its neighbours. 'The minds of all men are similar in their feelings and operations ... As in strings equally wound up, the motion of one communicates itself to the rest; so all the affections readily pass from one person to another, and beget correspondent movements in every human creature. When I see the effects of passion in the voice and gesture of any person, my mind immediately passes from these effects to their causes, and forms such a lively idea of the passion, as is presently converted into the passion itself.'[9]

Sympathy is based on a real physical process of resonance because the emotional mechanism of each person is the same.

But even as the strong natural force of sympathy gave rise to sociability, human nature is such that proximate forces move us more powerfully than distant ones. The passions everywhere were similar, yet the play of emotions took place within each person. Thus, we each have a natural tendency to be self-interested and to be partial towards those who are nearest to us. Hume had seemed to explain how people could be both sociable and selfish at once, but the customs and mores of civility had a further source. Sympathy could explain the power of benevolence, which conveyed feelings of approval towards regulatory social institutions once they had arisen. Those institutions that serve our nature come to be loved, but how did they arise in the first place? Hume observed that some virtues were natural, arising from pleasurable passions. All pleasures were not equal, however, and moral feelings must arise from disinterested rather than self-interested motives. Furthermore, moral feelings were transformative, creating feelings of love and pride for virtuous activities, and these became passions with their own force. Morality thus had a secondary force, involving love and hate, pride and humility. These additional feelings were learned. Besides the natural passions, which were given by human nature, there arose secondary passions that were artificial in that they were acquired by experience. The results of social learning were what Burke would later call our second nature. By a natural process, beginning with our given propensities and reinforced by long experience, morality could arise as conventional.

Justice was a conventional institution of this sort, which had both natural and artificial sources. Hume described it as 'an artifice or contrivance, which arises from the circumstances and necessities of mankind.'[10] It had additional special features. First, it was systemic, operating for the good of the whole society rather than for particular persons. What was just for a single person could be contrary to the interests of the whole. And while people had a natural sympathy for those with whom they came directly into contact, they had no natural love for humanity as a single whole. This led to the second consideration, that social institutions, like those required for justice, could not have arisen by deliberate action. As Hume's famous colleague would have put it, the hand that guided their formation was invisible to the actors involved.

Justice, for Hume, could be thought of as a coordination problem. A system was needed by which self-interested persons could come to follow common rules. The overriding interest that each person had in society was for 'security and protection, which we enjoy in political society, and which we can never attain, when perfectly free and independent.'[11] Political society was initially formed in steps: First, the rules of property, trade, and contract were discovered as necessary to meet the basic needs of life. Second, the moral goodness of these laws of nature (as Hume called them) came to be felt as a natural passion. This original system of natural laws became further generalized into the broader system of justice, providing additional rules of conduct. Finally, a government was formed to administer the evolved system of justice. These institutions served the passions and were artificial and conventional, but they were not rationally planned. The passions became regulated not by the greater authority of reason but by a system that naturally evolved to meet their demands. Thus justice for Hume had two foundations, self-interest and an acquired sense of morality. The first leads to initial levels of cooperation that are necessary to meet the needs of life, and the second arises as the rules of cooperation are recognized as being in everyone's interest. He concluded, 'After that interest is once establish'd and acknowledg'd, the sense of morality in the observance of these rules follows *naturally*, and of itself; tho' 'tis certain, that it is also augmented by a new *artifice*, and that the public instructions of politicians, and the private education of parents, contribute to the giving us a sense of honour and duty in the strict regulation of our actions.'[12] The rules of morality, once learned by a culture, must be passed on to each new generation. In this way, our cultural knowledge can live on.

Hume sought to correct the rationalistic strain in Lockean empiricism, according to which the unaided mind alone could acquire its ideas through a private mechanical process. One might say that Hume wanted to relieve Locke of his Cartesian loneliness. To do so, he showed that we are not monads, each a separate blank slate. The forces that wrote on one, by the mechanism of sympathy, would write upon all those with whom one is in communication. The similarity of human beings meant that each of us could learn from the other; among our most important conventions is a common language. Our ideas do not come from private sense data alone but are given by our culture. Our best, most complex ideas, about who we are and how we should live together, are customary and were passed to us from previous generations. In short, Hume brought to Lockean empiricism the new eighteenth-century idea of culture. The result was the idea that the telos of life came from the temporal order of one's culture. This was the central theme of the Scottish Enlightenment, in which modern conservatism was born.

Smith and the System of Natural Liberty

At the heart of Smith's *Wealth of Nations* is a simple argument. Under certain conditions, civility and productivity are mutually reinforcing. Civility represents the order of society, a hierarchy necessary for the distribution and production of wealth. As civility develops, society becomes more orderly. This order encourages productivity by creating interdependence and cooperation. Through the division of labour, productivity flourishes and society prospers, both in its wealth and in its cultural refinement. The more civil a society, the more orderly and wealthy it can become.

A corollary of Smith's system of natural liberty is that each stage of social and economic development has its appropriate mores, habits, and liberties. The morality of workers was simple and somewhat austere, as appropriate to their place in the productive order; that of the refined classes was more licentious, less disciplined. Similarly, the educational needs of the sexes varied according to their social roles – each to his or her given place. Religion was of interest as an institution of order. Some religious practices had a useful function in the progress towards civility, as did certain republican virtues. Without the institutions of social order, the processes of civility and productivity would fail. The machinery of the system of natural liberty would break down.

As long as the evolved level of civility and order is maintained, natural liberty can prevail. Under such a system, the sovereign need only attend to the duties of public defence, civil and criminal justice, and the maintenance of those public works that are to the general advantage of society.[13] Each of these duties is derived from the requirement that the evolved social order must be maintained because it is the essential precondition of the system of natural liberty.

Smith's philosophy centred morality in everyday human life. Happiness was in one's natural activity. In this he agreed with Locke. People do, they make; they are industrious. However, Smith recast the individualistic Lockean pursuit of happiness as a social process. The *Wealth of Nations* presented a naturalistic account of development through the material improvement not of individuals but of societies as a whole. He began by identifying the source of wealth in the division of labour, which, in turn, is based on the natural propensity to exchange. Individuals are by nature industrious, but they are also social. They naturally want to trade what they have made of their labour. The source of value is in labour, but the source of collective enrichment is in exchange. Atomistic self-reliance is eliminated through the division of labour, as workers specialize their skills and exchange their products. Productivity increases, and society grows together.

This was the vision that appealed so strongly to Marx – progress as collective productivity. But Smith's notion of social unity was different from that of Marx. According to Marxism, human nature would be transformed by the socializing process of unification. For Smith, human nature was a constant, the essential mechanism underlying the entire system. One could no more revoke human nature and still have a functioning society than one could repeal the laws of physics and still have a functioning universe. For Marx, following the tradition of positive liberty, the mutability of human nature was a foundational belief; for Smith, following the empiricist tradition of negative liberty, human nature was given. Marx thought the proletariat would outgrow the social order. For Smith, social order remained the prerequisite for productive freedom and unity.

The source of social order was also the subject of Smith's moral theory. His *Theory of Moral Sentiments* followed Hume in taking up the conception of morality as a problem of coordination among persons with given passions. Smith rejected the teaching of Hutcheson (under whom he had studied), who argued that we have a specific moral sense; rather, he argued that the idea of sympathy among common people was sufficient to produce moral sentiments. Because it is the same in each person, the mechanism of sensation produces feelings of sympathy. This occurs because the passions – the propensities of human nature to react to sensual stimuli in given ways – are common to all. According to the theory Smith took from Hume, these natural forces are strongest within each person, but the same forces will also resonate naturally within the soul of one's neighbour. This resonance was not just a colourful metaphor but a central idea of empiricist psychology.

Smith added that this natural resonance of feeling would occur most easily to one who was not already vibrating to a private tune. This was his idea of the impartial spectator – one who is not preoccupied by pre-existing feelings and who is, therefore, the best judge of virtuous action. We each carry within us the imaginative capability to be impartial in this way, and so we are capable of moral behaviour.

Certain virtues disposed people to be more sympathetic and, therefore, more sociable. Among these virtues were many that were learned. These conventions contributed to social unity. Smith claimed that there were two categories of virtue: those that disposed us towards the acceptance of our commonality with our fellows and those that led us to restrain our passions. Society required both cohesion and restraint in order to encourage the communicative process of sympathy. Commonality provided fellow-feeling, while self-command encouraged a sense of proportionality. Those passions indulged in too strongly or felt too weakly (as inappropriate or out of proportion to the events that caused them) would not find the sympathy of one's fellows. Inappropriate feelings were difficult to sympathize with, because their cause was not in proportion to the effect. Similarly, immoderate feelings would not be felt in the same way by all persons, so they would not cause sympathy. Propriety and proportion were prerequisites to the natural passage of feelings between persons with similar propensities.

Amiability and self-command are the marks of an orderly, harmonious society. Thus Smith concluded: 'And hence it is, that to feel much for others and little for ourselves, that to restrain our selfish, and to indulge our benevolent affections, constitutes the perfection of human nature; and can alone produce among mankind that harmony of sentiments and passions in which consists their whole grace and propriety.'[14] If the empiricist tradition, once secularized, tended implicitly towards licentiousness by exalting the human appetites, then Smith's answer was to add to this tradition the Stoic virtue of self-control. But he did not advocate total Stoic self-abnegation in favour of the interests of others; rather, he sought to reconcile moral self-interest, including partiality towards one's loved ones, with the needs of a harmonious society.[15]

Moral sentiments are contingent on a judgment of merit. We sympathize with the gratitude we observe others to feel for meritorious actions towards them. Morality thus involves a double feeling of sympathy. In observing the interactions among our fellows, moral approval arises when we sympathize, on one hand, with the benefactor's motive as appropriate to the occasion, and, on the other, with the beneficiary's appropriate feeling of gratitude. Each of these judgments is predicated on the similarity of the passions among all parties – benefactor, beneficiary, and observer – as the necessary precondition of sympathy. Morality based on sympathy is inherently judgmental of the appropriateness of the feelings and motives of others.

For Smith, merit was about just deserts, and propriety was about the appropriateness of emotions and motivations. When harmonized in a well-ordered society, good actions produced just results. The virtues necessary to prosperity were those that promoted success in business: industriousness, prudence, and circumspection. Similarly, the virtues of truthfulness, justice, and humanitarianism naturally were rewarded by the confidence and esteem of one's fellows. Although these rewards occasionally failed, nature often guided human society towards a distribution based on merit and just deserts.[16]

For Smith, this concordance of virtue and reward seemed better harmonized among commoners than in higher society, and so he became the champion of bourgeois virtues:

> In the middling and inferior stations of life, the road to virtue and that to fortune ... are, happily in most cases, very nearly the same. In all the middling and inferior professions, real and solid professional abilities, joined to prudent, just, firm, and temperate conduct, can very seldom fail of success ... The success of such people, too, almost always depends upon the favour and good opinion of their neighbours and equals; and without a tolerably regular conduct these can very seldom be obtained ... In such situations, therefore, we may generally expect a considerable degree of virtue ... In the superior stations of life the case is unhappily not always the same. In the courts of princes, in the drawing-rooms of the great, where success and preferment depend, not upon the esteem of intelligent and well-informed equals, but upon the fanciful and foolish favour of ignorant, presumptuous, and proud superiors; flattery and falsehood too often prevail over merit and abilities.[17]

Smith believed that a society based on privilege and favour rather than on merit and just desert would not be one that could continue without authoritarian intervention. He favoured the 'middle class' virtues of temperance and industriousness as being suitable to a naturally harmonious, well-ordered society. In such a society, the coordination problem of the passions could be solved by the invisible hand of virtuous self-interest; this famous phrase appeared in both of Smith's best known books.[18] Economic institutions, like those that Hume had described, did not arise and operate according to wilful design but, rather, evolved to meet the needs of the natural passions. The coordination problem could be solved, in morality as in economics, by the natural growth of institutions to serve the given ends of human nature.

If his idea of the good society required some level of equality among well-informed, sympathetic fellows, his theory did not lead to a classless society; rather, sympathy led to a desire for recognition, and this fuelled admiration towards those individuals who stood above the crowd. Following an observation of Hume, Smith argued that sympathy, far from being an egalitarian impulse, led to ambition and the distinctions of rank in society. The seeker of recognition would not desire to be lost in the egalitarian crowd. Except for the fallen and the philosophical few who had lost or given up the natural desire for the esteem of their fellows, the impulse of sympathy led to the love of advancement and distinction. This desire was the source of respect for, and emulation of, the wealthy and the great, as could be observed among the common folk. The phenomenon could not be explained by admiration for possessions themselves or by the unlikely possibility of reward but only by the given propensities of human nature. People seek recognition not in equality but in elevation.[19]

Smith believed in negative liberty but thought that the moral and economic processes of civility would coordinate free individuals. He was not an individualist but a social theorist, and his purpose was to establish that negative liberty could become systematic. His moral theory sought coordinating principles for the natural passions, while his economic theory aimed at harmonizing their productivity. The economic process of the market was natural, so the system itself was free in the negative sense: the free market would behave in its natural way as long as it was not wilfully obstructed. As an attribute of the market as a natural system, negative liberty came to be centred in the economy. This combination of naturalness and goodness – Smith's system of natural liberty based on the given telos of human nature – is precisely what defenders of positive liberty find objectionable about laissez-faire economics.

With its greatest philosopher, Hume, and its economic genius, Smith, the empiricist tradition was turned towards the study of culture. Challenges to the new ideas would come from an alternative tradition in Europe, which had culminated in the revolution in France. Among the loudest voices raised against those events was that of Burke, who called on the English tradition to resist contrary Continental ideas.

Burke's Temporal Conservatism

For Edmund Burke, society was a living whole, with a continuous existence across time. The good, for Burke, was centred in society as a natural process. Morality and economy were aspects of society as an extended entity in time and space. He was a lover not of the status quo, as such, but of the process from which it had arisen. Again: process, not status, was the essence of the empiricist teleology. Temporality, the natural flow of time, was its core concept. The good was what arose from this process; evil was what occurred when it was disturbed. While it began, with Locke, as a theory of personal morality, the early conservatives incorporated this teleology into a social theory. With his focus on social order not just among living individuals but across time, Burke was the first modern conservative politician.

Burke differed from other conservatives of his era. He was not the only counter-revolutionary to object to the events in France. The angry French writers, de Maistre and Bonald, reacted with anti-democratic, anti-liberal religious authoritarianism. Burke was different. His *Reflections* began as an answer to religious thinkers, including Richard Price and Joseph Priestley, who sermonized in celebration of the French Revolution. While religion had a place in his conservatism, it was not foundational. Moreover, he was not an authoritarian. In his own career, Burke was a Whig reformer who supported greater Irish legislative independence and the American Revolution. His objection to the French Revolution was aimed at its zeal for rationalistic change rather than at its advocacy of liberty. He felt that the French ideas were a perversion of true liberty, which depended on evolved social practices and institutions. The structure of society was foundational to liberty in two ways. Historically, it was the result of a long process of free interaction; politically, it was necessary to both regulate and coordinate the freedom of individuals.

Burke belonged to the school of Hume and Smith. As an active politician, his writing was typically more hortatory than analytical. Whatever their differences of style and interest, the family resemblance should be clear. To recapitulate, English political philosophy since Hobbes had been dominated by the idea of negative liberty as the free pursuit of one's given ends. The utilitarians would take this idea in a progressive, individualist direction, culminating in Mill's synthesis (following Humboldt) of negative and positive liberty. But other thinkers took the idea of the givenness-of-ends in the direction of social cohesion. Individuals were connected by the sympathy that naturally arose among persons with similar ends. Events that stimulated the natural passions would have the same effect on every person because human nature was everywhere the same. The sentiments of one person, if they were proportionate to their cause, would necessarily be felt by an observer, just as a note played on a string would naturally resonate on its similarly tuned neighbour. This resonance would occur most readily if the second string was not already playing its own tune, and so sympathy came most easily to an impartial spectator. Each of us has the imaginative capacity to be impartial in this way.

The Scottish Enlightenment had its own encyclopaedia. The *Encyclopaedia Britannica*, in its inaugural Edinburgh edition (1768-71), summarized the moral philosophy of this tradition:

> Man is admirably formed for particular social attachments and duties. There is a peculiar and strong propensity in his nature to be affected with the sentiments and dispositions of others. Men, like certain musical instruments, are set to each other, so that the vibrations or notes excited in one raise correspondent notes and vibrations in the others. The impulses of pleasure or pain, joy or sorrow, made on one mind are by an instantaneous sympathy of nature communicated to some degree in all, especially when hearts are in union of kindness. The joy that vibrates in one communicates to the other also. All passions, but especially those of the social kind, are contagious, and when the passions of one man mingle with those of another, they increase and multiply prodigiously.[20]

This school of thinkers emphasized the unplanned evolution of institutions as necessary to coordinating and regulating the natural passions. This institutional evolution was itself natural, so human nature became a process of the social whole. Social cohesion resulted from the mutual recognition of the goals towards which people naturally strove, but the forces of self-interest also came into play. People were made naturally sociable by the similarity of their passions, yet the passions played most strongly within each human breast. Morality was rooted in our common sense (read literally) but sympathy must be augmented by an acquired sense of justice. Civilization had to be learned. As improvements occurred in the institutions of society that favoured the given pursuits of human nature, people would learn to love them. Variations in modes of civility could occur among cultures, but progress was measurable against the constant standard of human nature.

The dynamic nature of society allowed for changes in status through personal achievement and gradual social mobility, but, at any given time, social distinctions would occur. Human nature included variations in the distribution of natural talents. In addition, people differed in their moral capacities, such as the willingness to forego current pleasures for delayed rewards. Moral sympathy and the legitimacy of society's structures were founded on the equality of human processes but not on equality of status. A more thorough-going egalitarianism would require the breaking of the bonds of social cohesion in order to level and rebuild this structure for each generation. For thinkers in this tradition, an egalitarian society would be disunited and amoral. They did not deny the value of equality but defined it as a process that occurred within everyone but that had an uneven outcome. The priority was on social order, which made all other goods possible. In some cases, as with the monarchy, the privileges of birth may be defended as embodying the political order.

The process of cultural growth was a long one, and the cohesion among individuals reached across ages. Locke's conception of identity, based on a continuity of ideas across time, belonged to societies as well as individuals. These ideas were what gave life its meaning. In the long process of social evolution institutions had developed, and the people of each generation came to find themselves placed within them. For the thinkers of this school, the status earned or inherited in one generation should be passed on to the next. The continuity of the social order meant stability and security for all.

An appropriate system of virtue would solve the coordination problem of the passions. The bourgeois virtues are central to the economic system as well as to the moral one. Their value, given the ongoing needs of human nature, is something we know by long experience. A social institution is a continuous idea, existing beyond the lifespan of any individual. These conventions serve to unite society over time. For example, private property was a kind of social glue in two senses. First, it is necessary for the growth of society across generations, so that we may pass on the benefits of our accomplishments to our progeny and each generation need not start anew. Second, it is central to the bourgeois virtues, beginning with the Lockean moral idea that one owns one's own actions. Property connoted benefit as well as responsibility for past actions. It is a moral institution that unites and coordinates individuals across time.

The temporal dimension allowed for social change but not for wilful creativity. Institutions should be respected as the embodiment of the right order of things, even if they appear inequitable from the standpoint of abstract status. Social mobility was possible through merit but only insofar as it took place within the rules of the social structure. Apart from these rules, the idea of merit had no meaning. We may succeed or fail against the evolved standards of society, but to replace those standards with our own private rules is to destroy the idea of merit. The natural pursuits of human nature, rather than the artifice of human will, provide the true source of social evolution. The limited designs of even the best human thinkers are inferior to the long process of social experience. As Burke put it, 'The individual is foolish but the species is wise.'[21]

This was the school of thought to which Burke belonged. He believed in 'the common nature and common relation of men,' and in 'the common feelings of nature [and] sentiments of morality.'[22] In his polemic against the French Revolution, he would highlight another of the major themes of his tradition: the value of evolved social order is threatened by wilful freedom (i.e., by the ideal of positive liberty that had flourished on the Continent). The empiricists before Mill, from Hobbes to Locke to Hume, had denied that freedom meant wilfulness. Burke believed that the ideal of self-creativity was a threat to the true liberty that social order made possible. Citizens had a right not to wilfulness but to the conventions that secured their freedom by regulating their passions. According to Burke: 'Government is a contrivance of human wisdom to provide for human wants. Men have a right that these wants should be provided for by this wisdom. Among these wants is to be reckoned the want, out of civil society, of a sufficient restraint upon their passions. Society requires ... that ... the inclinations of men should frequently be thwarted, their will controlled, and their passions brought into subjection ... In this sense the restraints on men, as well as their liberties, are to be reckoned among their rights.'[23]

Burke sometimes did not distinguish between passion and wilfulness as the greater threat to social order. Thus he saw Hobbes's 'mechanic philosophy' as itself a kind of destructive rationalism.[24] Burke would also have rejected the synthesis of positive and negative liberty of Humboldt and Mill. He warned against the divisiveness of romantic individuality, worrying that from 'the want of a steady education and settled principle ... the commonwealth itself would, in a few generations, crumble away, be disconnected into the dust and powder of individuality.'[25] But there was an extra quality in Burke's rejection of wilfulness. The passions could be regulated (so the empiricist worldview could be emended), but the Continental idea of freedom was fatally flawed. The passions were natural, even though they required the guidance of long wisdom, while positive liberty was purely arbitrary. Burke's contrast was between arbitrary wilfulness and natural passions. He belonged to those 'who have chosen our nature rather than our speculation, our breasts rather than our inventions, for the great conservatories and magazines of our rights and privileges.'[26]

The conventions by which the passions were regulated could be seen as a second kind of human nature – one that was acquired rather than inborn. This distinction, Burke claimed, had been understood by the ancients: 'They had to do with men, and they were obliged to study human nature. They had to do with citizens, and they were obliged to study the effects of those habits which are communicated by the circumstances of civil life. They were sensible that the operation of this second nature on the first produced a new combination.' The process of enculturation, the development of this second nature, was the acquisition of habit. 'Prejudice renders a man's virtue his habit, and not a series of unconnected acts. Through just prejudice, his duty becomes a part of his nature.'[27]

In effect, Burke distinguished among three categories of human motivation. The first category was natural, and Burke sometimes related it to religion: human nature was given by its creator. The second category was human convention, and to this belonged humanity's second nature of cultural learning (by which people acquired the habits of civility). This second nature was artificial but unplanned (though not arbitrary) because civility suited human nature. Humanity's second nature gave rise to the diversity of social practices and the variety of institutions observed in history and across nations.[28] Finally, the third category of motive was that of the free creative will, which Burke rejected as destructive and illegitimate. This wilfulness was what Burke called arbitrary power.

Richard Price had referred to the French Revolution as the legitimate overthrow of 'an arbitrary monarch.'[29] Burke agreed that royal wilfulness was illegitimate but replied that the problem was wilfulness not royalty. Acts of pure will, whether of king or of subject, are arbitrary in their essence. Arbitrary power is the rule of the 'occasional will,' or unguided whim, whether of the one or of the many. With power in the hands of the people, wilfulness took on a false sense of legitimacy. For Burke, 'It is therefore of infinite importance that [the people] should not be suffered to imagine that their will, any more than that of kings, is the standard of right and wrong.'[30] Wilful rule, if unguided by justice and social order, was arbitrary and illegitimate, whether the ruler was a man or a mass. This form of rule, Burke predicted, could easily culminate in terror.

The alternative to arbitrary power, whether in the hands of a person or a people, was to accept the conventions of justice and social order that formed the second nature of each nation. For Burke, the source of goodness was in the social order: 'Good order is the foundation of all good things.'[31] Social order provided cohesion for living individuals, but it also reached across the ages. It was this continuity in time that defined society as a single entity. In this figurative sense, society could be said to be based on a contract – but on one whose worth is rooted in time. The value of such a contract is not derived from the temporary will of each member but from the temporal flow of social life across the ages. The theme of temporal continuity as the foundation of society is among Burke's best-known ideas:

> Society is indeed a contract. Subordinate contracts for objects of mere occasional interest may be dissolved at pleasure – but the state ought not to be considered as nothing better than a partnership ... to be taken up for a little temporary interest, and to be dissolved by the fancy of the parties. It is to be looked on with other reverence, because it is not a partnership in things subservient only to the gross animal existence of a temporary and

perishable nature. It is a partnership in all science; a partnership in all art; a partnership in every virtue and in all perfection. As the ends of such a partnership cannot be obtained in many generations, it becomes a partnership not only between those who are living, but between those who are living, those who are dead, and those who are to be born. Each contract of each particular state is but a clause in the great primeval contract of eternal society, linking the lower with the higher natures, connecting the visible and invisible world, according to a fixed compact sanctioned by the inviolable oath which holds all physical and all moral natures, each in their appointed place. This law is not subject to the will of those who by an obligation above them, and infinitely superior, are bound to submit their will to that law.[32]

For Burke, freedom of choice was an inferior foundation for society. His rejection of consent as the basis for political allegiance was based on the primary value of society. Society cannot be contingent on free consent because it is prior in time, in logic, and in value to the freedom of its members. Hume had pointed out that tacit consent was too weak a concept to carry the weight Locke had assigned it,[33] arguing, instead, that the development of society was gradual, taking place through unplanned convention rather than wilful consent. Individual consent did not come into play because society grew on its own. Burke concurred, arguing that individual liberty was the consequence of social order.

The system of virtues had arisen through social convention, or cultural learning, for the good of all. Happiness was found by achieving the ends given, first by nature, and then by the second nature of one's cultural legacy. To yearn for inappropriate ends, given the facts of nature and social life, would lead only to unhappiness and unrest. Following Smith, Burke described 'the happiness that is to be found by virtue in all conditions; in which consists the true moral equality of mankind, and not in that monstrous fiction which, by inspiring false ideas and vain expectations into men destined to travel in the obscure walk of laborious life, serves only to aggravate and embitter that real inequality which it never can remove, and which the order of civil life establishes as much for the benefit of those whom it must leave in a humble state as those whom it is able to exalt to a condition more splendid, but not more happy.'[34]

The system of reciprocal obligations across ranks, which had evolved into what Burke had famously called the age of chivalry, had united society across classes. 'It was this which, without confounding ranks, had produced a noble equality and handed it down through all the gradations of social life. It was this opinion which mitigated kings into companions and raised private men to be fellows with kings. Without force or opposition, it subdued the fierceness of pride and power, it obliged sovereigns to submit to the soft collar of social esteem.'[35]

Burke did not deny the legitimacy of social mobility based on merit. But merit itself required that the climb be steep so that ascendance would represent a real achievement. 'The temple of honor ought to be seated on an eminence. If it be opened through virtue, let it be remembered, too, that virtue is never tried but by some difficulty and some struggle.' A more ambitious scheme of equality would require that the idea of social ascendancy be eliminated and, with it, the idea of merit. Equality is the enemy of excellence. Whatever scheme of organization was chosen for society, some criterion of ordering would be needed. Anticipating Michels' iron law, Burke argued that 'those who attempt to level, never equalize. In all societies, consisting of various descriptions of citizens, some description must be uppermost.'[36]

Equality, beyond that of natural processes, was for Burke unnatural and harmful to society. Property, he argued, by its nature was unequal, yet it was the necessary means by which social subgroups, such as the family and the church, could provide for their continuity.[37] Property was the most concrete of the ways in which society depended on the principle of inheritance to create bonds of belonging across generations. Civility, order, and rights were each a kind of social capital, to use the modern term, that society gave to each new generation.

Modern Conservatism

Modern conservatism is distinctive in its temporal vision of society. Civil society is the result of an evolutionary process; civilization grows but is not made. Institutions develop over time to meet the given needs of human nature, which are innate and vary only within certain limits. While an older religious conservatism remains with us, in which the good is given strictly by God, its ideas have currency wherever they are most useful in expressing the broader conservative worldview. The concept of original sin, for example, is a resonant image for conservatives, a way of encapsulating both the limits of human nature and the danger of wilfulness. The wilful freedom of Adam led to evil; his sinfulness remains part of our nature. For mainstream conservatives, however, the divine source of goodness, while rarely forsaken completely, is usually complemented by other teleological concepts. Tradition and the processes of nature may be understood as consistent with the divine order, but conservatives differ in their religiosity. While this worldview may appeal strongly to those with certain religious beliefs, it is based on social ideas that belong to the secularism of modernity.

In a study of political ideas in post-war America, Melvin Thorne identified two central themes as consistently held by modern conservatives.[38] The first is that human nature is fundamentally unchangeable. This does not mean that our nature is the source of goodness. In fact, it may be understood as fallen or, at least, as a source of selfishness. While ideas like normality and nature have retained their approbative meaning, they do so negatively: what is abnormal or unnatural is bad. The source of goodness is more complex. Thus the second theme, that human beings require the guidance of objective moral order. We need order before we can be free. The social order is a product of civilization, which grows up gradually over time. Progress is possible as an evolutionary process of society. Social planning, however, is contrary to the limits of our nature. Social improvement is learned incrementally, and we are always in danger of sliding back. Morality must be reinforced by protecting the social institutions within which it is embedded. The state has a role, but it is to augment the social order rather than to replace it with rationalist designs. Human nature cannot be transcended, but people can learn to be good.

In some thinkers, the roots of modern conservatism are especially clear. The moral themes of the Scottish Enlightenment have recently been taken up by James Q. Wilson, who located the source of the moral sense in Darwin's evolutionary biology.[39] Sociality is natural but must be reinforced by convention, and the given inclinations, including sociality, must be guided by evolved social institutions. Evolution is the natural process of development, through social learning, of conventional institutions. This process is based on the internal resources that nature has given each individual. The result is an argument in support of those social institutions, beginning with the family, that nurture and regulate the given inclinations of human nature. Sociability can be misguided, and the institutions for its proper guidance can be destroyed by wilful meddling, but the essential features of the good society are given by the ongoing processes of human nature in each person and in society as a whole. Wilson's arguments will sound like common sense to many citizens. Modern political discussions continue to include some who follow Hume, Smith, and Burke, seeing the fundamental social good in terms of continuity, structured cohesion, and civil order.

To other modern citizens, these themes will sound like a thin apology for the privileges of the rich and powerful. Those of a more egalitarian persuasion, whether they define equality in terms of opportunity or of result, will be dismayed that some thinkers, and a segment of their fellow citizens, continue to see social order as the fundamental social good. Conservatism, for these readers, is based on an unreasonable fear of change, or is a remnant of religious/social anachronism, or is little more than a self-serving legitimation of patriarchal/economic power.

Among the most frequent of objections to conservatism is the suspicion that it is implicitly racist. This belief may take stronger and weaker forms. Some anti-conservatives think that the idea of social order based on human nature necessarily implies an acceptance of a racial hierarchy. In this view, racism is the reductio ad absurdum of conservatism, which defends all social differences as natural. Even for those who do not think conservatives are necessarily racist, the objection may remain that conservatism is not actively opposed to racism. The conservative worldview, it may be argued, simply lacks any resources to resist this social evil. Conservatives can become active anti-racists only if they abandon the core of their ideology and act on the basis of more enlightened values.

It is true that conservatives defend social order as natural and good. It is also true that this order seems inevitably hierarchical. However, it is an overstatement to say that nothing in conservatism is contrary to a racial hierarchy. The commonality of human nature is among the deepest ideals of conservatism. While this nature is held to include a range of capacities, the idea that such differences correlate by race does not follow from the conservative worldview. It is a contingent assertion, and conservatives may deny it as well as anyone. Even if the higher talents were unevenly distributed, for conservatives human nature is about the given inclinations and ordinary needs, and less about intellect and creativity. The latter abilities are idealized more in the tradition of positive liberty, and it is only differences in these talents that might justify social differences based on merit. Conservatives believe these talents are less important because they do not see society as the product of creative human intellect. Intelligence is less important than common sense, and common sense, by definition, belongs to all. Similarly, the common passions are equal in all, while the ordinary virtues by which they are regulated can be acquired by anyone. In the conservative vision, success in life is due more to one's virtue than one's intellect. The bourgeois virtues especially, like hard work and the postponement of gratification, are the product of habit and inculcation – they are learned – and it is these that modern conservatives admire as securing one's place in society. A conservative will feel closer to an honest, hardworking person of virtue, regardless of race or other status, than to any advocate of moral self-creativity. They look to the processes by which the social order arose rather than to the status of anyone within it. What is important to conservatives is the commonality of moral order, which they believe, more than others, must transcend racial differences.

For anti-conservatives this vision of society is illegitimate. Having rejected the evaluative basis of conservative anti-racism because it conflicts with their own deeply embedded system of values, the charge of racism appears plausible. Racism is a limitation on positive liberty: to deny this freedom to anyone is to be politically suspect. The defence by conservatives against this charge cannot be based on good reason. If conservatism were legitimate, then our own evaluative assumptions would be false or at least limited in some way. The possibility is too troubling to consider. The refusal of conservatives to remake society on racially egalitarian grounds is pr oof of the charge. Indeed, they do not even see that racism is among our leading problems; instead, they worry about irrelevancies and misconceptions like the alleged moral breakdown of society and supposed state interference in social affairs. Can they not see that progress towards racial harmony requires the moral remaking of society?

The argument of democracy goes on. Meanwhile, conservatives have their own ways to mis-characterize their opponents. For example, the ideal of human progress is sometimes called utopian, and the givenness of human nature is sometimes expressed as a rejection of human perfectibility. However, the improvement of human nature does not require perfection. There is a difference between perfection and progress. Only by setting the goal impossibly high does the charge of utopianism seem to stick. Moreover, the ideal of self-creativity is not to achieve a perfect end: it is an end in itself. Nietzsche did not see the transvaluation of values as a route to a higher good. He did not envision morality as a series of steps, in which the goal at each stage was to reach the next level. There were no moral plateaus in Nietzsche's vision; he detested anyone who would rest anywhere. Nor did he have a sense of up and down. For him, the good was in transvaluation for its own sake. Similarly, self-creativity will always require the overcoming of what exists. There is no final destination because all of the value is in the travel. Progress is its own end.

As political ideals vary, so do the diagnoses of social ills. Just as we differ in our evaluative priorities, we diverge in the urgency we assign to social problems. The great political issues for conservatives, including crime, national defence, and the rate of immigration, are each centred on the security and sanctity of society as an orderly whole. Conservatives see crime not just as a series of offences against particular victims but as a threat to the social fabric itself. Each criminal act is an offence against the whole of society. This is the point missed by those who argue that the public's outrage against crime is not justified by the actual risk to each person. For conservatives, crime is not just about personal insecurity, it is about the rightful order of society.

Common norms, in this view, are not just guides to individual behaviour, they are the essential link between each individual and the whole. The sense of belonging, for conservatives, comes from the sense of rightful order. When the order of society appears under threat, the sense of belonging, which gives meaning to life, is directly endangered. Thus the perceived threat to social institutions brought about by advocates of social change is capable of producing strong emotions. Unlike egalitarians, conservatives do not seek a sense of belonging by overcoming social differentiation; rather, for them, to belong is to find one's place within the social order by building a secure place within it. Conservatism is not a mere apology for the privileges of the powerful. The idea of social order, of acknowledged roles and obligations, remains meaningful to many people. If conservatives are too sanguine about hierarchy, they may still be right that a mass is not a society. Hierarchy is inegalitarian, but it is also a system of reciprocal obligations. The well-off have an obligation to support the poor, but misfortune should not license indolence. The essential connection between benefit and responsibility, they believe, should not be severed by unqualified charity. Hume spoke for conservatives about the responsibility of those who give: 'Giving alms to common beggars is naturally praised; because it seems to carry relief to the distressed and indigent: but when we observe the encouragement thence arising to idleness and debauchery, we regard that species of charity rather as a weakness than a virtue.'[40] For conservatives, social stability, coherent identities, and a network of mutual obligations are exactly the features missing from modern life.

On economic questions, modern conservatives may find themselves allied with certain liberals. The market as an organic or holistic entity is a conservative idea,[41] while the slogan 'laissez faire' seems to capture both poles of liberal individualism with its colloquial meaning, 'let us be,' and its literal translation, 'let us make.' The ideal that Max Weber identified too narrowly as the Protestant ethic is both individualistic and moralistic at once, allowing a coalition of conservatives and liberals to arise in favour of the free market. This coalition naturally hinges on the idea of negative liberty, as in notions like the sanctity of contracts (with which the state should not interfere even for the good of a contractor). Among the strongest guarantors of freedom and security, for this coalition, is the institution of private property. Similarly, the popular desire to 'get ahead in the world' is both liberal and conservative. On one hand, it expresses, in a materialistic way, the positive desire for self-creation. As Isaiah Berlin wrote, 'Creation is of man's essence; hence the doctrine of the dignity of labour.'[42] On the other, it implicitly acknowledges a social ladder upon which one can climb. If it relies on a somewhat shallow version of these ideals, the belief in economic self-improvement is not *just* materialistic. In the working world, ideals like fruitfulness and self-improvement have been made available to ordinarily talented people.

But a coalition is not a consensus, so liberals and conservatives will come to disagree on many economic policies. Conservatives, for example, may worry more about the stability of markets, in some cases advocating protectionist measures to secure the order of the whole. Some conservatives may distrust capitalism in general, seeing it not as a system to coordinate our natural wants but as an unnatural force disruptive of social life. Liberals, meanwhile, may celebrate individual economic freedom as a means to personal growth and fulfillment, and seek to extend these benefits to all. Thus liberals may advocate policies like day-care to ease women's entry into the workplace, while conservatives would see this as interfering with traditional roles. Similarly, many liberals will support affirmative action policies as a route to true equality of opportunity, while conservatives will see them as contrary to merit. While coalitions are often possible in a pluralist world, consensus is not.

On some issues, conservatives may resort to individualistic language. For example, foes of abortion may frame their objections in terms of the rights of the foetus. But individualist 'rights talk' cannot capture the conservative complaint that abortion is but one symptom of the breakdown of sexual morality – the humanistic interference with natural, traditional, or God-given gender roles.[43] For feminists, abortion rights are at the very centre of a woman's freedom from social and biological constraints, and they represent her positive liberty to create her own social role. For conservatives, abortion represents the breakdown of the traditional, natural, or theological system of differentiated obligations and privileges of gender. Abortion, for conservatives, is not just about the rights of the foetus but about the ideal of womanhood within the social order.

Still, the idea of the rights of the foetus is not entirely alien to conservatives because the innocent, in the proper order of things, are those who have few obligations but many rights. Innocence is a conservative idea, the necessary opposite of moral guilt. Original sin may set the limits of human innocence for some conservatives, but the ideas of guilt and innocence remain implicit in their conception of moral order. The innocent are those who have few obligations, and the guilty are those who have few rights. The distinction between guilt and innocence is fundamental, and so conservatives may oppose abortion while favouring capital punishment. On the other side of the argument, for those who worry that women have been excluded from the power of self-creation and who reject the constraints of conservative order, the ideas of guilt and innocence are, at best, fuzzy. If the existing moral order is viewed with suspicion, then the distinction between guilt and innocence will appear less clear. Advocates of the positive conception of liberty may see capital punishment as the worst evil, as the destruction of a unique individual, while abortion is the mere termination of the self-creative process before it has really begun; that is, before the foetus has become an autonomous, or self-sufficient, being.

If a significant segment of the citizens of modern democracies find meaning in conservative ideas, and if conservatism conflicts with other legitimate evaluative orientations that people may reasonably hold, then democracy is not about evaluative solidarity among the citizenry; instead, it is about continuous contestation among citizens who have non-trivial differences in their visions of the common good. Some believe in the priority of solidarity, others in individual rights and freedom, and others in social order. Conflict, not consensus, defines modern democracy.

In Chapter 5, liberal individualism was described as the synthesis of autotelic power and telic security. With their focus on the individual as the source of value, liberals downgrade the value of community. In a parallel way, conservatism may be described as the synthesis of telic security and community, resulting in the rejection or downgrading of autotelic power. But if negative liberty can be a communal rather than an individualistic ideal, then might not an alternative sense of social belonging be found in the idea of positive liberty? To answer this question, we must look to the history of socialism – the third major ideology deeply rooted within modern democracy.

7
Socialism and the Power of Social Unity

If the greatest philosopher of the British empiricist tradition was David Hume, then his counterpart on the Continent was Immanuel Kant. The latter's role in the development of the idea of positive liberty, centred on the secular value of the free human will, was surveyed briefly in Chapter 3. But Kant was neither a pure romantic nor an egoist who celebrated wilfulness for its own sake. His goal was more difficult: to reconcile positive, wilful freedom with reasoned self-government, thereby completing the Rousseauvian project. To understand the ideal of collective empowerment, we must return for a moment to Kant and then move on to Hegel and Marx. The theme uniting these thinkers was that positive liberty could belong to society as a progressive whole. The community could be the self-creative source of value.

Kant's political vision was the mirror-image of that of his near contemporary, Burke. While Burke's best known book was an answer to the rationalism of the Enlightenment, Kant's *Foundations of the Metaphysics of Morals* (1785) was a reply to the empiricists whom Burke followed. Where Burke saw the purpose of society in the need to regulate the passions, and wilfulness as the major threat to the institutions that performed this social function, Kant believed that free will was the source of value and that reason was necessary to regulate it. For him, the given inclinations of human nature were the primary threat to rationality. In short:

- Burke accepted the passions as natural but in need of regulation, while rejecting wilfulness as corrosive of society.
- Kant saw the will as the source of value but as needing regulation, while renouncing the natural inclinations as an obstacle to progressive self-governance.

Beginning from different conceptions of liberty, the two writers ended with symmetrically opposed theories of a well-governed society.

Like Hume, Kant's importance in the history of political thought has not been widely recognized. In politics, he was a proto-socialist whose goal was to reconcile the positive freedom of each citizen with the harmonious progress of the community. This was, and remains, the overriding objective of socialism. Because Kant thought he had resolved it, he could sound like a defender of individualism, but his political theory was about the self-improvement of humanity as a whole. According to Kant: 'The end of *man* as an entire species, i.e. that of fulfilling his ultimate appointed purpose by freely exercising his own powers, will be brought by providence to a successful issue.' The starting point for this collective progress was mastery over the natural passions that caused conflict: 'Although the ends of *men* as individuals run in a diametrically opposite direction ... the very conflict of individual inclinations, which is the source of all evil, gives reason a free hand to master them.'[1] Human nature caused problems that reason would seek to overcome. In solving these initial difficulties, reason became stronger. Over time, it would become dominant and bring social cohesion.

Kant's political vision was about peace, progress, and cosmopolitan harmony. His concept of liberty was positive, based on each person's creative will as the source of goodness. Nothing but the will could be good in itself. But reason brought the will into social harmony. People were free, but people were also enlightened – or could become so – as history moved forward. Enlightenment would bring unity to positive liberty. The first step was to overcome human nature.

In politics, Kant followed Rousseau: 'Every legislator [should] frame his laws in such a way that they could have been produced by the united will of a whole nation, and to regard each subject, in so far as he can claim citizenship, as if he had consented within the general will. This is the test of the rightfulness of every public law.'[2] However, he was not a totalitarian. On one hand, his focus was on the freedom of the individual, including both self-creativity and interpersonal inviolability. Here Kant was a forerunner of Humboldt and Mill – a liberal, perhaps the first. But on the other, Kant's goal was to put each free will on the same rational path. Each will, if it ruled itself rationally, would rule universally. Freedom leads to harmony. The ideal constitution would not limit individual freedom but unite it:

> A constitution allowing the *greatest possible human freedom* in accordance with laws which ensure *that the freedom of each can co-exist with the freedom of all the others* (not one designed to provide the greatest possible happiness, as this will in any case follow automatically), is at all events a necessary idea which must be made the basis not only of the first outline of a political constitution but of all laws as well. It requires that we should abstract at the outset from present hindrances, which perhaps do not arise inevitably out

of human nature ... The more closely the legislation and government were made to harmonise with this idea, the rarer punishments would become, and it is thus quite rational to maintain (as Plato does) that none would be necessary at all in a perfect state ... For no-one can or ought to decide what the highest degree may be at which mankind may ... stop progressing, and hence how wide a gap may ... remain between the idea and its execution. For this will depend on freedom, which can transcend any limit we care to impose.[3]

Kant and the Regulation of the Will

Kant's theory of liberty was about the creative will, which would be regulated and coordinated neither by respect for the negative liberty of others nor by conventional morality but by the power of reason alone. Rationality, for Kant, played the role that class-consciousness did for Marx, unifying the creative forces of the human species. It would develop with the progress of history. Kant's political theory must be understood as socially holistic, consistent with the line of thinkers to which he belonged. Rousseau, Kant, Hegel, and Marx – through them we can trace the lineage of the socialist tradition within modern democracy.

The essential difference in the developing ideals of positive and negative liberty was in the relationship between human wants and human will. For the early modern advocates of negative liberty, the wants were taken as given, and volition was one stage in the natural mental process of action towards those ends. The will was not free, in the sense of complete independence from natural influences; rather, it was one part of the natural causal process as it took place within the human soul. Freedom was natural, and the will was part of human nature.

For the proponents of positive liberty, freedom was not about achieving predetermined wants; rather, it was about the power to determine for oneself what one wants. Wilfulness was not about *having* wants but about deciding *what* to want. Positive liberty is the freedom to determine one's own ends. In doing so, we create ourselves as evaluative beings. Value emanates from each human soul. As Kant put it, human value was not based on our natural desires but on our freedom to determine our own desires. It was not 'that faculty which makes man dependent upon nature (through impulses of sense), that is, not that in respect of which the worth of his existence is dependent upon what he receives and enjoys. On the contrary it is the worth which he alone can give to himself ... in the *freedom* of his faculty of desire, and not as a link in the chain of nature.' A person driven by natural inclinations or passions is not free in the positive sense. Positive liberty is autotelic, the freedom to create one's own telos. Thus, the free will is the self-contained, human source of value *ex nihilo*. Kant continued: 'In other

words a good will is that where man's existence can alone possess an absolute worth, and in relation to which the existence of the world can have a
final end.'[4]

In the concluding half of the *Critique of Judgment* (1790), entitled the 'Critique of Teleological Judgment,' from which the preceding quotation is taken,
Kant presented an alternative to the empiricist teleology of nature. We should
not look for the source of human goodness in physical causality: to do so is
to confuse physics with metaphysics. If we are unable to do without a teleology, then this is because we are so constituted as to see nature in terms of
design.[5] As an alternative to physico-teleology, from which could be inferred only an external prime mover, Kant suggested a moral or ethico-
teleology whose law could be known. Moral responsibility was possible only
if people stood apart from the causal order even as they existed within it.
'Now we have in the world beings of but one kind whose causality is teleological, or directed towards ends, and which at the same time ... determine
ends for themselves.'[6] Our earthly telos was in the positive liberty of humankind, which Kant sought to describe as communal. Our cultural self-
development is the true end of nature:

> As the single being upon earth that possesses understanding, and, conse-
> quently, a capacity for setting before himself ends of his deliberate choice,
> he is certainly [a] titular lord of nature, and, supposing we regard nature as
> a teleological system, his is born to be its ultimate end ... Such an end,
> however, must not be sought in nature ... The production in a rational being
> of an aptitude for any ends whatever of his own choosing, consequently of
> the aptitude of a being in his freedom, is *culture*. Hence it is only culture
> [that] can be the ultimate end which we have cause to attribute to nature in
> respect of the human race. His individual happiness ... [is] ruled out.[7]

Kant explicitly recognized the distinction between positive and negative
liberty, although he defined them in his own way.[8] Independence from outside causation was an inadequate definition because liberty required not
the protection but the remaking of human nature. In the *Foundations of the
Metaphysics of Morals*, he argued that the negative concept was not so much
wrong as too limited. If the human will were to be defined as 'a kind of
causality ... [then] freedom would be that property of this causality by
which it can be effective independently of foreign causes determining it.'[9]
This was the negative concept of liberty, the freedom of natural causation
in the absence of foreign or imposed causes. But the empiricists' internalization of causality was, for Kant, an inadequate solution. To be ruled by
predetermined objectives is heteronomy not autonomy. Internalized causality was still causality set in motion by external sources; instead, the will
should be seen as a supernatural causality. The will, and nothing external

to it, was the prime mover, or first cause, of human action. Rather than being ruled by causal laws, the will gave law to itself. 'The preceding definition of freedom is negative and therefore affords no insight into its essence. But a positive conception of freedom ... must be [of] a causality according to immutable laws, but of a peculiar kind ... What else, then, can freedom of the will be but autonomy, i.e., the property of the will to be a law to itself?'[10]

Kant described positive liberty in terms of self-given law rather than self-determined ends – autonomy rather than autotely. The difference was precisely that the former was guided by reason: autonomy equals autotely plus rationality. The will was defined by Kant in terms of its end-creating power, and the rational will was the source of moral goodness. Morality was not based on the consequence of promoting happiness, given the inclinations of human nature; rather, the foundation of Kantian morality was the creative act of willing, limited only by rationality. 'The good will is not good because of what it effects or accomplishes or because of its adequacy to achieve some proposed end; it is good only because of its willing, i.e., it is good of itself.'[11] Morality was not about achieving one's given ends but about giving one's ends to oneself, guided only by reason. With this codicil to the human will, autotely became autonomy.

The regulation of human freedom, defined as wilfulness rather than unobstructed inclination, was uppermost in Kant's ethical theory. Because he believed that the will, since it was the source of goodness, must be superior to the human passions, he discounted the force of sympathy among persons with similar inclinations. He rejected the view of the Scottish philosophers: 'Beneficence ... resides in the will and not in propensities of feeling ... and not in tender sympathy.'[12] Instead of being regulated by common feelings or cultural experience, the will was to be regulated by reason alone. If he had chosen to paraphrase Hume, Kant might have said that reason should be the slave of the will – but a slave whose function was guidance. Reason was subservient to the will, but it served by showing the way. 'Reason is given to us as a practical faculty, i.e., one which is meant to have an influence on the will.'[13] Rather than moral sentiments and social institutions, freedom, for Kant, was to be regulated by the force of reason.

For Kant, moral actions were those performed from pure duty rather than from self-interest or from a given inclination that the actor sought to satisfy. Moral action had nothing to do with the contingencies of human nature or with any other empirical information about the existing state of the world. 'Empirical principles are not at all suited to serve as the basis of moral laws. For if the basis of the universality by which they should be valid for all rational beings without distinction ... is derived from a particular tendency of human nature or the accidental circumstance in which it is found, that universality is lost.'[14]

Moral duty must be determined by universal reason rather than by empirical contingencies. Moral laws are those that apply to rational beings as such. Their generality transcends the nature of individuals. Rational morality stands above the empirical world and, therefore, cannot be inferred from experience of any sort, especially not from the facts of human nature.

Hume may have distinguished between facts about the physical world and facts about human nature, but Kant drew a clear line between 'ought' and 'is.' Like the new moral language of value, the fact-value dichotomy belongs to the tradition of positive liberty.[15] For the empiricists, like Locke and Hume, who saw human life in terms of a given teleology, the language of virtue remained natural. One's virtues were in the way one performed one's given social roles. By describing human nature, we define the virtues appropriate to it. Values, by contrast, are chosen. The revolt against ethical naturalism came with the idea that the human will is the spontaneous source of goodness.

For Kant, the 'ought' of life came with the recognition of an imperative. The imperative of morality was distinctive in that it was generalizable, or categorical: 'Act only according to that maxim by which you can at the same time will that it should become a universal law.'[16] However, generality was only a *formal* criterion of goodness. The categorical imperative did not tell you what to will; it did not prescribe the *substance* of a good act. To the contrary, the substance of goodness must remain undetermined because its source is in the act of willing. In this sense, the will is prior to the good. Freedom is to be unconstrained by a pre-existing good. It was Kant's great innovation to seek a formal rather than a substantive criterion of morality. In this way he could address the great dilemma of positive liberty as the source of value: how to distinguish good acts of will from bad ones. Under the categorical imperative, the lawfulness of morality was in its formal generality rather than in its substance. The 'ought' of life, the decision about what one should do next, remained a free creative act of will. In this regard, will was superior even to reason, which could provide the form but not the substance of a good act.

Generality, according to Kant, is the essence of law. A law of nature, for example, is one that is true in all similar cases. Positive law differs from natural law by defining the universe of cases to which it applies, but within its defined limits it, too, is universal. Positive laws apply to a particular group or class, but, for Kant, humans are that class of beings who have freedom of will. By having a will, each person belongs to a common group to which the law of morality must apply generally.

Our moral duty is the law we give to ourselves but only if it fulfills the following formal criterion: it must be applicable without contradiction to all beings similar to ourselves. My self-given law must be law for all wilful creatures. A perfectly rational being would not find such a law to be a constraint upon its will, since a purely rational will would always produce universally applicable laws. Only those who are distracted from their duty by the self-interested inclinations of human nature would find the categorical imperative to be a constraint on their will. In the *Critique of Practical Reason* (1788), Kant introduced the following distinction to explain his theory: the *pure* will belongs to every person who is free but limited by human nature, while the *holy* will is pure and without self-interest.[17] For a holy will, moral obligation would be no constraint.

Where Hume had seen equality of feeling as giving rise to a morality of common sympathy, Kant envisioned equality of the will as leading to a morality of common reason. To summarize his moral theory, if generality is the essence of law, then self-given laws must apply in all like cases. Free persons are not unique egoists but are essentially similar in their freedom. The will of one member of humanity is equivalent to that of another because wilful freedom is the defining attribute of human beings. When we rule ourselves, we rule all those who are like us. Autonomy is self-rule, but it produces universal laws. The creative will remained the core of Kant's moral theory: autonomy is generalizable autotely. Each person is the source of value – the will is the human attribute that alone can be self-sufficiently good[18] – but rationality guides the free will towards universality and harmony.

Kant's theory was an attempt to solve the basic political problem of positive liberty – how wilful people should live together. His theory is fundamentally egalitarian in that everyone is similarly wilful, equally the source of good. This vision remains with us today in every political theory that sees democracy as progressive solidarity. If only we were to communicate freely and for long enough, we would come to agree on the public good. If the sources of distortion are eliminated, then rationality will remain. The community can become autonomous and rationally self-creating; democracy can change human nature. Self-creativity will converge into harmony, but first we must reform the institutions that distort rationality. The preconditions of democracy are clear: first, eliminate the sources of irrationality; second, remake human nature. After the revolution, then democracy – but first, the revolution. The quiet professor of Königsberg was no radical, but the socialists of today are his children. Most see economic reforms as the first necessary step, but their common goal is the autotelic community.

For Kant, the source of goodness began as the free individual will but easily became 'humanity as an end in itself.'[19] Rationality was our highest guide not just in morality but in politics – an attribute of common citizenship in which the individual was a 'legislative member in the realm of ends.'[20] In his characterization of the political goal of the Enlightenment, self-rule became thoroughly collectivized: 'The touchstone of everything that can be concluded as a law for a people lies in the question whether the people could have imposed such a law on itself.'[21] Wilfulness was at once common in every person and an attribute of a single collective entity. The people were a rational whole endowed with positive liberty, the power to will its own ends. Positive liberty became power in social unity.

Kant articulated this goal in another way in his *Idea for a Universal History with a Cosmopolitan Purpose* (1784).[22] There he depicted reason as the developing power by which humanity came to deal with the problems that arose from its nature. The contingencies of individual human nature led to difficulties, but the grand purpose of nature as a totality could be discerned from the progress of the species. Reason was presented with challenges at each stage of human progress in something like a Hegelian dialectic of development. 'By virtue of the good they contained, [they] served for a time to elevate and glorify nations ... Conversely, we should observe how their inherent defects led to their overthrow, but in such a way that a germ of enlightenment always survived, developing further with each revolution, and prepared the way of a subsequent higher level of improvement.'[23]

The great telos of nature was not in the freedom of individuals but in the progress of the human race: '*The history of the human race as a whole can be regarded as the realisation of a hidden plan of nature* ... After many revolutions, with all their transforming effects, the highest purpose of nature, a universal *cosmopolitan existence*, will at last be realised as the matrix within which all the original capacities of the human race may develop.'[24] Kant's theory of progress, not of individuals but of the human whole, led him to see the French Revolution as evidence 'of a *tendency* within the human race as a *whole*, considered not as a series of individuals', to move towards cosmopolitan harmony.[25] In contrast to Kant, liberals like Humboldt and Mill were concerned with individual development. This was not Kant's theory. His theory was about the progressive unity of the social whole. He was not a liberal but an early socialist.

In summary, Kant sought to give a philosophical foundation to the idea of a common creative will, which Rousseau had imagined but had left undeveloped. The human will was the new, secular source of goodness, regulated only by the socially unifying dictates of reason. The fact that individuals often acted badly proved nothing about rationality and morality as such, but showed only the corrupting influence of self-interest. The negative concept of liberty, which the English and Scottish empiricists had embraced, was the source of social, moral, and political problems. Their conception, with its acceptance of human nature as given, was precisely what rational morality should seek to overcome.

Because it drew individuals away from the unifying dictates of rational creativity towards the selfish interests of their own inclinations, human nature in its given form was seen by thinkers following Kant as a threat to social cohesion. The natural inclinations must be overcome or transcended, rather than merely regulated. Hence, a central theme in this political vision was the mutability of human nature. Negative liberty, founded on the acceptance of human nature as given, was its bête noire. With Kant, after Rousseau,[26] the transformation of human nature through social change became a political goal.

Hegel and the Positive Freedom of the Whole

While his great dialectical system of thesis, antithesis, and synthesis remains the best known feature of Hegel's philosophy, the trend in Hegelian scholarship in recent decades has been to de-emphasize his metaphysics. Among left-leaning intellectuals in the West who were becoming dissatisfied with communism, Hegel's reputation underwent a rehabilitation. As one reviewer put it, this revision was motivated by 'the need for a new Marx.'[27] The problem of communist authoritarianism was attributed to scientific materialism, which had led Marxist dictators to sacrifice humanity to history. The solution was a return to the earlier, less scientistic Marx, whose most famous predecessor was Hegel. The need for a friendlier Marx inspired a search for a sympathetic Hegel.

Hegel's philosophy is difficult not only in its systematic nature but because his social ideal was unusually demanding. He sought to show that a society can be self-created by willing itself into existence. The theme of his system was communal positive liberty. He belonged to a tradition that saw freedom as an internally generated, spontaneous process of social development. Society in this view was a living, growing whole. Like Kant before him and Marx after him, Hegel was among the most important contributors to the emerging tradition of socialism.

The Kantian marriage of rationality and wilfulness gave issue to a theory of social harmony. But humanity, as a harmonious whole, would emerge only in its maturity. In childhood, humanity remains a self-interested creature, capable of understanding its duty but experiencing morality as a constraint. By contrast, a being with a perfectly rational will would not feel morality as conflicting with its inclinations because it would be naturally good. Kant's theory of social progress was inspired by Rousseau, but Rousseau had seen the people as a polity, while Kant saw the people as a species. In his version, the human race as a whole would grow unified. With maturation, Kant suggested, humanity would be united in the wilful rationality of moral freedom. Even if this goal is not entirely achievable because of the regrettable limitations of human nature, society might move incrementally towards it. Social progress was a self-creative movement towards egalitarian unity.

After Kant, progress towards wilful unity became the master idea of Hegel. His project was to describe the historical process by which humanity became united as a single will. Where Kant's theory had motioned towards the growing unity-in-will, Hegel made it his central idea. History would culminate in the communal positive liberty of society as a single consciousness, which he called *Geist*. In German, *Geist* means both spirit and mind; for Hegel, it was the immanent destiny of the universe, embodied in the coming-to-consciousness of the communal will. With the emergence of the self-aware *Geist*, the human will as a single entity would become godlike, comparable to the divine will in its self-sufficiency. We are free when we are our own source of being: '*Geist* is Being-in-itself (self-contained existence). But this, precisely is Freedom ... I am free when I am within myself. This self-contained existence of *Geist* is self-consciousness ... It is the judgment of its own nature and, at the same time, the operation of coming to itself, to produce itself, to make itself (actually) into that which is in itself (potentially) ... World history is ... *Geist* striving to attain knowledge of its own nature.'[28]

Imagine, Hegel suggested, we are able to see history in its completeness before us. Each moment in the history of humanity is visible as part of a single entity. A historically complete view of a tree, for example, would include at once the seed, the sapling, and each stage of growth up to the fully mature plant. Just as the tree was a unity across time, humanity was a single historical whole. The continuity of its development in time was evident in its pattern or design, which Hegel called the Idea.

Each stage of human progress informed the next, just as the growth of a tree could be known by the information contained in its seed: 'As the germ bears in itself the whole nature of the tree, the taste and shape of its fruit, so also the first traces of *Geist* virtually contain the whole of history.'[29] The contradictions apparent at any particular moment in history were a symptom that the organism had outgrown its current form. Like a new branch bursting from an old tree limb, human progress was a continual process of self-becoming, driven forward by the internal pressure to grow. Contemporary conflicts in politics and ideas were signs of potential growth, indicating that the existing state of society was about to be transcended in accordance with history's plan.

This plan, called the Idea, was the genetic code for the development of Nature. Idea's design and Nature's materials together would become a final whole as *Geist* matured. Recall the Aristotelian contention that the soul is to the body as eyesight is to the eye. The Idea gave a purpose, or telos, to Nature. Together they were *Geist*, just as soul and body together made a person. The fully developed person was one whose faculties or purposes were perfectly realized, just as a fully developed eye would have perfect eyesight. The *Geist* was the perfection of the human telos of Idea and Nature together.

The process of development was historical, yet the unity of the whole was immanent throughout its developmental stages. History was not just the process of completion of the Idea; it could not be completed in the way that a blueprint might be completed. Since the blueprint of social development was contained within humanity itself, the endpoint would come when humanity became conscious of its own design or purpose. Because its purpose was its own creation, in maturity it would become aware of its power of self-creativity. The fully developed Idea, Hegel claimed, would end in the coming-to-consciousness of *Geist* as the creative, self-aware will of humanity – the communal will that had created itself. The telos of humanity was self-creativity as *Geist*.

Hegel's *Geist*, in other words, would come into awareness of its positive liberty. In this way, Hegel completed the conception that Kant had worked towards by following in the latter's footsteps and then taking his own. He began by describing freedom in the Kantian way as the wilful capability of transcending the given ends of human nature. 'The will ... involves the dissipation of every restriction and every content either immediately presented by nature, by needs, desires, and impulses, or given and determined by any means whatever. This is the unrestricted ... thought of oneself.'[30] Through creative, wilful thought, one determined one's own personhood. The will was the self-sufficient thought of oneself, which depended for its existence on no external source.

Like Kant, Hegel understood the role of the passions and of natural causality in the negative concept of freedom. But the freedom to achieve the given ends of human nature was incomplete, and so he called it mere subjective freedom. True freedom was objective, found only in the realization of the true, self-given ends of humanity. 'Freedom ... does not *exist* as original and natural. It must first be acquired and won; and that is possible only through an infinite process of the discipline of knowledge and will power.'[31]

Kantian autonomy described freedom as rational self-determination, but, for Hegel, freedom even in this form was not yet complete. The will would not be unified by the secondary means of rationality but would become a social whole in itself. Final freedom would come when the creative will was realized as an attribute of the social whole. For Hegel, 'realize' and 'actualize' were active verbs. They meant 'to make real' as by an act of will. To self-actualize is to create oneself. *Geist*, for Hegel, was our self-actualizing communal soul, our collective mind and spirit. The process of its self-development is what we call history, and the end of history is communal self-awareness.

The will became free in three stages, by achieving first negative, then positive, and finally perfect liberty. The first two stages were individualistic, but perfect freedom belonged to the whole. First, the will freed itself from outside causation. Each person became independent. Second, it became self-actualizing in the individual. Finally, it became more perfectly actualized as a single will centred in humanity as a social whole. Freedom in this form was the essence of humanity as it created itself, as the will became self-aware: 'Freedom ... comprises within itself the infinite necessity of bring-ing itself to consciousness and thereby, since knowledge about itself is its very nature, to reality.'[32] Perfect freedom would belong to the will of *Geist*, which had become conscious of its own end or purpose.

As Kant had hinted, liberty grew from negative to positive to communal as history became complete. The stages of history had corresponding social institutions. For example, the family served the natural needs and senti-ments of the individual but gave way at the proper time of life to the more cooperative practices of civil society. Commerce teaches respect for law, so individuals in commercial society could begin to learn the value of law as necessary to coordinate freedom. Respect for law by self-interested indi-viduals would lead to the recognition of the value of autonomy, or self-given law. Finally, autonomy would become harmonized in the unified state, in which the distinction between state and society would disappear and collective autonomy would be achieved.

The developmental process continued in the life of states. Just as indi-viduals came together as peoples, the peoples of the world would unite. National Spirit would become World Spirit. The collective autonomy of each state, which Hegel described as the mind of the nation, became unified through interactions among nations, resulting finally in the harmonious universal State. By being naturally harmonious, its freedom would take the form not of law-abiding autonomy but of pure autotelic wilfulness. Thus Hegel defined 'the *State* as freedom, freedom universal and objective even in the free self-subsistence of the particular will. This actual and organic mind (a) of a single nation (b) reveals and actualizes itself through the inter-relation of the particular national minds until (c) in the process of world-history it reveals and actualizes itself as the universal world-mind whose right is supreme.'[33]

Hegel was not simply a statist. His conception was of something much larger, more theological than political. History was the process by which *Geist* wills itself into creation. In this way humanity as a whole became godlike. 'In contemplating world history we must thus consider its ultimate purpose. This ultimate purpose is what is will in the world itself. We know of God that He is the most perfect; He can will only Himself and what is like Him. God and the nature of His will are one and the same; these we call, philosophically, the *Idea*. Hence it is the idea in general, in its manifestation as human spirit, which we have to contemplate. More precisely, it is the idea of human freedom.'[34]

Freedom was the process of humanity collectively willing itself into exist-ence. This was positive liberty writ in the largest way possible. Hegel's *Geist* was creative in the theological sense, as the foundational source of all value, as well as being the source of its own existence. Human goodness was col-lectively self-generated as *Geist* created its own end. With the completion of history, humanity would be revealed to itself as its own creator. In its potentiality, *Geist* was ever present in history, driving forward to its own completion, whereupon it would come fully into consciousness. Having attained perfect freedom by achieving its own purpose, humanity would know its own will.

Kant's progressivism had hinted at the eventual unity of the human will, but Hegel finished the project. In doing so, he found a place for both individualistic romantics like Humboldt and communal romantics like Herder. Each saw positive liberty as primary but differed in attributing it to individuals and to the German people as a whole, respectively. Hegel's greatness was in extending political theory to accommodate each of the three great political themes of eighteenth-century Continental thought: positive liberty, cultural nationalism, and rationalistic universalism.

However, Hegel did not satisfy all the thinkers of his day. For some, he seemed too ready to accept the current state of political affairs as appropriate to the age. Among his followers were some who stressed the givenness of the historical telos. With this focus, they became conservative, upholding the legitimacy of the social order of the time. But others stressed the wilfulness at the centre of his vision. These Young Hegelians were more romantic and more progressive. Some were especially creative, striving not just to understand the world but to change it by will. To do so, they overturned the Hegelian system, creating a self-sufficient worldview of their own.

Marx's Labour Theory of Value Creation

With Marx, the socialist tradition matured. Before the dominance of Marxism, nineteenth-century socialism 'was a highly competitive enterprise,'[35] to borrow from a recent ironist. Marx was able to dominate egalitarianism because he found a simple way to normalize Hegel while retaining the socialist idea of freedom. It is a familiar story that Marx inverted Hegel so that materialism replaced idealism, and economics replaced philosophy, as the engines of progress. But Marx's idea was founded on a more basic substitution. He simply redefined positive liberty, the new secular source of value, not as will but as labour. His central innovation, borrowed from Adam Smith, was the labour theory of value. Marx's inversion worked by giving to labour the place that his predecessors had given to the creative will. The progress of history was not a movement towards communal wilfulness, as Hegel had written, but towards communal labour. The end was the same – humanity would emerge with a common productive consciousness – but the process was driven by a different kind of creativity – that of the ordinary worker.

Capital is no more than the name of a special kind of surplus value that is left over once labourers have been clothed, housed, and fed. The genius of industrial capitalism was to allow the surplus value from labour to become self-creating as the tools of production. Capital is a tool used for the creation of further surplus value, which, wrongfully, is controlled by capitalists. The alienation of labour from its own value – the value of which it is the initial source – would eventually come to an end with the coming-to-consciousness of the proletariat. The capitalists would be overthrown, and the tools of production would be retaken by labour. The alienation of labour from its value would end, together with the superstructural conventions of capitalism. Labour would become self-ruling, conscious of itself as the true source of value. All that was needed to initiate this process was agitation by a few leading figures. These apostates of the ruling class would lead the revolution by anticipating the true desires of the proletariat. They could become the midwife of history.

For Marx, pre-history was the era of the non-productive collectivity. Early peoples subsisted, consuming all that they produced. Their labour did not create surplus value, and society remained united in its productivity and consumption. In order for value to become self-productive, labourers and their product had first to become alienated. The first stage of this process was early agriculture, which created more than was consumed. Value for the first time was created as a thing in itself; it could be accumulated and exchanged. Labour began to divide. With the rise of specialized workers, some of this created value was exchanged for tools. With the accumulation of the tools of production, capitalism arose. In capitalism, society had discovered the magic of self-creating value, but society was further disunited. Industry grew and the production of value flourished. As capitalists accumulated wealth, they caused alienated labourers to collect in large industrial groups. Finally, in a stage yet to come, accumulated value and collectivized labour would be reunited upon the overthrow of the capitalists. Under communism, collectivized labour would produce value in common – value for all to use. History would be complete and humanity again would be whole, creating and enjoying value in full consciousness of itself as a single productive entity. Class-consciousness of workers, rather the self-conscious *Geist*, was the destiny of humanity as a completed whole. This was the story, adapted from Hegel, that Marx told by substituting labour for will as the source of value.

Marx thought Hegel had almost seen the true essence of the human being as labourer but had erred in describing the dialectic as operating in the realm of ideas; instead, history was the process by which labour and labourer became alienated from each other before being reunited. Hegel was not entirely wrong, merely too abstract. As such, he had mistaken the limited work of philosophy for the true productive activity of physical labour. 'The only labour which Hegel knows and recognizes is *abstractly mental* labour ... In short, within the sphere of abstraction, Hegel conceives labour as man's act of *self-genesis* ... the coming-to-be of *species-consciousness* and *species-life*.'[36] To transform Hegel's vision, Marx would come to see, one need only replace his abstract conception of self-creativity with the labour theory of value. The motive force of history was not in an ethereal philosophy but in the hard economic reality of the common labourer.

Physical labour was related to the self-creative lifeforce itself: 'The productive life is the life of the species. It is life-engendering life. The whole character of a species – its species character – is contained in the character of its life-activity; and free, conscious activity is man's species character ... Man makes his life-activity itself the object of his will and of his consciousness. He has conscious life-activity.'[37] This was the view of the early Marx, contained in the *Manuscripts* of 1844, which show that the economic turn in his thought was not a late consideration. For him, labour was value-creativity and was related to the power of will.

From that basis, Marx began his study of history. Economic development was the story of the alienation and then reconciliation of labour with its own vital force. Production developed first in agriculture and then in industry as labour learned to create surplus value. But as long as humanity remained estranged from the product of its labour, this life-activity was merely instrumental, necessary to maintain life but lacking its true conscious meaning. Under capitalism, labourers would be given nothing more than was necessary to subsist, with capitalists taking the rest. Only later, when labour and product were reunited, would humanity be truly free in the positive, creative sense. This freedom, for Marx as for Hegel, was inherently communal. With his inversion of Hegel, Marx took up the story of history as the self-creation of society through the collectivization of positive liberty: 'Since for the socialist man the *entire so-called history of the world* is nothing but the begetting of man through human labour, nothing but the coming-to-be of nature for man, he has the visible, irrefutable proof of his *birth* through himself, of his *process* of *coming-to-be*.'[38]

In his mature theory, Marx differentiated between labour as value and labour as the source of value: 'Human labour-power in motion, or human labour, creates value, but is not itself value. It becomes value only in its congealed state, when embodied in the form of some object.'[39] When this object was a tool or industrial process, capital was created. Capital was objectified labour, a productive force that had become estranged from its source. But the objects in which this value became crystallized were special: the tools of production were created but also creative. Productive tools, or capital, represented congealed value in itself but were also value creating. In short, capital was value-creating-value. The magic of capital was in 'the power or activity which creates value by value existing for-itself – which lies in the concept of capital.'[40] As value-creating-value, capital allowed the productive forces of industry to be unleashed.

In its early stages, labour created value in its 'congealed state' when artisans made and used their tools and farmers worked their own plots of land. Private property in these primitive forms marked the beginning of the alienation of labour and the first accumulation of capital. Value-creating-value had come into being. What was alienated could be owned, and at this stage the tools of production were self-owned by the labourer. But production thereupon 'flourishes, it lets loose its whole energy, it attains its adequate classical form only where the labourer is the private owner of his own means of labour set in action by himself.'[41] Alienation was necessary for production to create value where once there were only raw materials.

Marx, while among the most forceful critics of capitalism, also understood it as providing the preconditions for labour's eventual emancipation. He hated the rich who owned capital, but he saw capital as creating value. Unless alienated in this way, labour cannot become productive: 'Capital's ceaseless striving towards the general form of wealth drives labour beyond the limits if its natural paltriness, and thus creates the material elements for the development of the rich individuality which is all-sided in its production as in its consumption, and whose labour also therefore appears no longer as labour, but as the full development of activity itself.' Although subjugating workers, capitalism creates the wealth for their eventual liberation. But more than that, it creates society as a single productive entity: 'All combined labour in a large scale requires, more or less, a directing authority, in order to secure the harmonious working of the individual activities ... Their union into one single productive body ... [is] not their own act, but the act of the capital that brings and keeps them together ... As co-operators, as members of a working organism they are but special modes of existence of capital ... The capitalist mode ... [is] a necessary condition to the transformation of the labour-process into a social process.'[42]

Capitalism created the class-consciousness of the proletariat, which would emerge as a single productive entity with full self-awareness of its creative power. 'The life-process of society, which is based on the process of material production, does not strip off its mystical veil until it is treated as production by freely associated men, and is consciously regulated by them.'[43] Marx was notoriously vague about the organization of society after the revolution, but his history, like Hegel's, was teleologically holistic, with an end in which all social questions were resolved in the creative unity of the whole. Once the goal of value-giving solidarity had been achieved, for Marx as for Hegel, no social problems would remain. History was the process by which those issues were worked out, and the end of history was their resolution. By definition, the post-historical period would be without social ills. The answer to all problems was the creative power of solidarity.

Modern Socialism

The essence of socialism is equal participation in the creative will of society as a whole. The core idea that ties together community and positive liberty is solidarity, the sharing of creative social power. Socialists put more emphasis on equality than do other political thinkers, but equality of material conditions is not their ultimate goal because socialism, at its heart, is not materialistic; rather, true egalitarianism is about the equality of power, the equality of will, the equality of participation in the creative forces of life. Inequality of material conditions is taken as proof of the absence of the equality of power but is not, in itself, the central problem. Marx's rallying cry at the end of his pamphlets is not 'Equality' but 'Unite!' Equality, beginning with the distribution of productive resources, is a necessary means to the true socialist end, which is solidarity as self-creative power-in-unity.

Some liberals will agree with the ideal of full equality of power. The Dworkin-Kymlicka ideal of the egalitarian plateau is a move in this direction. Any properly liberal theory, according to these egalitarian liberals, must promise equality of respect and dignity and, therefore, of power and resources. But Dworkin and Kymlicka are still individualists. Socialists believe not just in equal power but in common power. They want unity in the creative forces of life, the progress not of individuals alone but of society as a single whole. Socialism is essentially holistic, promising a sense of full belonging in the common life of a growing, progressive society.

The economic failures of Marxism have been a major setback for socialism, but non-economistic alternatives will retain their appeal. The concept of democracy as a collective, self-developmental ideal, by which society may be transformed and the vagaries of human nature transcended, is socialistic at its core. The goal is to create individuals anew, altering the given ends of human nature in order to bring people together. Creativity should not be an individual's private goal but should be the common objective of society itself. Society should be self-creative, the means by which human nature is transformed and united.

For example, the participatory democracy of Carole Pateman and Benjamin Barber argued for Rousseauvian self-governance as a collective transformational goal. As Pateman wrote, 'Rousseau's theory provides the starting point and the basic material for any discussion of the participatory theory of democracy; the good society creates its own model citizens through "socialisation," or "social training" ... in order that the necessary individual attitudes and psychological qualities can be developed. This development takes place through the process of participation itself.'[44] Barber's view was similar: 'Autonomy is not the condition of democracy, democracy is the condition of autonomy ... Freedom, justice, equality, and autonomy are all products of common thinking and common living; democracy creates them.'

Again: 'We can learn how to become creative individuals *within* the families, tribes, nations, and communities into which we are born, or we can remain heteronomous pawns of such associations.'[45]

For thinkers of this school, true democracy is based on communal autonomy, but self-given laws are not simply about governance; rather, they are the tools with which we define ourselves. The freedom in which we are to be united is autotelic. Individuals create themselves through democracy, overcoming their private, given inclinations in order to come together in a common, self-given good. For solidarity theorists, negative liberty is the problem to which communal positive liberty is the solution. Rousseau is its first exemplar, and the Lockean view of human nature remains anathema. As Barber summarized, Locke's view of human nature 'reduces the role of will to one of obstinate resistance. Hence it obstructs common willing – what Rousseau called general willing – where communities essay to disclose common purposes or discover common ground through the political interaction of active wills. The very idea of sovereignty, construed as the paramountcy of a common will, cannot exist in a setting defined by the primacy of the right of the individual to unlimited resistance (that resistance being seen as a property of essential – and hence rightful – human nature).'[46]

Among the most interesting non-economistic socialists is Charles Taylor. In his early work, Taylor properly locates the source of resistance to communal thinking in the alternative empiricist tradition: 'The exclusion of this possibility of the communal comes once again from the baleful influence of the epistemological tradition for which all knowledge has to be reconstructed from the impressions imprinted on the individual subject.'[47] Descartes, and then the English empiricists, sowed the first seeds of modern individualism. In Taylor's philosophy, they are among the villains who led modern politics astray. He also recognizes that negative and positive liberty may be combined into a single political idea, as J.S. Mill did in following Humboldt. Individual self-realization requires that one be free from the imposition of others, thus negative liberty is instrumental to the positive liberty of individuals. But, taken as an ideal in itself, the negative conception causes individuality to devolve into self-interest and atomism. Thus, Taylor is among the most forthright of those who argue against negative liberty.[48] To summarize his project, Taylor wants to overthrow the negative concept of liberty and rehabilitate the positive notion, taking it back from individualistic liberals. His goal is to reassert positive liberty as communal freedom. As such, Taylor is among the clearest, most self-aware representatives of modern, non-Marxist socialism.

A short introduction to Taylor's project is the booklet, *The Malaise of Modernity*.[49] Against Rousseau's concept of freedom, with its variants in Hegel and Marx (each of which can become totalitarian), Taylor suggested the ideal authenticity. This is derived from Herder, according to whom 'each of us has an original way of being human ... Being true to myself means being true to my own originality, and that is something only I can articulate and discover. In articulating it, I am also defining myself.'[50] Authenticity is not just self-rule but self-creation, positive liberty in its purest form. Taylor moved quickly from individual authenticity to its communal form, which he called the 'culture of authenticity.' Self-definition is not a private matter because it requires the resources of a public language: 'We become full human agents, capable of understanding ourselves, and hence of defining an identity, through our acquisition of rich human languages ... No one acquires the languages needed for self-definition on their own. We are introduced to them through exchanges with others ... The genesis of the human mind is in this sense not "monological," not something each accomplishes on his or her own, but dialogical.'[51]

The focus on social interaction gives rise to Taylor's concerns about the need for egalitarian recognition. In traditional society, one's identity was given by one's place in the social order, but in the culture of authenticity, where one creates oneself through interaction with others, social recognition is the necessary precondition to the acquisition of an identity. Equality of recognition becomes an essential demand because, without it, we are robbed of the means of creative self-definition. Having gazed in the modern mirror of individual self-sufficiency, and having found no true source of value there, Taylor's suggestion is that we look for it in the eyes of our fellows.

Taylor is not a mere reactionary against liberal individualism because he sees that it shares a core value with his own communal ideal of self-creation. While liberalism sometimes takes the debased form of negative libertarianism, it may also appear as a moral ideal when it leans, instead, towards positive liberty. Liberals of the latter sort have his sympathy, though not his agreement. They are his allies, however, against the misguided values of conservatives and right-leaning liberals. 'The struggle ought not to be *over* authenticity, for or against, but *about* it, defining its proper meaning.' Thus legitimate political discourse is limited by Taylor to include only versions of positive liberty. All else is beyond the pale. The threat to authenticity comes from 'an alliance of people with a disengaged scientistic outlook, and those with more traditional ethical views, as well as some proponents of an outraged high culture.'[52]

The latter description comes in a paragraph calling for dialogue and sympathetic engagement, yet it is clear that Taylor does not hope to extend the discussion to thinkers animated by political traditions much beyond his own. That his system is based on dialogical equality and inclusiveness, yet excludes those with other evaluative priorities, is a symptom of the conceptual tension inherent to modern socialism. An ideal based on unity in a disunited world, it must exclude those whom it sees as the source of fragmentation. The completion of the socialist project is for the future. For today, it is an activity for insiders only, the private pursuit of an intellectual elite. Socialism today excludes the majority of the people because they cling to other ideals. Taylor knows that in an era dominated by liberal individualism, to talk of the single will of the community is to be misunderstood. While he occasionally hints at this goal,[53] his argument is that of a sage who knows the mass is against him. If he hesitates to state his case outright, it is because of its inherent difficulty. His is a project whose completion cannot yet be envisioned either by its beneficiaries or even by its prophets.

Among political ideologies, socialism is conceptually the most demanding. Not only do its best defenders see freedom as self-creation – as difficult as pulling oneself up by one's bootstraps[54] – but they centre it in society as a whole. Among some of its originating theorists, like Hegel and Marx, society was expected to emerge in time as a single consciousness. For those outside the German idealist tradition, and even for those who struggle within it, this is a challenging concept. There is an additional political problem for socialists. This problem is related to the first but occurs in practice rather than in theory. On one hand, their ideal is based on inclusiveness in decision making: no voices should go unheard. On the other, dissenters are by definition a threat to harmonious decisions. In modern politics, one symptom of this tension may be seen in the fact that socialists view themselves as the ultimate democrats but attract relatively few voters. The result is a kind of Manichean politics of denunciation against the villains who are misleading the people. Much of the intellectual energy of socialists is expended in unmasking false prophets rather than on building on the comparative appeal of their core values. A comparison of values is contrary to their vision because to compare values is to accept the evaluative diversity of modern democracy.

Since their ideal is communal consensus, the problem of legitimate dissent is particularly acute for socialists. By contrast, the political ideologies that include negative liberty do not seem as inimical to political pluralism and dissent. Conservatives recognize the political realm as limited and, therefore, as excluding questions about ultimate ends. Society, they suggest, works out these issues in the course of its natural evolution, unless it is distorted by the meddling of wilful politicians. Liberals, meanwhile, consign the problem of tensions among ends to the individual's own conscience. Only socialism makes harmony in politics central to its ideal.

The ideal of harmony is sometimes defended in contrast to totalitarian unity, for example by Benjamin Barber: 'The aim is harmony: the discovery of a common voice. Not unity, not voices disciplined into unison, but musical harmony in its technical meaning ... In music, harmony is not a matter of a single voice but of several voices, of distinct notes, which complement and support one another, creating not the ennui of unison but a pleasing plurality. Harmony is not monism, and the consensus reached by democratic deliberation and action has nothing in common with the unity imposed by the collectivist demagogue armed with a plebiscite.'[55] But before we can join the chorus, we must be willing to be remade. The mutability of each singer is the first requirement of Barber's ideal: 'The participating citizen, however, is a being with a mutable nature, whose evolution is in part a function of its social habitat ... Participation entails change – a faculty for self-transformation – for the community as well as for the participating member.'[56] Harmony requires that we change our tune.

The difficulty of socialism may be illustrated by comparing Taylor with his Oxford teacher, Isaiah Berlin. Although a defender of the idea of negative liberty, at times hinting at its primacy among liberties,[57] Berlin was a thoroughgoing value pluralist. His central idea is that there are many ideals and values, each with its unique legitimacy. Tyranny arises only when one ideal is imposed over all others. Even negative liberty may become tyrannical if it comes to occlude all alternative ideals.

Taylor, by contrast, returns occasionally to the question of pluralism in the ends of life, but he does so in the way the tongue returns to an aching tooth. For example, his notion of deep diversity suggests that, in a nation like Canada, some citizens may be defined as rights-bearing individualists, while others may belong to a more cohesive collectivity.[58] This collective entity presumably would be allowed to take certain actions to ensure its own flourishing.[59] While some regions allow each person to choose his or her own way, other regions may be more culturally unified. The individualistic solution to pluralism, Taylor suggests, is shallow diversity. Real diversity exists when some groups are allowed not to be internally pluralistic. True pluralism should allow a unity of goods among its legitimate ideals. This is an important and useful idea because the individualist approach to the fact of pluralism does in fact downgrade the value of community. The solution to the problem of pluralism, Taylor suggests, is a kind of non-universalistic solidarity for some and liberal individualism for others. Conservatism, of course, is unacceptable to Taylor. His diversity may be deep, but it is not wide.

Elsewhere, Taylor dissociates himself from the 'utopian monism of radical thought, in order to take account of the real diversity of goods that we recognize.' But he also wants to order these goods, which requires a common scale of valuation. 'A single coherent order of goods is rather like an idea of reason in the Kantian sense, something we always try to define without ever managing to achieve it definitively.'[60] This is asymptotic monism but monism nonetheless. Near the end of *Sources of the Self*, he hints that a 'publicly accessible cosmic order of meanings' might become possible in a less individualistic age.[61]

In direct response to Berlin's value pluralism, Taylor writes, 'I still believe that we can and should struggle for a "transvaluation" (to borrow Nietzsche's term *Umwertung*) which could open the way to a mode of life, individual and social, in which these demands could be reconciled.'[62] His rejection of universalistic solidarity for a more nuanced view, whereby each culture may find its own way, is consistent with the ideal of self-creativity that reached a kind of completion with Nietzsche. But the ideal of transvaluation is itself a value, lying near the core of positive liberty. To assert the supremacy of this value is to be a monist. Taylor's monism is implicit in his socialism. His ideal may be defined as a particularistic version of communal positive libertarianism. His concession to value pluralism is to recognize that others may want to be excluded from the ideal, but he clearly believes they would be choosing a less valuable life.

Non-universalistic socialism is an important amendment to the tradition, given the current reality of a pluralistic world, but Taylor's is not the only alternative. Another approach is that of Paul Hirst, who suggests that socialism should resituate itself as primarily a social goal rather than a governmental one. Society includes a great range of voluntary associative groups, and socialists should form their own. Voluntaristic socialism, co-existing with other social groups, is what Hirst calls associative democracy.[63]

A major theme of Hirst's work is the pluralism of contending goals pursued by various groups within a single nation. These groups are best served by the institutions of civil society, which can be pluralistic in a way that the institutions of government, which presumably must share a coherent policy vision, have greater difficulty achieving. A healthy pluralism of values is enabled by a variety of voluntary associations, including multicultural groups and goal-oriented assemblies of like-minded citizens. Differences do not become cleavages until they are politicized, so the proper domain for the expression of political diversity and value pluralism is in civil society, which thereby may become a kind of policy adjunct to the state:

> The claim made here is that 'pluralization' of the state is compatible with the project of associational socialism, with devolving the tasks of social organization and economic activity to self-governing voluntary associations of citizens ... Socialism must be built in civil society, by voluntary and autonomous efforts. It must return to the associationalist tradition and create its own institutions, in the way that the cooperative movements, the friendly societies and the Arts and Crafts colonies attempted to do. Seeking to monopolize centralized state power, seeking to make socialism a compulsory social project, has been the ruin of socialism.[64]

Hirst's solution will not satisfy those, like Taylor, who continue to be attracted to the creative possibilities of politics. For them, Hirst will have missed the point. The creative unity of the people is inherently political, defined by the process of collective self-governance. Hirst's suggestion will seem to them at best an interim solution, educative and transformative but not suitable as a final goal in itself. The endpoint of socialism should be solidarity, not the fragmentary multiculturalism of plural associations.

Whatever their differences, writers like Taylor and Hirst show that socialism remains difficult but not impossible to conceptualize. Its problems lie in its height of ambition, in seeing society as a self-creative whole. This ideal may continue to mature as simplistic materialism and authoritarian alternatives are abandoned. Since its roots mingle deeply with others in the history of modern democracy, its intellectual and historical depth will allow socialism as a political ideal to continue. It will be strong among many theorists, several activists, a number of politicians, and some voters.

But its importance may not lie entirely in its theoretical strength. In an individualistic world, where evolved social institutions have lost their meaning for many people, socialism promises a new source of belonging. Its theoretical proponents may want to emphasize the meaninglessness of social life because its transformation is their goal, so the malaise of modernity may appear strongest to those predisposed to certain values. Nonetheless, the strength of this worldview may not lie in its descriptive accuracy or its theoretical clarity but in its evaluative resonance. Socialism may take its most coherent form as a consistent value orientation rather than as a fully developed political philosophy. It is more an ideal than a theory.

The need for social belonging may attract adherents to less intellectualized versions of the socialist ideal. An example is the popularity of new-age spiritualism and therapeutic movements that promise to provide a new meaning to life through group belonging. A related phenomenon is the modern tendency of some to define themselves as the victims of outside forces. The embrace of victimhood may seem at first to be an abdication of human will, but its ideological force is in seeing causality as something foreign and dangerous: If it were not for the harmful forces within me, imposed *against* my will, then my true creative spirit would emerge. Adherents to such beliefs identify the causal order not in terms of the givenness of human nature but as the source of spiritual oppression. The popularity of Freudian ideas, among some left-leaning political thinkers and among ordinary people, may be due to its relation to the ideal of belonging through self-creation. Through consciousness-raising or some other collective process, one's true self-creativity may emerge in a new group-derived identity. Human nature may be transformed through belonging, whereupon the meaning of life, our creative growth together, will become clear.

This is a modern story of compelling force for those who see each person as the original link in a great chain of being. This ancient idea, now secularized and humanized, continues to provide meaning to many lives.

Every soul, in this view, is a source of value, the way a flame is the source of light. Goodness emanates from each person – or would do so, if illicit influences did not get in the way. We ought not ask how the unfortunate arrived in their current state because historical contingencies are irrelevant. The creative potential of each person begins in the present moment. Questions about personal responsibility belong to an alternative tradition. In this one, the light from each soul shines anew with every moment. Each person is good or has the potential to be so; evil is contingent, artificial, unnecessary.

From this belief, it is a short step to see human goodness as a single thing. The prophets of individuality, who properly understood each soul as the source of a special light, failed only to recognize the similarity of their glow. It is only our given nature that sets us apart, that distorts our enlightenment. Since moral growth is our essence, we can only grow better by growing together. The problem is to eliminate the obstacles to communal progress. These begin in human nature, which is neither as rigid nor (certainly) as righteous as is supposed in the alternative tradition of negative liberty. We must overcome this tradition as a first step towards the achievement of internally generated common good. In this shared sense of self-creativity, by which we define ourselves as a community, an authentic self-generated sense of communal belonging can be found.

In politics, this view can take the form of participatory politics as discursive democracy, industrial democracy, or some other mode of enlightened self-determination. In economics, it leads to an egalitarianism of resources, which are understood as the materials necessary for self-development. Some forms of religious association are socialistic in their nature, especially where religion is seen as the route to self-fulfillment. Wherever spiritual growth is valued more than duty towards a given morality, religion turns towards positive liberty. Religions that stress progressive communality are socialistic; those that focus on communal morality are conservative; those that leave the choice to individuals are like the fitting rooms of enlightenment. (Adorned with beliefs that suit us perfectly, we express our authentic selves to the world.) In personal spiritualism, the socialist ideal may take the form of therapeutic movements. These may be further animated by political goals, like the consciousness-raising groups of the early women's movement. In self-creativity, the personal is political. Some of these groups may emerge as broad social movements, providing a sense of living purpose to their members. For these citizens, the search for greater inclusiveness is overriding. Social growth becomes an end in itself, providing a shared sense of self-becoming. In general, anyone for whom the community is a source of self-growth may be attracted to the socialist ideal.

Socialism is especially difficult because of its focus on inclusion. As a political theory, socialism is complicated by its consensual ambition, but as a set of values it is vigorous in modern society. The idea of social progress is one that may appeal to many liberals, especially those alienated by modernity, even if they would not take the step to a fully holistic conception of society. The most important political effect of socialism may be in its leftward pull on the liberal individualist majority. Democracy is large and contains multitudes, including socialistic movements and ideas. Its core values go deep in Western history, and as one of the ocean currents of modern democratic politics, socialism will endure.

However, if value pluralism is true, then many potential socialists will also recognize the attraction of alternative ideals. According to the theory of value pluralism, each of us can see the unique value of competing ideals. These values are incommensurable: they cannot be measured on a single scale because each good is unique. Good things are good in their own way. Liberty is good as liberty, not as equality or justice. Goodness is not a monistic quality. The more we try to define it, the more it splinters into subsets, each with its own unique quality. Plato was wrong: the Form of the Good is variety. Pulled from the cave, we see many suns. Goodness contains multitudes – that is value pluralism at its simplest. The harder we look for the common good, the more it divides into a variety of goods. Diversity is in the details, increasing with each order of magnification. The deeper we go to justify our choices, the further we are pulled apart. The endless diffusion of the good into distinct goods – this entropy of value – is the reason socialism is so difficult.

8
Democracy as a Pattern of Disagreement

We began by asking why people disagree about politics. Deep disagreement is the most obvious feature of politics today, but we do not yet have an explanation for this fact – at least, we have no explanation that respects the basic evaluative complexity of our culture as legitimate. Sources of evaluative error are not hard to adduce: perhaps the people are blinded by self-interest, are ideologically distorted, are falsely conscious, or are unwitting victims of systemic social forces. Alternatively, perhaps the people have been seduced by the licentiousness of a counter-cultural vanguard class whose vices exemplify our moral decline. Just as we have divergent values in our culture, so we have a variety of theories explaining why the people are wrong.

Each of us wants to believe that our fellow citizens share our own evaluative priorities, or would do so if only they saw things clearly. We all want to live in a community that reflects our self-understanding. It is painful to imagine that our fellows reject our views. Can it really be, when we hear an opinion we cannot share, one that offends against our own defining ideals, that such a view can be reasonably held? What kind of community are we – what kind of person am I – if such statements, contrary to our deepest values, are not denounced categorically as false? If I am right to hold my views, whose truth gives purpose to my life, then those who contradict me are plainly wrong. Their views are offensive and so is any theory that says they are legitimate.

Pluralism, among those who work hard for their opinions, is a theory that invites rejection. After all, politics is already painful and divisive. We do not need a theory that would solidify our evaluative differences. Whatever our own political views, we may join in the hope that pluralism is false. We should favour, instead, the contrary hope for progress towards a common good.

Unfortunately, hope is sometimes the enemy of truth. The most obvious fact about politics is that people disagree about the common good. As far as history can be traced, the best thinkers in each age challenged each other's understanding of the good. Each of the great political philosophers found followers, but across schools, dissensus was the rule. Within schools, consensus was ephemeral, rarely outliving the founding thinker. Free thought, it seems, leads inevitably to disagreement. Today, in every political community of freethinkers, the only consensus is that most people think most people are wrong.

Political thinkers tend to splinter into poorly connected groups, rather like clubs for the like-minded. Within these clubs, people disagree within a more narrow range of opinion. The more general the definition of this shared vision, the more inclusive the group can be. Political beliefs are not just abstract values; they are *our* beliefs, the highest defining good that we share. Our club is right, the others are wrong. The truth of this feeling is so visceral, so central to our identity, that it remains only to work out the details among us. Yet, when discussions go beyond broad principles, agreement about specifics becomes elusive. Even among the generally like-minded, dissensus is never far away. The art of maintaining consensus (as every committee head knows) rests on limiting the depth and breadth of discussion. The more sophisticated the group, the more numerous the disagreements. And so, we remain polite, we stay on the surface, we refrain from mentioning all the small ways our fellows are wrong.

Every community protects its certitudes from evaluative entropy by limiting the topics of conversation. Our taboos unite us by protecting the illusion of approaching consensus. With every move towards specificity and concreteness in politics – as we close in on the common good by descending from national myths, to constitutions, to political platforms, to public policy, to legislation, to enforcement – the conflict of goods becomes more acute. Each step towards concreteness requires an additional increment of authority, the monopoly of force by those in charge at that level.

However, if politics involves conflict, this tells us nothing about the truth of the pluralist theory as presented here. Why should we believe that the full range of values surveyed in the previous chapters are equally legitimate? Just because an evaluative worldview is historically grounded and continues to have adherents today, it does not follow that this worldview is true or good. For example, taking a side of the debate for illustration, racism was founded on a conception that can no longer be thought reasonable; why not reject other social atavisms? Perhaps the only legitimate pluralism is among versions of emancipatory politics, whether of the liberal or socialist families. Modern, progressive pluralism is about accommodating differences within a common emancipatory framework. It should not include freedom-denying political visions that accept human nature as given. If negative liberty was founded on the archaic scientism of Galilean physics, then why should we respect such an outmoded belief today? In the march towards a pluralistic politics, we must leave some old ideals behind. Pluralism is deep, but it is not so wide.

The history of ideas may be of interest for its own sake (a critic might continue), but to suggest that the essence of an idea may be contained in its source is to commit the genetic fallacy. For example, the fact that people share genetic ancestors with other primates does not mean we are 'really' just monkeys. Evolution moves onward and sometimes upward, in ideas and values as among living things. Obviously, values change over time. New, more developed beliefs come to replace older, less progressive ones – not just because they are new but because they are better. How can it be denied that positive liberty, with its corollary about the inherent dignity of each human soul, is more compelling than the cold, lonely worldview of negative liberty? In the case of positive liberty, something of the old story remains true: moral goodness belongs potentially to each wilful being. Each human will is like a light that cannot be doused, though in unhappy circumstances it may be eclipsed. Pernicious events sometimes get in the way of a good will, but, in their potential, all souls are *inherently* good; evil is a matter of a harmful environment. To reject this truth is to lose the highest good that we have. History helps us see that some traditions are enriching and good; others should be forgotten. Positive liberty provides a better narrative of modern life than does negative liberty. We should retain one and reject the other. This is the true lesson of history.

Can this objection be reasonably met? In fact, it is tautological, having persuasive force only if one accepts the evaluative priorities upon which it is based. There is no Archimedian, value-superior viewpoint from which we can judge between political values. The value of positive liberty is undeniable, but it is not the only value we have. The belief in the ultimate dignity of all persons, regardless of events in their lives, is contested as a matter of fact. Is it *legitimately* contestable, or are those who contest it merely confused? This is a question of competing values. Some people believe that the right to life itself can be forfeited. Depending on how one asks the question, this belief may belong to a large majority of citizens. A survey that puts the question in the context of an egregious evil – Should Hitler have been executed, if caught? – may achieve near unanimity. For most people, some human evils are too great to be excused as caused by pernicious events. Sometimes the human will is the source of evil. The light of every human soul does not burn with equal goodness; some people are not a source of value. Those who do great evil by conscious and deliberate acts of will have lost their inherent dignity, or perhaps they never had it. If our starting point is a context of great human evil, then the inherent dignity of each human being is less sure. It depends on where you begin and on how the conversation develops. It is the sort of thing about which reasonable people may disagree.

The alleged superiority of positive liberty is a popular bias among modern intellectuals and artists, whose preferred pursuits are those requiring self-creative talent. The modern university, for example, is a broadly anti-conservative institution whose purpose is to allow a new generation to develop its own self-creative powers. Universities are institutions of social mobility; they are where students go to find their own telos. Members of these institutions may vary in their understanding of this wilful choice – whether one's ends should be uniquely self-created; whether they should be chosen from a range of pre-existing alternatives; or whether they should merely be examined and endorsed without necessarily changing. Views vary in their radical import, but the ideology of the modern university is skewed in a certain way. We create ourselves through our self-expressive freedom, dismantling old mores, ideas, and values by putting new ones in their place. To the extent that they see this as their role, academics are positive libertarians.

Although there are exceptions (who must pay the price of disfavour for their views), among academics there are not many who are open to the gut-level moral force that conservative and negative-libertarian ideas have for many people. Religious conservatives, for example, are beheld with incomprehension at best and, at worst, with fear and loathing. Economic libertarians may be seen as less overtly dangerous but are dismissed as promoters of selfishness. In the modern university, the dominant range of political values is narrower than it is in the broader culture. It is an important institution within our culture, but it is one with its own mission and its own systemic ideological bias. The breadth of value pluralism tends not to be recognized by academic political thinkers because their club has certain ideological entrance requirements. In the broader culture, there are many clubs, each with its own characteristic club-talk. Democracy is bigger than a university.

The certitudes of positive liberty are most obvious to those for whom they are the founding club-talk. Every normative argument is founded on definable evaluative grounds. Intellectuals are cleverer than others in justifying their normative priorities, but they, too, begin with values taken from our common culture. Our reason is the slave of our priorities. Like everyone else, intellectuals must sort out the ultimate conflicts among our values as best they can. It is in the nature of political theory that the explanatory edifices we erect eventually obscure the complexity of our foundational values. Political theorists are like bricklayers who assume that the earth beneath them is flat. This assumption allows them to build upward at perfect right angles; otherwise, how could we know where to place the next brick? But, in fact, our foundational starting points do not line up perfectly with each other. Building upward from an uneven surface, small differences on the ground become large distances between higher stories. At the surface, we were close neighbours; in the clouds, we are far apart. And now, looking back to earth, our initial differences are hard to see because the edifices of competing theories obscure the ground below. Which theory stands truest? There is no way to say because our values plumb differently at the ground.

So, in answer to the criticism that positive liberty presents a better story about how to live, and that the pluralist theory presented here is illegitimately broad, the answer is a plea to open your sympathies a little wider and to include more of your fellow citizens – not as you wish them to be but as they actually are. When it comes to understanding political conflict, the safer bet is towards breadth, but for those with fixed priorities, any truly pluralist theory will seem too wide. Those committed to the priority of positive liberty have their own gut-level beliefs and will not accept the visceral certitudes of others. And so politics goes. Among the committed, it is a duel of incomprehension, an unwinnable war of conflicting certitudes; for those with unresolved views, it is a bewildering contest of common goods; for the uninterested, it is a disreputable waste of time. Democracy has something for everyone.

The understanding of politics presented here is based on the theory that its values are the basis of a culture. There is no further foundation for our values; our values go all the way down. If cultures are ways of life, and if values are ideas about how to live, then the values of a culture are its essence.[1] Values may be understood as divergent themes within a single cultural story. Because a culture is neither a single mind nor an arithmetic aggregate, its defining themes can be many and conflicting. Characters and plot lines vary over time, but these themes retain their animating power. The culture examined here is a diffuse one, which grew from ancient Greece and Rome, spreading through Europe and on to other continents. For convenience, we may call it the culture of the West, but it is the most likely candidate to grow into a global culture. For those of us who belong to it, because we share conflicting values, we have a common culture.

The history of ideas is the story of our stories. It tells us that our stories are many and that their themes conflict with each other. The logical stories of our most careful thinkers are especially useful in showing the divergence of themes because they magnify our differences by drawing their architecture in straight lines. If we work our way back downward from the edifices of theory by tracing the history of ideas, we discover no firm foundation. All thinkers built upon the stories they knew; we never reach the ground level; beneath our ideas we will find only more ideas. Perceptions matter, evidence counts, logic must be followed. The end product, however, must be a story that people can live by, one that helps us make sense of our lives. Our stories are all that we have. In fact, we have many. What we do not have is a super-story that resolves all the conflicts among them.

Because we lack rational criteria of judgment between ultimate options – because there is no super-value among the ultimate values of our culture – there are limits to which our priorities among them can be defended by reason. Moral philosophy has no final answer to the problem of how best to live. Its ancient conceit is to believe there must be a single best answer, which we may find using our powers of reason, but this promise has never been fulfilled. The problems of life are not solved by appealing to rational philosophy but by incremental judgments of priority among goods in par-ticular cases. Little by little, as we make these judgments over the course of our lives, we become what we will be. Each judgment establishes the con-text for the next difficult decision we must make. We are who we are be-cause we live a certain way, going in one way instead of another. Our self-understanding is built upon a long series of previous judgments among conflicting goods. Reason under-determines our actions not only because goods conflict but because our judgments depend on our accumulating self-understanding; that is, on our previous judgments. We do not live accord-ing to a philosophy but arrive at a philosophy in the course of living. The Owl of Minerva flies at dusk, tracing landscapes that grow by the day.

Using the divergent themes of our common culture, we try to make sense of our lives. We judge among goods based on our self-understanding, and each judgment adds another layer to who we are. Our self-understanding consists of the accretions of our judgments. They provide the frameworks of meaning within which we live, and these are created not by reason but by small rationally under-determined judgments among goods. Each judg-ment adds another stratum of grounding. We do not build our lives by rational blueprints taken from a common philosophy; instead, our self-knowledge accrues upon previous judgments, like choral islands growing from a common sea. And yet, we build upward and apart. Our materials are common, but we diverge.

People make sense of their lives in different ways. To arrive at a self-understanding is to have life-determining preferences from among the rich-ness of cultural possibilities that we share. Our common values or cultural themes, while meaningful to all of us, take us in different directions. In order to make sense of things, we are forced to prioritize values. We under-stand ourselves, and the world around us, according to these priorities. Some of our fellow citizens live by different structures of priorities, or hierarchies of values, and their beliefs contradict our own. And so we come to the basic question of politics – What should we do together? – with opposed views. Political conflict is about differences of priority among shared values.

However, the need to judge among goods does not mean that the free-dom of choice among goods is our highest value. This freedom is the high-est good only in the context of a certain self-understanding. For some, the persistence of open-ended choice would diminish the meaning of life by undermining a given structure of values. Among the competing ideals in our culture is a story about the life of permanent commitment. To say that people must choose because life is about choosing is to narrow the full range of options open to us. Choice is the highest defining value only in terms of a certain evaluative hierarchy. The life of endless possibility makes sense in its own way, but it is exclusive of some good alternatives, like the life of settled conviction. Pluralism does not mean we must venerate choice. Some of the normative stories that make up our culture are not based on choice as the ultimate good. The alternatives are not endless – our culture is not infinite – but, within common horizons of meaning, we have reasons to disagree even about the priority of the freedom of choice.

If values are basic to one's outlook, and if our common values are many, then there will always be room for disagreement in politics. At the bottom of many political conflicts is the fact that we disagree about what it means to be a good person. The priority of the value-creating will, and the inalienable dignity of each human soul, is one such vision. But there may also be legitimate alternatives, including some that place a higher priority on permanent responsibility for one's past actions. Can one's basic dignity be diminished by one's own deliberate acts? Should we distinguish, for example, between the deserving and undeserving poor? Do our misdeeds become part of our identity, or is each moment a new moral beginning? Is crime merely a matter of bad circumstances, or have some of us made ourselves into bad people? Is the accumulation of wealth a mark of oppression, or is it a sign of success in pursuit of happiness? Much of the argument of democracy revolves around these sorts of value-based questions. Positive liberty suggests one kind of answer, but there are others alive in our culture. Democracy is not the pursuit of harmonious self-determination but the contest among positive liberty and other values.

If the permanence of evaluative conflict may be resisted from the point of view of positive liberty, it is also objectionable to those who see our hierarchy of values as given. For example, it might be argued that the approach taken here, the history of ideas, is subversive, destroying our common morality by a subtle process of reductionism. Concerns about the genetic fallacy may arise from more than one side. However, to trace the history of our values is not to unmask them as mere narratives, or to provide a genealogy of groundless morals, but to show why they are meaningful and enriching to modern citizens. The historical-cultural depth of our values demonstrates not their fallaciousness but their authenticity. Does it matter that positive liberty was born from the secularization of divine-command morality? No, because divine-command morality was a real morality, which taught generations of our forbears how to live a good life. Its modernized version continues to do so. Does it diminish the legitimacy of negative liberty to know that it was born from the marriage of Galilean physics and post-Aristotelian ethics? No, because the idea of a natural human telos provides an account of our proper goals that makes life meaningful for many members of our culture. The ethic of self-spontaneous human goodness, and the ethic of responsibility based on self-ownership, are both true ethics whose force every member of our culture can feel – unless, of course, they have been educated into hardened views. Those who have made final judgments may deny the reality of the ideals they have gone against, but for most people the conflict of goods is an ongoing fact. The philosophy of ordinary life is always a work in progress.

Democracy may be defined as the collective decision-making process by which we temporarily decide what to do together by choosing among conflicting goods. Because no single answer is the right one, democratic decisions are never final. Good reasons can always be adduced to revisit collective decisions, so there will always be a back-and-forth quality to public policies produced democratically. Because these decisions are always imperfect, there are limits to what we can do together, but the criteria and location of the line between state and society are among the central questions we will always revisit. Public policies will always be wrong in some way, and so we will always have to try again. However, the political pendulum swings within certain limits because our common values are not infinite in number. Democracy is circumscribed by certain values – to know those values, and the conflicts among them, is to know democracy. It is not a common philosophy but a system of ideas in permanent tension with each other. Democracy is not a single theory but a regular pattern of disagreement.

So enduring is this pattern that a ubiquitous metaphor has arisen to capture the inherent ideological tensions of democracy. Although no one has been able to define it, all political observers know what it means to say that someone is of the left, centre, or right. This metaphor is as old as modern democracy and has survived only because it captures, in a simple way, something about its permanent essence. The inherent oscillations of democracy may give rise to predictions about the demise of left-right tensions, but fluidity should not be mistaken for shapelessness.

Democracy is a culturally specific form of government, deeply rooted in Western values. If any culture seems likely to become global, it is the culture of the West. It may become more complex and convoluted in the process but not less so. Democracy could become more pluralistic as it grows, but to grow is not to be uprooted. As the culture of democracy expands globally, its inherent values will spread with it. Every democratic nation will have a recognizable core of ideological similarities. Local variations may enrich the mixture, but certain lines of arguments will always arise. Every emerging democracy will share the familiar pattern of disagreement. Future cultural developments may complicate these arguments, but left-right differences will remain at the core. If other systems of government arise, rooted solely in cultures other than that of the West, they will not be democratic. Were a mono-ethical culture to replace the culture of Western modernity, politics would become unnecessary and democracy would disappear. Until that happens, democracy will be about value pluralism, and politics will never be less than a three-way argument of left, centre, and right.

Before showing how the values of liberty provide the substructure of the left-right spectrum, let us summarize their history.

Reprise: Two Concepts of Liberty, Three Political Ideologies

Democracy is the rule of the people, but the people disagree about the common good. Democratic politics is copious – or incoherent, depending on how one understands it. (Pluralism conjugates pluralistically: My politics are broad and complex; yours are complicated and thorny; theirs are contradictory and confused.) If deep disagreement about the common good is an observable fact, does this mean that the work of democracy has not yet been done, or should we define democracy in a way that accepts deep divisions among the people? This enquiry began to address this question by examining the nature of civil society. The modern distinction between political and civil society was born in reaction to the universalism of the eighteenth century. Two contrary traditions arose, both of which saw each people as unique. One envisioned these differences in terms of cultural self-creativity, the other in terms of social conventions and modes of evolving civility.

At the heart of these two visions of civil society are two competing conceptions of what it means to be free. On one side is the tradition of positive liberty, which arose with the transition in moral language from virtue to value. The ancient virtues were based on the teleology of given social roles. The first step in the transition from virtue to value came with Neoplatonism, in which the source of good was a self-sufficient God. The good emanated from God like an unquenchable light that was the source of all things and . that had no source outside of itself. Next, the idea of emanation was replaced with that of intentionality. The good came deliberately from God's will rather than emanating from his essence. In the morality of divine command, the good was whatever God valued. Unlike virtue, value is not just a noun but a verb, describing both the product and the process of a creative act. With modernity, this idea became secularized, and the good became that which humans wilfully value.

In this tradition, the human will had become the *self-sufficient* source of goodness. Only the good will, Kant said, could be *good in itself*. Rationality was a formal criterion for morality, but the generative source of good acts was the will. *Self-creativity*, for those who sought this kind of freedom in its deepest sense, was the truest liberty. To define ourselves is not just to give a value-neutral self-description; it is to choose our own ends. Nor is positive liberty merely the freedom to do the things one wants; rather, self-determination is about deciding what to want. It is the ability to give one's defining purpose, or telos, to oneself. At its purest, positive liberty is the idea that one's defining ends are self-created. Although often called autonomy, or self-governance, at the core of this ideal is the *autotelic power* of self-creation.

Like its cousin, negative liberty is a modern idea, born of the secular revolution and the search for meaning in more human-centred terms. This view began with the medieval rediscovery of Aristotelian naturalism, which led to the idea that the causal order was a process put in place by God. This worldview took momentum from Galileo, whose discovery provided the causal mechanism underlying all nature. God made the world to unfold of its own momentum, without requiring his further interventions. Just as divine-command morality was a transitional religious stage in the tradition of positive liberty, Deism, or natural religion, was the precursor in the development of negative liberty. Nature was a causal process originating from a divine source.

In this view, the purpose of human life is in the natural flow of things. In the empiricist version of Aristotelian teleology, the internal life of each person is part of this flow. Our drives and motives belong to the *causal process of nature*. In this view, our defining telos – the ends towards which we are made to strive, those that mark us as human – are given by our part in the flow of nature. Good living depends on the ability to distinguish good ends from bad ones in the context of the *flow of one's life*. This internal process, summarized by Locke as the *pursuit of happiness*, belongs to each of us and should not be hindered by others. Anything that interferes with the natural flow of our lives thereby limits our freedom. To impose change upon us is to threaten our liberty.

Negative liberty is the freedom of continuance, the liberty to act as one naturally is given to do. In this view, 'natural' is a term of moral worth. Good living leads to fulfillment, as Aristotle had understood, but, in the modern version, the telos of human life is to be found in the ordinary pursuit of happiness. By fulfilling our ordinary needs, we live a good life. Negative liberty is about *telic security*, the freedom to follow our given ends. This is a view opposed by those in the Kantian tradition, for whom goodness is found in the free will. Among late-flying owls, it may be an unfamiliar landscape, but it is one upon which many ground-dwellers find meaning.

For the great thinkers among our predecessors, the search for meaning sometimes led to new combinations of ideals. The modern idea that ties together the ideals of autotely and telic security is individualism. Each individual is both self-defining and inviolable. Whatever tensions may arise between self-creativity and the givenness of one's ends, these are left to the 'black box' of the individual to decide. (In this sense, individualism may be seen as a response to the problem of value conflict in general, but it is an answer that defers rather than resolves. The deference to individual choice, we will see, leads to new evaluative conflicts.) Liberalism is the ideology centred on individualism. Among liberals, some may lean more towards creativity and others towards security in human ends, but, as liberals, they see the individual as the highest good. With this simple solution to the problem of conflicting values, liberalism became the dominant ideology of the modern era.

Our most important secondary ideologies are socialism and conservatism. Socialism vests positive liberty in society as a self-creative, growing whole. The people become one as they collectively define their common good. Conservatives see society as an ordered whole, a set of evolved institutions that coordinate and regulate the given ends of human nature. Neither socialists nor conservatives deny the worth of individuals, but they each see society as having its own independent value. The value of community for them, unlike for liberals, is not reducible to the value of the individuals who belong to it. Although their visions of the good society are deeply different, socialists and conservatives agree that individuals should often defer to the greater good of society. They believe that individuals have value but that they are not the only locus of value.

By focusing on the social whole, socialists and conservatives, in effect, reopen the black box of the individual, forcing onto the political agenda the divisive question of whether human ends are given or created. Socialists, in their creative desire to remake society, must reject the central idea of negative liberty: that the given ends of individuals are inviolable. The vitality of society requires the remoulding of individuals in the name of political and social growth. For socialists, negative liberty is the illegitimate veneration of resistance to this growth. Conservatives, meanwhile, see wilfulness, or change for the sake of creativity, as the great threat to evolved social institutions. Positive liberty, the wilful bursting of traditional social bonds for the sake of self-caused growth, is anathema to them. Liberals, finally, diminish the independent value of community in either guise because they see it only as the sum of its parts. For them, community is at best a derivative value and is not a good in itself.

The underlying values of positive and negative liberty, then, are central to the major ideologies of our time, arrayed left to right.

Value Pluralism and the Left-Right Continuum

Although it resists precise definition, the left-right spectrum remains the most common way of describing political differences.[2] As a first step toward a graphic depiction of the pluralist model, the values it identifies may be mapped onto the left-right continuum.

Figure 1

The values of democracy along the left-right continuum

Left		Centre		Right
Solidarity	Positive liberty	Individualism	Negative liberty	Social order

Solidarity is to socialists as individualism is to liberals, and as the social order is to conservatives. Socialists are ideological neighbours to liberals because they agree on the value of self-creativity, although each side sees it as embodied in different forms. Socialists see the united will of the community as self-determining, while left-liberals see the individual will as the self-sufficient source of value. In a corresponding way, right-liberals are neighbours to conservatives, agreeing on the meaning of freedom as negative liberty but disagreeing about whether the value of social institutions takes priority over that of individuals.

One of the advantages of this specification of the left-right spectrum is that it has an identifiable centre. Democratic centrists, if this theory is correct, are not just confused or indecisive; rather, they are liberals who may lean left or right on particular issues, depending on their own priorities. However, in the modern era, the pull of the centre is strong for most people. Most modern citizens are liberals, although they may lean, with varying degrees of consistency, either towards self-expressive creativity or towards the ordinary pursuit of happiness. Although they share the centre, we may distinguish between left-liberals and right-liberals. But, because they see the highest good as the freedom of the individual, however they define it, these centrists remain ideological liberals. While priorities may shift over time and vary across nations, modern democracy is such that citizens' ideological preferences typically peak somewhere in the centre range. Liberal individualism is the dominant ideology of modernity.

For some people, individualism may be tempered by the acceptance of a communal vision of the good. Although most of us tend to put ourselves first, we may also search for community in our different ways. Like individualism, community is an ideal that can take left- or right-wing forms. Communitarians, like individualists, cleave left or right between liberties. Solidarity is a communal value, as is social order. They involve communal conceptions of freedom based on positive and negative liberty, respectively.

However, the search for community is not depicted in the preceding figure. If we add the dimension of community to the model, then we can

Figure 2

Two continua of democratic conflict

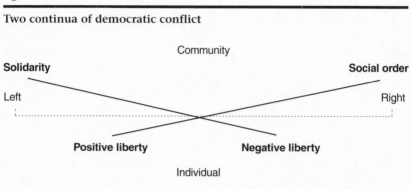

show that there are two distinct continua of conflict embedded within the left-right spectrum. As depicted in Figure 2, solidarity is in conflict with individualistic negative liberty; social order is opposed to individualistic positive liberty. These continua are not quite parallel, but they are related. Left and right remain important terms of distinction, but they arise most commonly in the context of arguments about two distinct issues. Much of the argument of modern democracy is about the conflict between (1) solidarity and the negative liberty of individuals, and (2) social order and the positive liberty of individuals. Each of these two issues may be described in terms of left- and right-wing positions.

Except among philosophers, contests among values rarely occur in pure form; rather, they are played out in arguments about public policy. Taking each continuum in turn:

(1) Solidarity, the ideal of socialists, is inimical to negative liberty, the belief that the human telos is given. Socialists take it as doctrine that before we can come together, we must remake human nature. This was a foundational belief for Rousseau, Kant, and Marx, and it remains a central assumption for socialists today. For them, the pursuit of happiness is not an idealization of our telos but an ideological problem to be overcome. This continuum of conflict, therefore, is largely between those who seek to overturn the ideal of *homo economicus* and those who see it as right and good. Marx's influence had a reinforcing effect on the economistic nature of this debate, but other socialist theorists also saw economic equality as the essential prerequisite to creative social unity. At the other end, economic libertarianism is founded largely on the belief that each individual is a satisfaction-maximizer – that human ends are given and that liberty consists in the natural pursuit of happiness, the ongoing process of achieving those ends. Since happiness is in the pursuit more than in the result, equality

of results does not trump equality of freedom for right-libertarians. Economic egalitarians, by contrast, are those who see material equality as the necessary prerequisite to the sharing of creative social power. Economic inequalities are problematic not just on their own but, more important, because they represent gradations in social power. By remaking human nature, we can come together as powerful creative equals. This is the ideal of solidarity.

(2) The second continuum, between social order and positive liberty, is about social and moral traditions versus personal moral liberation. Is emancipation from social constraints the first step to our liberation, or are our given social institutions the necessary means to enabling our freedom? Progressives believe in social change as necessary to creative growth, whether of individuals or of society. The latter issue, whether individuals or society should be the locus of creativity, separates individualist progressives from socialists, but they are allied on the value of self-creativity as the essence of liberty. Traditionalists, meanwhile, favour the sanctity of the evolved institutions of social order because they see these as the natural outgrowth of legitimate human striving. Wilfulness, to them, is destructive of the social and moral bonds that give meaning to our lives. The second continuum of conflict, in short, is about the legitimacy of social change – whether society should evolve slowly and only within the limits set by human nature or whether social relations should be reformed more quickly and creatively. The tension between self-creation and traditionalism is sometimes referred to as a kind of 'new politics,'[3] but this dimension of politics is centuries old. The self-expressive ideal is a deep tradition in democratic politics. Before the postmaterialists were the Flower Children and the '1968ers'; before them were the Beat Generation and the Angry Young Men; before them were the Lost Generation and the Bloomsbury group; before them were the Transcendentalists and the Decadents; before them were the Romantics and *Sturm und Drang*. The idea of self-creativity is not original to our times; rather, the 'new politics' is based on an old ethic of newness, an ideal that has long been in democratic tension with the alternative ideal of social order. The tensions that culminated in the French Revolution, in which the left-right terminology was born, were not merely about industrialism and the economic politics of class. The idea of personal self-determination, and the antithetical concerns about the sanctity of social institutions, have been politically contentious since the time of Rousseau, Kant, and Burke. In recent wealthy decades, the ethic of newness has become more common and less elitist, but it is not new.

In Figure 2, these two continua of ideological conflict are not pictured as orthogonal (that is, at right-angles) to each other. The intent is to suggest that they are not entirely independent. A respondent's position on one continuum will tend to be related, according to this theory, to his or her location on the other. Particular cases will vary, but, in general, those who favour economic equality will also favour expressive freedom. Those who see value in our inherited institutions will also tend to favour negative economic liberty. The overall polarity of democracy remains as depicted in Figure 1. However, Figure 2 shows that the left-right continuum means more than one thing. Left and right remain useful summary terms, but their meaning shifts with the topic of the argument.

In empirical studies, these two continua of conflict seem to be present in many democratic nations. Based on his study of Japanese voters, Flanagan argued that the dimension of conflict over economic issues was complemented by a libertarian-authoritarian dimension.[4] Kitschelt and Hellemans studied environmental activists in Belgium and found support for the multidimensionality of left-right orientations (despite the widespread belief among these subjects that left and right are obsolete terms).[5] Among Dutch voters, Middendorp found two stable dimensions of conflict, one based on redistributive economics and the other on social traditionalism.[6] Knutsen studied eight European nations and found that postmaterialist politics played a role in addition to redistributive questions and older secular-religious dimensions.[7] He determined that older orientations were not replaced by new values but existed within a rich mixture of value conflicts, each of which was positively correlated with left-right self-placements. Among British voters, Heath, Evans, and Martin used a pair of indices to measure socialist-laissez-faire and libertarian-authoritarian values.[8] In a year-long panel study and in the 1992 British Election Study, these two continua were consistently related to each other, to left-right self-placements, and to party preference. These various models each are formally similar to that in Figure 2. Typically, one continuum, involving economic solidarity versus economic individualism, was found to coexist with another that concerns social politics and cultural traditions. Politics seems to involve common dimensions of conflict within a number of modern democracies.

If new issues come to be articulated in politics, must they necessarily displace old ones? Some empirical analysts have proposed and tested, in contrast of Ronald Inglehart's theory of value replacement, a thesis of value pluralization. The findings of Kitschelt and Hellemans, using a sample of activists, as well as the eight-nation comparative study of Knutsen,[9] favour the pluralization thesis over the theory of value replacement. According to these studies, the left-right distinction is neither singular in its meaning nor is it becoming meaningless. To the extent that values are emerging within democracy, these are added to, but do not replace, existing ones. This suggests an emergent, persistent pluralism in values. If this conclusion is true, then democracy is becoming more conflictual over time. The movement is not towards democracy as solidarity but away from it.

However, the assumption that today's trend will continue tomorrow is a perilous one for social scientists. If the movement of democracy is not towards socialism, then we should be cautious about concluding that the final demise of egalitarianism is in sight. An alternative interpretation is that, in the normal to-and-fro of political arguments, issues wax and wane at irregular intervals. The best explanation for this phenomenon may have been given by John Stuart Mill, who observed that, 'in political and philosophical theories, as well as in persons, success discloses faults and infirmities which failure might have concealed from observation.'[10] In the post-Second World War years, egalitarian politics rode a wave of success in Western nations as the welfare state grew. The 'equality fatigue' in some nations may be driven by the successful implementation of egalitarian policies, allowing the cost of the welfare state to become apparent, both monetarily and in terms of foregone societal alternatives. If these policies are reversed, then the perceived need for them among citizens may return.

The Structure of Ideological Diversity

The theory of democracy as diversity may be depicted in a final, more complete, way, as shown in Figure 3. Here socialism and conservatism are presented as ideological neighbours divided by a sharp apex. Each is based on a vision of the good centred in society as a whole. In their different ways, they share the value of community. But if liberalism is dominant in modernity, then an ideology that asserts the ascendant value of community (shown

Figure 3

Democracy as diversity: A model of ideological pluralism

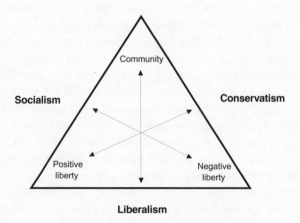

as the peak at the top of the model) will be difficult to maintain. The communitarian apex is precarious and difficult to ascend and cross because the gravitational pull of liberalism is strong.

The advantage of the model in this more complete form is that it shows the lines of synthesis along the perimeter as well as the lines of antithesis. The previous depiction, presented in Figure 2, is embedded within this model in the lines of antithesis between socialism and negative liberty on one hand, and between conservatism and positive liberty on the other. In addition, the tension between the liberal individual and the authority of community is included. In this form, the model has a kind of structural integrity, suggesting the stability and longevity of ideological conflicts within democratic culture.

Each of the corners of this triangular model may be thought of as a cleavage point dividing ideological neighbours. As noted in previous sections, left-liberals may agree with socialists about the importance of positive liberty, but they differ on whether it should be a social or individualistic value. Conservatives and right-wing liberals may agree about the naturalness of negative liberty but differ about the relationship between individual wants and evolved roles and rules. The dominance of liberalism in modern democratic cultures, however, means that individualism in most cases has a presumptive advantage in these disputes.

It means, further, that the cleavage between socialism and conservatism is especially pronounced. A holistic ideology, based on the predominant value of community, is difficult to maintain in its pure form. By contrast, it is not unusual to encounter a romantic ideology focused solely on wilful self-sufficiency (like existentialism or postmodernism) or a libertarian affirmation of negative freedom above all else (like reductionistic theories based on economic self-interest). To most of us, these ideas may seem narrow or dogmatic, but they do not usually invoke a visceral reaction. But communitarianism in its pure form, in which the good of the individual is presumed to be entirely secondary to the good of the community, is difficult for modern thinkers to tolerate. While we can allow that some people may voluntarily choose to belong (for example) to a traditional religious community, it is their individual choices that matters most. The only allowable subjugation of the individual is self-subjugation. We believe they have chosen to give up their individual freedom for their own reasons, so individualism remains the primary consideration. Modernity means that, in almost all cases, the individual's good trumps that of the community. Pure communitarianism is too illiberal to be given credence. Putting the same point another way, communitarianism is an especially sharp cleavage point, one upon which few thinkers can perch without falling eventually towards either socialism or conservatism. Furthermore, if the communitarian corner is especially sharp, then few people are likely to cross between conservatism and socialism. The party of conservative socialists will have few members.

The model in Figure 3 is more complete than those in Figures 1 and 2. It presents, in a concise way, the stable structure of values and ideologies inherent in modern democracy. But by being more complete, it may appear to understate the presumptive dominance of liberal individualism and to exaggerate the 'cross-over' potential between socialists and conservatives. This effect disappears, however, if we think of the triangular model as standing vertically. Modernity provides a downward pull away from community and towards individualism. The cleavage between socialists and conservatives is especially pronounced because of this gravitational effect. To illustrate this feature of the model, we must understand the inherent ambivalence of holistic, or anti-individualistic, ideologies.

The Two Faces of Community

The history of the twentieth century gives us one reason to believe that holistic ideologies, centred on the primary value of community, may be particularly difficult to sustain within democratic nations. These movements, including communitarianism, populism, republicanism, nationalism, and fascism, may be understood as having two different aspects, conservative and socialist, between which they are torn. When both faces are combined in a single political vision, the results can be foreboding. Fascism, whatever its other attributes, may be seen as the admixture of communal security with communal romanticism. Hence, it is both defensive and aggressive, both insular and ambitious. Fascism is an extreme case, which venerates authority and thus can resist the pull of modernity with force. However, each of the holistic ideologies is torn in two directions at once. Those holists who refuse the rule of force are likely to slide eventually towards familiar socialist or conservative ideas.

Holistic political movements arise because modernity pulls against community, which opens an ideological space for political entrepreneurs. Over time these movements, if they are democratic, will be drawn either left or right by the same modern pull, the 'gravitational' force of individualism. While romantic and libertarian movements may also feel left-right pressures, for communitarians in a liberal age, this cleaving force will be particularly intense. In politics, holistic movements will be unstable. The political value of communal belonging is real, but for politicians seeking an electoral advantage, it will be especially elusive. Over time, the political value of community will ebb and flow, but its tidal surge will rarely crest. Unless a political community comes under real threat, the final wave will not rise.[11]

The ideological history of holistic political movements is too large a job to be completed here, but some evidence for these assertions may be found in a series of recent works. For example, in a seminal collection outlining the communitarian reaction against liberalism, Michael Sandel includes left- and right-wing critics of individualism, each of whom struggled with this ambivalence.[12] Alasdair MacIntyre argues that each person's life must be considered as a single narrative quest and that no life can be understood apart from its constitutive traditions. But the idea of tradition quickly becomes something creative rather than evolutionary: 'What I have called a history is an enacted dramatic narrative in which the characters are also the authors.'[13] While he began with traditionalism, MacIntyre cannot sustain both the traditional and self-creative sides of his holism. Forced to choose, his idea that traditions are constitutive of identity turns out to be hollow. His argument turns against conservatism,[14] and, thereafter, he backs away from the idea that traditions have prescriptive force. Tradition becomes only a context for future voluntarism: 'It is rather the case that an adequate sense of tradition manifests itself in a grasp of those future possibilities which the past has made available to the present.'[15] Where he tries to have it both ways, MacIntyre's argument becomes convoluted: 'Notice that rebellion against my identity is always one possible mode of expressing it.'[16] Faced with the choice between creativity and heritage as the theme or telos of the human story, MacIntyre chooses the path to the left.

In the same collection, Peter Berger compares the ideals of individual dignity and social honour. The former is independent of any social role, but the latter takes its force from society itself. 'The social location of honour lies in a world of relatively intact, stable institutions, a world in which individuals can with subjective certainty attach their identities to the institutional roles that society assigns to them.'[17] He recognizes the ideal of individual dignity as liberating and accepts the romantic idea that social roles are partly self-defined, but his own ambivalence is clear. Berger's main concern is for stability and order: 'Stable identities ... can only merge in reciprocity with stable social contexts ... Put differently, there is a built-in identity crisis in the contemporary situation.'[18] Where MacIntyre turns away from the authority of one's heritage towards the romantic goal of creativity, Berger sides with tradition.

The tension between the conservative and progressive sides of the holistic ideal is also evident in the popular communitarian book, the best-selling *Habits of the Hearts*, an extended critique of American individualism by a team of social scientists. They describe their vision as counter-individualistic, as 'an ideal of society as a reality in itself, not as something merely derived from the agreement of individuals.'[19] A recurring theme throughout the book is the role of traditional morality as a source of unity among Americans. However, in the concluding chapter, entitled 'Transforming American Culture,' the socialist side of this vision suddenly arises. In the introduction to the updated edition, the authors take pains to distance themselves from moral conservatism, yet in the original work, 'moral' is among their most common adjectives. The interesting ambivalence of the book appears in the fact that these writers could find something of value in the idea of traditional moral order, even against their own voluntaristic, socially tranformative political goals.

Another example of this tension comes from the scholarly literature on poverty. Socialists and conservatives each can find a social justification for collective assistance to the poor. Liberals may agree with these policies for individualistic reasons. But if a coalition was once possible in support·of welfare payments, today these policies are criticized from both the left and the right. The character of this tension can be seen by reading together two accounts of its history in the United States. Frances Fox Piven and Richard Cloward, who advocate the egalitarian restructuring of the economy, argue that relief programs expand only to restore civil order after massive economic dislocations and then retract, abandoning the poor when order returns.[20] In their view, social order is the secret reason that the welfare state arose. Marvin Olasky, who advocates the resurgence of socially unifying compassion and charity, faults the welfare state for its egalitarian refusal to make distinctions based on desert.[21] For him, the welfare state had been founded upon the egalitarian refusal to make moral judgments. Neither side in this debate about the deficiencies of the welfare system draws on individualistic arguments, but their evaluative premises are symmetric and contrapuntal: the egalitarians criticize the welfare state as conservative, and the moralist condemns it as socialistic. How one defines the problem of poverty, or any other social issue, depends on one's hierarchy of values.

That the holistic ideal of belonging can take either a conservative or a socialist form is demonstrated in a different way in Isaiah Berlin's well known essay, 'Benjamin Disraeli, Karl Marx and the Search for Identity.'[22] Both men were alienated from their Jewish roots and sought to regain a sense of belonging in ideology, one in conservatism and the other in socialism. Berlin wrote that 'one of the sources of the vision of both Disraeli and Marx – what made the former see himself as a natural leader of an aristocratic elite, and the latter as the teacher and strategist of the world proletariat – was their personal need to find their proper place, to establish a personal identity ... It was an attempt on the part of those whom history and social circumstances had cut off from their original establishment – the once familiar, safely segregated Jewish minority – to replant themselves in some new and no less secret and nourishing soil.'[23] Men without people, these two alienated, deracinated individuals sought a new sense of identity and belonging in these two non-individualistic ideologies. Berlin would be the last to reach a reductionistic conclusion – that values are really just psychological needs – from this fact; rather, his central point in this essay, repeated often in his writing, is that belonging and identity are among our truest ideals. For Marx and Disraeli, for whom these values were manifested in ideology, the available alternatives were socialism and conservatism.

The apotheosis of reactionary anti-individualism in this century, the excesses of which give individualism much of its presumptive strength in our day, is fascism. The core of fascist ideology is its holistic statism, in which the good of the state is the highest ideal. This was the idea, for example, taken from Giovanni Gentile by Benito Mussolini. In *The Doctrine of Fascism*, Mussolini expressed his ideal, including its antithetical relation to liberalism, in unmistakable language.

> Being anti-individualistic, the Fascist system of life stresses the importance of the State and recognizes the individual only in so far as his interests coincide with those of the State, which stands for the consciousness and the universality of man as an historic entity. It is opposed to classic Liberalism which arose as a reaction to absolutism and exhausted its historical function when the State became the expression of the consciousness and the will of the people. Liberalism denied the State in the name of the individual; Fascism reasserts the rights of the State as expressing the real essence of the individual. And if liberty is to be the attribute of living men and not that of abstract dummies invented by individualistic Liberalism, then Fascism stands for liberty and for the only liberty worth having, the liberty of the State and of the individual within the State.[24]

Fascism is neither a right-wing nor a left-wing movement; rather, it is both at once. Unlike other holistic ideologies, fascism builds outward from its anti-individualist core in both directions at once. Fascism is neither conservative nor socialist but both at the same time, combining the collective goals of growth and security together; hence its inevitable bellicosity. As Alan Ryan observes, 'The most interesting feature of Nazi ideology was its ambivalence about revolution ... Nazism was the apotheosis of this ambivalence, simultaneously presenting itself as counter-revolutionary and yet revolutionary.'[25] National Socialism was the most racialized of fascist movements, but its combination of aggression and defensiveness was common in fascist thought. Fascists idolized the will to power, yet rejected both rationalism and individualism. In place of universal individualism, they sought a source of collective particularity in an idealized past. The fascists were truly Janus-faced, looking forward and backward at once. Where Hitler sought to restore the greatness of the First and Second Reich, Mussolini was inspired by ancient Rome. The proto-fascist Georges Sorel, whom Berlin described as 'dominated by one *idée maîtresse:* that man is a creator, fulfilled only when he creates,'[26] turned this romanticism towards the restoration of former glories. Another historian wrote, 'As Sorel himself put it, the myth of the general strike was not a description of something that might occur but rather the expression of a determination to act. The workers' participation in this myth ... performed the function of creating solidarity among them for the never-ending battle with their enemies. In Sorel's view, the vital thing was to bring back "grandeur" to human affairs.'[27] Again, Sorel, in his own way, combined socialist and conservative ideas in the form of creative myth-making and nostalgia for the glorious past.

Nationalism provides a final example of a dualistic ideology balanced on the fulcrum of holism. Given the experience of this century, liberals are right to worry that nationalism may hide an incipient fascism, but it need not do so. A socialistic nationalism would be inclusive and egalitarian, while a conservative nationalism would be insular rather than expansionist. In practice, problems would arise, and either movement might be captured by factions drawn by power itself, but in neither case do the ideas themselves seem to require the glorification of hostility. Fascism is unique in its combination of aggressiveness and defensiveness, of security-through-aggression on a collective scale.

Canada has seen the best example of these two sides of nationalism. As David Cameron points out, in Quebec during the Quiet Revolution,

> a strategy of *survivance* has been replaced by an energetic and effervescent *épanouissement* [blooming], that the minimal desire for survival has been supplanted by a demand that French-Canadian society be permitted to blossom, to expand and develop ... Prior to 1960, self-preservation meant resistance to change, keeping apart from external influences that would threaten to alter the composition of French-Canadian society. After 1960, self-preservation meant the acceptance, even the welcoming, of change, for it was realized that if French Canada ... was to preserve itself it had to take control of its destiny and become the initiator of change.[28]

With the exception of fascists, who combine security and power with force, the theorists of holistic ideologies must eventually choose between communal creativity and the regulatory force of given rules and roles. For those who find a primary source of goodness in community, the good ultimately must be wilfully created or given as part of one's heritage, but it cannot be both at once. If the will is to have creative power, then it must overcome given rules and roles; if given prescriptions are to be secure, then wilfulness must be curtailed. Creativity and givenness are irresolvably in conflict: the good either exists as it is, or it is continually overcome and remade. For anti-individualistic theorists, the liberal answer – that these questions are a matter of private choice – is not available.

If these value conflicts exist not just for theorists but are endemic to democratic culture, then ordinary voters will face similar questions. Debates over public policy are not just about the best means to the common good, they are about competing visions of the good. Political parties that attempt to ride the wave of holism must eventually go either left or right, or become divided and disappear. The left-right cleavage inherent to democratic politics is felt within all parties but acts with special force upon those that appeal to the primary value of community.

Berlin's Theory of Value Conflict

Two themes characterize the theory presented here, both of which are best known in the work of Isaiah Berlin. The first is about the tension between positive and negative liberty, and the second is the more general phenomenon of value pluralism.[29] The theory represents an attempt to refine the definitions of his two concepts of liberty. If he was right, then most of us make sense of things not by constructing a consistent theory in which all true values fit together but by finding a way to choose among conflicting values when faced with the necessity of deciding. We prioritize and choose as best we can, without always having perfect reasons.

Moreover, his theory is one of legitimacy. Our ultimate values, sometimes incommensurable and often conflicting, are nonetheless legitimate and real. They are human values, so that anyone entirely incapable of seeing their appeal must be considered less than human. As Berlin put it,

> The possibility of understanding men in one's own or any other time, indeed of communication between human beings, depends upon the existence of some common values, and not on a common 'factual' world alone ... Moral categories – and categories of value in general – are nothing like as firm and ineradicable as those of, say, the perception of the material world, but neither are they as relative or as fluid as some writers have too easily, in their reaction against the dogmatism of the classical objectivists, tended to assume. A minimum of common moral ground is intrinsic to human communication.[30]

As a theory of legitimacy, pluralism differs from relativism. The former holds that our values are common but that there are conflicts among them. A relativist, by contrast, cannot say anything about human commonality. Relativism at best is the claim that one's own views are constrained by a particular paradigm. Values in this view are private or, at best, parochial. Berlin's theory by contrast leaves open the possibility that some core human values are universal yet do not fit perfectly together.

The impossibility of consensual harmony does not occur because people differ in their values but because our common values conflict with each other. Priorities differ because of this irresolvable conflict, but human values are common. As Michael Ignatieff summarizes Berlin's position: 'People disagree in society, Berlin argues, not because each is enclosed in a subjective web of relativistic conviction impervious to argument; in fact, they are able to break out of this subjective web and enter into the moral worlds of those with whom they are in conflict. The disagreement occurs because the goods that men contend about – for example, equality versus liberty, justice versus order – are themselves difficult to reconcile in practice. Berlin stresses that we disagree not primarily because we fail to understand each other, but because we seek goals that are in conflict.'[31]

Pluralism holds that there exists a core of ideals, values, and beliefs that humans are capable of appreciating, though we may choose among them differently. One way to understand pluralism is to see appreciation as one sort of evaluative activity, choice another, and advocacy a third. In this view, it is in the character of human beings to be able to understand the appeal of our core values, but it is in the character of our values that they conflict. In short, pluralism accepts our values as real in themselves, as non-material but nonetheless objective entities, shared in our common appreciation but not always combinable in our practical choices.

The reason values do not just conflict but are often incommensurable – that is, they cannot be measured on the same scale – is because there is no overriding value, such as happiness, against which all other values may be judged. Pluralism denies that any one value always takes precedence so that other values may be judged against its standard. Happiness sometimes conflicts with justice, and justice with mercy, and mercy with merit, and merit with happiness. Pluralism may be understood as the breakdown of transitivity among our core values due to the absence of a common scale by which conflicting values can be weighed. Since pluralism holds that we can have no such scale, there can be no impartial decision procedure, and no abstract priority rule, for settling many conflicts.

In Berlin's best known essay, 'Two Concepts of Liberty,' which he first presented as a lecture in 1958, he sought to sharpen the distinction between positive and negative liberty as a central example of value pluralism.[32] His argument can be simplified by leaving to one side, for the moment, the collective form of positive freedom known as self-government. To paraphrase, negative liberty is the security of non-interference, and positive liberty is the power of self-determination. These labels, security and power, are borrowed from Humboldt rather than Berlin, but they capture much of the distinction Berlin wanted us to make. He argued that power and security are conceptually distinct, even if they are related in practice, and that the failure to recognize this distinction will lead – and has led, in many nations – to the loss of freedom altogether.

Berlin believed that, historically, the neglect of negative liberty has been the more common error. But he should not be taken as asserting the primacy of negative liberty. 'I am not offering a blank endorsement of the "negative" concept as opposed to its "positive" twin brother, since this would itself constitute precisely the kind of intolerant monism against which the entire argument is directed.'[33] Berlin was not a right-libertarian but a pluralist.

Despite his essay's title, Berlin suggested a critical third aspect of liberty. If positive and negative liberty are distinct ends of free individuals, then the matter is more complicated when we consider people in the collective. As such, positive liberty becomes the collective right of self-government. The latter, he suggests, tends to conflict with the freedom of individuals. Berlin argued that wherever well-meaning leaders claim to have found the single legitimate way of life for the group, positive liberty easily sanctions coercion so that liberty – both positive and negative – disappears altogether. Negative liberty is the great bulwark against the collectivization of positive liberty and, therefore, is essential to the freedom of individuals. Berlin's political priority, in short, was towards liberalism, but he was not a liberal of theoretical purity. He did not deny that communal belonging has legitimate value as an end in itself:

> When I ask myself what I am, and answer: an Englishman, a Chinese, a merchant, a man of no importance, a millionaire, a convict – I find upon analysis that to possess these attributes entails being recognized as belonging to a particular group ... We may refuse this goal the title of liberty; yet ... I can, by using words which convey fraternity and solidarity, as well as some part of the connotation of the 'positive' sense of the word freedom ... · describe it as a hybrid form of freedom ... yet one which no existing term seems precisely to fit.[34]

Since he delivered this lecture in 1958, the term communitarianism has emerged to fulfill the ideological function that Berlin described. While he was concerned about the way positive liberty comes to take on a collective meaning and thus threatens the negative freedom of dissenters, it is possible to see the sense of belonging as a distinct end in itself, just as negative and positive liberty are distinct.

The essential elements of the value-pluralist model of democracy, in short, are borrowed from Berlin. How well they have survived the usage of the borrower is an open question, but the inspiration behind the theory should be clear. (The reason for discussing their source near the end is to avoid a contaminating back-flow of judgment. Berlin's vision is larger than the one contained here. If it should be judged that the present theory is misguided, then the failing is not due to something implicit in Berlin's views.)

A final point might be made about Berlin's own location along the ideological spectrum. As a historical analyst, he was a pluralist, but his own politics were liberal. He advocated negative liberty not because he believed in its supremacy but because he recognized that those thinkers who denied its value too easily became authoritarian. The threat of totalitarian monism, as fascism or communism, was the overriding problem of his century. By its nature, positive liberty is more likely to inspire authoritarian ambitions. He emphasized that negative liberty is the essential value standing in the way of communal positive liberty. Nonetheless, he admired the romantic freedom of positive liberty for its own sake. He was an individualist, a vacillating centrist, and an ordinary liberal. His insight was that those who pursued the dream of solidarity were driven by authentic ideals and values whose worth he understood and affirmed. The threat of totalitarianism arises from among our highest ideals. If negative liberty is a Maginot line against certain communal forms of positive liberty, then it is one Berlin thought we continue to require.[35]

Pluralism versus Liberalism

If politics cannot unite us, then why not leave evaluative decisions to the individual? Value pluralism may seem to favour liberal individualism if it is taken to mean that in the absence of decisive reasons in favour of any particular value, choices must be left to the conscience of each person. However, individualism is itself an evaluative concept, and, as such, it has challengers. Some of our fellows are not liberals. To impose liberalism upon those who have contrary evaluative priorities, whose lives are made meaningful by a social understanding of the good, is not a democratic solution. Furthermore, although we may vary in the priority we give to community, the value of social belonging is difficult to deny. Liberalism tends to occlude this holistic value, but our political language would be diminished without it.

We have all had the experience of coming together in a group in such a way that our personal identity seems to melt a little at the edges into something larger than ourselves. Human relationships are misrepresented if we limit ourselves to talking about the sum of the individuals involved. For example, to belong to a couple is to be part of a whole. A couple is a thing with its own beginning and end, and its own purpose. It has a kind of life of its own, a character that cannot be described in terms of the aggregate attributes of two autonomous persons. When a couple breaks up, the loss is felt as grief, as if something unique has died. A couple is something qualitatively different than just two people bound together. It is a single thing, ontologically distinct and basic. Larger groups are real entities, too, although their defining purposes are more complex. The individual members of a set are unique entities on their own, but together they are a single thing, defined by the quality of their relationship.

If human relationships are holistic, this does not tell us anything about the moral or political priority of the individual to the group. The decision to give priority to the individual does not mean we must deny the independent value of holistic entities. This value is not derived from the separate worth of each member but belongs to the group as such. Only the most committed individualists will refuse to see the inherent worth of communities, societies, cultures, nations, and so on. Respect for individuals requires only the recognition that the value of community is not necessarily an overriding one. By recognizing the pluralism of values, we recognize the competing value of individuals and of groups. But once we realize that the question is one of priorities among worthy entities, we may further wonder whether other kinds of rankings might also make sense in their own way.

In times of peril, the voluntary subjugation of the individual to the group is a remarkably common phenomenon. With astonishing frequency, people throughout history have been willing to die during wartime to protect their fellows. Individualistic explanations are insufficient in these cases, but they can be explained if we recognize the inherently holistic value of belonging. We vote, or participate in collective action groups, because it gives us a sense that we belong to something *greater than ourselves*. In some cases, the hope that the group will survive after I, individually, am gone is sufficient to justify my self-sacrifice. If the group survives, then my identity will live on within it because it was the source of my value.

Rather than *deriving* its value from its members, the group *confers* value upon them. In collective action problems, participation itself is the reward, conferring value *from* the group *to* the individual. The group is prior in value to the individual. The thing we belong to must be greater than ourselves or no true value can come from belonging. Belonging can be valuable only if the group has an independent, non-derivative value of its own.

We belong to groups not in the merely additive sense, the way a tree belongs to a forest. Under the additive conception, if we cut down a few trees, we still have a forest, although a smaller one. Belonging in the individualistic, or additive, sense means that each individual's contribution is dispensable to the existence of the whole. A more holistic sense of belonging may be seen in the way the branches, the trunk, and the roots belong to a tree. Under this conception, our failure to participate in the group would not result in a smaller group but in a group that would be fundamentally changed by our absence. We vote, or belong to collective action groups, because we want to feel part of something larger than ourselves, something whose value lies outside of ourselves. A stronger sense of belonging can come only from the feeling that our contribution is part of the essence of the group.

If modernity has a bias towards individualism – a bias for which we may have good political reasons – it is still a mistake to believe that holistic understandings are dispensable. And pluralism helps us see that if individuals often come into conflict with their groups, the value of each is nonetheless real. Whether its source is defined as solidarity or social order, the need for individuals to understand themselves in holistic terms of belonging means that liberal individualism will always be challenged in politics. Since democracy is about more than individualism, democracy is not the same thing as liberalism. The latter may be the dominant ideology of our day, with its place in the centre giving it a permanent advantage in electoral and policy contests. Nonetheless, democracy is a broader concept, with room for socialists and conservatives as well.

When we consider the entire constellation of our common values, the outcome of particular discussions depends on priorities. Like a simple outline drawing of a cube, the surfaces of which seem to jump between foreground and background, our vision of politics shifts depending on the aspect that solidifies first in our perception. By focusing on the freedoms of the individual, political questions make sense in one way, but if we focus first on the prior value of the group, then things jump suddenly into an alternative alignment. The possibilities are not endless: our perceptions remain within a common range, and the cube never becomes a pyramid or a sphere. Some solutions are plainly wrong, but among the true visions, there is no single best answer. And the true visions conflict with each other.

Libertés! Égalités! Fraternités!

The future need not be like the past. Despite the reality of our imperfect world, is it not possible that a better future may be created? While perfection may not be possible, does the evidence of history not suggest that progress is sometimes possible? Might we not find a way to reconcile the great ideals or at least find a better way of making decisions than engaging in endless partisan bickering? Even if it were true that the modern West is divided in its ideals, why should other cultures, or another epoch, not be more harmonious?

One source of unity is hardship. A nation at war, or a group fighting for survival against natural calamity, may be united by common adversity. Labour unions, for example, are united by their adversarial position vis-à-vis management. Is this the best model of political solidarity? The problem is that oppositional unity is anchored by the permanent need for a foe, without which unity disappears. A common foe may unite us, but this is not the kind of solidarity that egalitarian democrats seek. Their belief is that unity may be achieved not by external threat but by mutual flourishing. Is it possible that a harmonious political community can arise where unifying hardships have been eliminated?

If pluralism in evaluative stories is the basis of our culture, then democracy is not solidarity. As the defining ideal of one group within democracy, solidarity may be an understandable belief, but as a definition of democracy, it leaves out most of the people. And since democracy is the rule of the people, solidarity is not democracy. In real existing democracies, while equality has had its successes, these have been achieved in competition with other values. Democracy is rich with competing values, in which equality has a place but is not supreme. Nor has any other political ideal reached supremacy. The core of democracy is not liberty but liberties, not fraternity but fraternities. Still, some may argue that the fact of pluralism itself justifies the supremacy of equality. Despite the practical difficulty of implementing egalitarian policies, might it not still be true that pluralism implies that everyone should be treated equally? If we have no way of choosing among groups or individuals with different priorities, does this not imply that all individuals and cultural groups are equal and should be respected as such? Should not equality, despite its difficulty, be given priority simply because pluralism is true?

This argument rests on a confusion. The equality of values and the value of equality are different things. If our core values are equally ultimate, then equality remains one value among many. The equality of individuals and groups is among our ideals, but this value often conflicts with, among other values, their freedoms. If the relative priority of equality is one of the basic differences that characterize democratic citizens, then their evaluative differences cannot be used to sanction the priority of one value. To uphold the equality of values is not to choose among them. We respect people as evaluators by respecting their priorities, not by imposing our own upon them. Some may favour versions of liberty at odds with solidarity; others may see equality as the enemy of excellence; yet others may understand themselves in terms of their place in a traditional, hierarchical community. People vary in ways that matter, and few are thoroughgoing egalitarians.

If there is an 'egalitarian plateau' among political thinkers, then it is either wide enough to hold those with competing priorities, or it is high enough to make equality the supreme value. Equality is a single ideal only if we define it in a very general way. As soon as we try to squeeze policy prescriptions from that definition we begin to narrow its terms. The egalitarian plateau becomes higher and narrower as we build towards actual legislation, and erstwhile allies fall away. To pretend that the plateau remains as wide after we have dredged and piled our way upward is to ignore the changes in meaning we have made. The equality of Hobbes and Locke, based on the commonality of natural human processes, is not the shared self-creative ideal of Dworkin and Kymlicka. One is about self-ownership and the givenness of one's place in the social order, while the other is about transcending the order of things as they are. Both ideals remain with us, and each represents a different priority of values.

Solidarity theorists have taken the idea of diversity to heart, with the goal of diminishing those inequalities in social power based on irrelevant differences like skin colour. Further, they envision a society in which important differences, including legitimate cultural values and practices, should all be equally honoured. For them, the ideal of equality provides a framework for the recognition of differences. All cultural groups should be made equally creative and powerful. Positive liberty should be shared. This ideal is important and honourable, but pluralism must be understood more broadly. A diverse society is one filled with more than differently enculturated social democrats. We differ more significantly in the meaning we make of the world, and this varies with our political priorities.

The supremacy of equality is perfectly clear to egalitarians. In order to eliminate value conflict, they seek to define other values in terms of equality. An example is Charles Taylor's 'politics of recognition.' For him, the highest freedom is positive liberty, the creative power to define oneself. But in his view, the tools of self-definition are communal. We define ourselves through our interactions in a common language with others. Therefore, to be free (in the positive sense) we must be recognized as equals by our fellows. In this view, equality is the prerequisite to freedom: equality comes first and liberty later. Taylor sees this priority as necessary and undeniable, which is to say he is an egalitarian.

Taylor's story of what it means to live a good life is profound, but it has its greatest appeal only to other egalitarians. They are convinced that they alone deserve to be called democrats, but they are wrong. The problem with their story is that it leaves out most of the people. It is an elite-driven theory not of democracy as it is but as it would be if only the people were different. Were theoretical egalitarians to put their beliefs to the electoral test of democracy, as Taylor deserves credit for having done, their success would be no greater than his. This result occurs not because the people are shallow thinkers, seduced and confused by the business media or by the enticements of capitalism, but because they are complex evaluators who live in a richer world than that of egalitarians.

In the wider world of politics, citizens have various priorities. Right-libertarians define equality as the formal right of everyone to protection from interference based on the situated equality of self-ownership. For liberal individualists, equality comes when everyone has a private space within which to be free in both senses. Conservatives see equality as the shared benefit of common institutions, including the natural differentiation of social roles. The meaning of equality varies with one's political priorities. As with liberty and fraternity, democratic discourse is fractured on the question of the true meaning of equality. Democracy is not about equality but equalities. It is a tragic richness of conflicting stories about liberties, equalities, and communities.

If democracy is not egalitarian solidarity, then what is it? Democracy may be defined as an institutionalized argument over the proper meaning and relative importance of liberty, equality, and community. Certain institutions, including partisan competition, elections, and legislative debates, are at the very heart of democracy. Every democracy will have institutions of evaluative contestation. Democracy is an unending institutionalized contest of values, which has settled into a familiar pattern of ideological conflict.

The Future of Democracy

Within democracy, the successes that egalitarians achieve in policy must be won through evaluative contestation rather than through overthrowing the system in favour of 'real' democracy. The argument of democracy is won in steps, and each of these can be reversed in future decisions. Egalitarians' policy victories will be inconsistent, partial, and reversible, as will those of activists with other evaluative priorities.

In the irresolvable democratic conflict among core values, liberal individualism has a centrist advantage because it is opposed by no single ideological alternative. Some of this advantage is due to the fact of pluralism itself, as liberalism has the simplest answer to the challenge of pluralism: leave evaluative choices to the individual. This advantage has been reinforced by the events of the twentieth century, which helped to cast suspicion on holistic political visions. However, liberalism also has a conceptual cost, leading to a kind of alienation and loneliness. This leaves other ideals with room to grow.

Socialism and conservatism have adherents, but each is at a disadvantage due to the individualistic bias of modernity. The distribution of voters from left to right depends on many political factors, but some level of support for parties representing each of the major ideologies will always be available in democratic nations. In many cases, socialistic and left-liberal visions may be balanced within a single party, as may conservative and right-liberal ideas. National variations in ideologies will occur, but evaluative similarities will be recognizable in the left-right politics of all democratic nations. Winners may emerge on certain issues, and trends in public opinion may continue for some time, but these victories and trends may later be reversed. The balance between left and right may vary across nations, and within nations across eras, but democracy includes the full continuum. Neither the right nor the left will disappear.

The pluralist model suggests that coalitions may form around a core value on either side of the political spectrum. On the right, economic libertarians will tend to be comparably supportive of conservatism, despite the resistance of the purists among them. Similarly, conservatives tend to support economic freedom, although some will resist for their own evaluative reasons. Both ideologies share the priority of negative liberty, although they see it embodied in different forms. The positions are not identical and arguments within the political right will emerge, but right-leaning activists often will have enough in common to form effective political coalitions.

Similarly, on the left socialists and progressive individualists tend to have related priorities because they share the ideal of positive liberty. They will have their disagreements, but they will often be able to work effectively together. Democratic politics will often be about forming coalitions among those whose agreement is incomplete. Some of these coalitions become institutionalized as political parties.

The role of political parties in democracy is to embody evaluative differences. They do not just provide a way of choosing a governing elite or act only as a disciplining mechanism by allowing us to 'throw the bums out.' Their purpose is not just to ensure responsibility by maintaining an alternative government-in-waiting. Parties perform these functions as well, but the essence of partisan differences is ideological. As was rightly noted by a recent team of analysts, 'Political parties are not simply vote maximizers. They are also, in a celebrated phrase, communities of co-believers, at the level of activists committed to distinctive bodies of belief, to differing conceptions of the role of government in society and the economy, to alternative interpretations of the master values of democratic politics like equality.'[36] Parties exist because activists come together around mutual concerns, and they evolve in certain directions because of the ideals and beliefs of their supporters. The privilege of contestation goes to those parties that successfully match the common evaluative priorities of citizens. While the supporters of fringe positions may complain that they have been shut out, it is more likely that their evaluative orientations are simply too narrow or arcane for most people. Although electoral systems produce distortions, the partisan system remains the best tool we have for expressing the evaluative priorities of citizens.

The assertion that partisanship is essential to democracy does not suggest that the institutions of democracy are never without defects or that reforms are unnecessary; rather, the claim is that, even if politicians were saintly and the rules of electoral competition were perfectly unbiased, the competition among visions of the good society would remain. Partisanship, at its best, is a reflection of this fact. Were we to replace the party system with some other means of reflecting the citizens' beliefs (for example, with a constituent assembly), then a similar pattern of ideological differences would emerge over time. Where there is democracy, there is ideological conflict. Democracy is the method of governance in which people find a way to live together despite their irresolvable differences of priority among common goods.

Apart from these general considerations, does it matter how we define democracy? Why not let politicians and theorists continue to define it in their own ways, as part of the back-and-forth of politics? This suggestion, in most cases, is a reasonable one. In contexts in which the institutions of contestation are well established, people indeed may call things what they want. Those who claim that they are more democratic than others because they are more egalitarian should be free to make their case. However, the danger that monistic visions, based on equality or any other value, pose to democracy occurs only when the institutions of contestation have not yet been established and entrenched or when their existence is threatened. Illustrative examples may be taken from the context of Canadian politics.

What would it mean for Native groups in Canada to achieve self-government? Clearly it would not mean the return to purely indigenous traditions. The arguments of the self-government movement are thoroughly saturated with Western values and political beliefs. The ideas of human rights; of national identities; of written treaties; of the rule of law; of judicial systems; of land as property; of collective self-determination; of economic justice; of equalities, liberties, and fraternities – all these ideas have been absorbed by Native peoples. Unless one believes that these values developed simultaneously on different continents, one must conclude that they represent a kind of assimilation. No other group in Canada has been assimilated more thoroughly into the habits of rights-talk. The rhetoric of self-government evokes an ideal of evaluative harmony, but it too is an ideal that has been assimilated from the spreading global culture of democracy. The problem is that it seems to have been taken up as an unexamined romantic mythology.[37] The Rousseauvian myth of natural egalitarianism is appealing to those with certain political priorities, but whatever its cogency, it came from across the Atlantic.

We do not know the values that might have flourished here in isolation from the culture of democracy. The record of what went before is an oral one, but its tellers belong to today. There can be no Rosetta stone between orality and literacy. When the written word joins the spoken voice, the message changes permanently. If some traditional values have survived, then they exist in addition to the values of democracy. Perhaps value pluralism among Natives is more complex than it is among other Canadians, but it cannot be less so. If Natives have absorbed some Western values, then, because stories can cross cultures, they will absorb others. This process may go both ways, so modernity may learn from indigenous peoples, but the trend can only be towards value pluralism.

Native self-government, if it is to be democratic, must be allowed to be ideologically pluralistic. If collectivist values should become legally entrenched so that they are enforced to the exclusion of other values, then legitimate dissent within Native communities will be silenced. The danger, if we pretend that the range of evaluative possibilities is narrower for Natives than it is for other people, is that we will allow an anti-democratic system to be imposed upon them. The belief in natural harmony may be strong among many Natives, but the complexity of their communities, like that of any other, must be respected. When a belief is used to justify a regime of power it should be scrutinized critically for its political dangers.

The central problem with the Native self-government movement in Canada is that it is almost entirely elite-driven, and elite rule is never democratic. This problem becomes especially acute when this elite is financed by Ottawa. For Natives, as for anyone else, it is perilous to confuse the interests of the leadership with the interests of the people. The great lacuna in Native politics is ground-level political activity. Until that occurs, self-government will not be real; when it arises, it will be pluralistic. To the extent that the organizational rules of self-government hinder this fundamental level of politics, they are contrary to the interests of the people. Democratic self-government must come from the bottom up, and when it does so, it will include (at a minimum) the familiar range of democratic beliefs. The myth of natural harmony is damaging to true self-government because it suggests that Natives are naturally univocal and, thus, that they can be ruled by a single voice in a monistic way. This is a myth of the powerful over the people, but it is not democratic self-governance.

Similarly, the politics of the wider Canadian community should be recognized as legitimately pluralistic. Politics at its best is about the contest of visions of the good society, but this vision of democracy has recently been challenged by an anti-pluralist myth. A political decision procedure that usurps the essential role of contestation about core democratic values is thereby anti-democratic. With the adoption of the Charter of Rights and Freedoms, a belief in Canada has arisen that we now have a definitive answer to our value conflicts. The Charter is understood by some as defining a hierarchy of values for all Canadians, with the result that the contentious work of basic evaluative contestation is no longer required. If democracy is inherently pluralistic, then this understanding of the role and meaning of a constitution is false.

Because value pluralism is true, constitution writers could not possibly have been super-planners who were able to craft an ideal hierarchy of values for an entire nation. In truth, they were only rival politicians with varying beliefs and competing priorities. They were the sort of people we see in politics today, imperfect individuals struggling to attract support for their ideals. Constitutional conventions, at best, are meetings of people mired in irresolvable evaluative differences. They search with great difficulty for common themes but settle by necessity for hortatory generalities. Constitutions can be no more than general statements of undefined ideals that everyone may accept precisely because they are imprecise. Every constitution, of necessity, is full of holes (as it were) where its writers refused wisely to judge. They exist because it is impossible to impose a hierarchy upon our ultimate values.

Constitutional abeyances exist because framers knew, through their experience or instincts as practising politicians, that to acknowledge the fact of their disagreements would imperil their imagined unity. British, American, and Canadian constitutional history is in each case the story of unresolved conflicts among political visions.[38] The constitutions that resulted are not systematic, coherent wholes but mixed packages of carefully undefined generalities. Michael Foley writes,

> They may include contradictions, tensions, anomalies, and inequities, but the fragility and, at times, total illogicality of such packages are kept intact through a convention of non-exposure, or strategic oversight, and of complicity in delusion ... Abeyances should not be thought of as empty constitutional 'gaps' to be filled in through the normal course of legal interpretation and political development ... The habitual willingness to defer indefinitely consideration of deep constitutional anomalies, for the sake of preserving the constitution from the severe conflict that would arise from attempts to remove them, represents the core of a constitutional culture.[39]

The theory of abeyances describes political ideals as colliding with each other during a nation's founding, just as they do in its maturity. Abeyances are not imperfections; they are the secret to the continued vitality of a constitution. Precisely because they do not seek to resolve ultimate value conflicts, constitutions allow us to continue living together even as we disagree about the precise form and substance of our common polity. Nationalism has been described in terms of 'the imagined community.'[40] Constitutional abeyances allow us to imagine that we live in solidarity, even though we disagree about ultimate priorities. They make political community possible in a pluralistic world. We can live together with the feeling of communal belonging and acceptance precisely because we are not forced to confront our political differences.

Constitutional rationalism – the belief that a hierarchy of values can be discovered in a constitution – is a threat to this community. Rationalists see abeyances as imperfections in need of correction. Driven by their misunderstanding of the deeper significance of abeyances, rationalists set out to eliminate them by discovering the 'true' meaning of the constitution. Forcing evaluative coherence onto a document in which it does not belong, constitutional rationalists undermine, in small steps, the abeyances that allow us to live together. Believing they can and should be overcome, rationalists force us to face the permanent differences that the framers had learned, through the contentious political process of constitution building, must be avoided for the sake of the imagined community.

The belief that a constitution contains a nation's defining system of values is one that may appeal to those that it empowers, but it is deeply anti-democratic. If the meaning of constitutions is as much in their silent wisdom as it is in their explicit content, then attempts to interpret them as substantive political blueprints will be both arbitrary and autocratic. Where evaluative differences do work their way onto the political agenda, it is the job of pluralistic institutions to decide among them. And those decisions will be incomplete, revisable, contentious, and democratic.

According to Foley's historical analysis, historically, US Supreme Court justices have had, with temporary exceptions, the wisdom (born of experience) to respect constitutional abeyances.[41] In doing so, they have nurtured and protected not only the documents they are responsible for interpreting but also their own ill-defined place within the American political order. On one side, they encouraged the myth of constitutional rationalism as central to their own influence; on the other, their knowledge of the conflicts entrenched as abeyances taught them to respect the limits of their role because to encroach those limits would have been to draw attention to them. Canadian courts have had less experience than American courts with the subtleties of constitutional interpretation. With our new Charter, our courts seem to have adopted the American myth of constitutional rationalism without having learned its limits.

The defenders of rationalism argue that the courts are merely doing their job by interpreting the values in the Constitution. In one sense, they are right. Constitutions do contain values, but they do not contain a hierarchy or a system of values. While it is possible to give an egalitarian spin to the Charter, for example, by an inventive reading of a phrase like 'free and democratic society,' the interpretation always belongs to the reader. Constitutions contain a range of conflicting ideals, so adherents of various political visions will be able to find support for their priorities contained within them. By reading the Charter as though it contains a single priority of values, the interpreters are putting in something of their own. The large and liberal reading of the Charter as though it contains not values but a system of values is not interpretation but inventiveness.

In the course of everyday politics, the lack of evaluative consensus in a nation is less problematic because regular elections and the evolved institutions of partisan politics allow today's losers to consent provisionally to decisions in the hopes of winning tomorrow. Consensus in a pluralist democracy might be defined by the consent of the governed to go along with decisions despite their disagreement. However, when constitutional rationalism leads to judicial activism, whether from the political left or right, this consensus will be threatened. The policy of *stare decisis*, appropriate and necessary to the rule of law, offers no hope of reversal, at least until the Court itself changes. Losers must either abandon their ideals or work to change the Court. Pluralism suggests that legitimate values are not easily given up, so losers will often not go away. Therefore, rationalistic activism will tend to lead to the politicization of the appointment process. When the courts become political, the political process will work to reclaim the courts.

To the extent that constitutions include specific instructions, such as an enumeration of citizens' rights, they must be interpreted by the courts. Rules are abstract by necessity. Additional rules may be added to guide interpretation, but these second-order rules also require interpretation, and so on in endless iteration. This is not to suggest that rights have no core meaning or that they should not be respected. Once they are entrenched in a constitution and accepted by citizens as their own, rights become powerful tools of political contestation. Like treaties, bills of rights must be respected by subsequent governments if the state is to have credibility. But it is a misunderstanding to see a list of rights as a definitive hierarchy of values. Democratic nations may choose to enumerate certain rights, but their interpretation will always be a political activity requiring con-testable evaluative judgments. It is the job of the courts to do this, but in doing their job they are engaged in politics. The more assertively they act, the more political they become.

These two myths – the belief in natural harmony among Natives and the vision of constitutions as definitive hierarchies of national values – are re-lated in a central way. They are examples, among others that can be ob-served in Canada and other nations, of a failure by elites to understand the people. While it is beyond the purpose of the present work to go more fully into specific political questions, these examples belong to a general prob-lem, which is the anti-democratic, elitist strain in the understanding of modern politics. Many of our best intellectuals, legal scholars, judges, edu-cators, and cultural leaders – a broad range of elites, with the notable excep-tion of those disciplined by electoral approval – have come to misunderstand the evaluative basis of democracy.

This misunderstanding amounts to disrespect for the complexity of the people's values. When elites seek ways to rule in the name of their own evaluative priorities because they dislike the full range of the people's views, the danger is to democracy itself. In every case where the institutions of governance are implicitly monistic, treating some ultimate values as higher than others, democracy is threatened. This is neither a left-wing nor a right-wing argument; nor is it centrist. It is, rather, a recognition that political views vary and always will. The belief in the march of history towards solidar-ity is ideological, based on certain evaluative priorities. The problem is that this ideology is not the only legitimate option. The marchers travel their own way, but the citizens of democracy do not march to order. Democracy is not a long march but a complex parade of colliding pathways. It does not go forever in one direction but travels back and forth upon the same ground.

It is possible that the centre of democratic gravity can be made to shift over time. If we envision democracy as a triangular model of ideological conflict, then perhaps it will topple to the left or right so that another ideology will replace liberalism to attain a presumptive democratic advantage in a new political era. If so, then this gain will be achieved only through the contest of goods. There are no Archimedian levers to tip the balance of democracy apart from the political values that people know. Democracy cannot be recentred from the outside but only through internal shifts of momentum. The first step, for those who would do so, is to understand the nature of the task.

At the turn of the millennium, the dominance of liberalism appears to be long-lasting. Certain decades-long trends in democracy may be adduced, such as the successes of the international human rights movement. This might be interpreted to indicate the dominance of left-liberalism, as citizens of democracies increasingly demand positive liberties from their governments. However, with the move away from the electoral politics of the welfare state towards the elite-driven authority of human rights law, this trend may have hardened into scholastic dogma. Against it is the more recent movement away from socialist economics, with the increasing tendency of new generations to look for ordinary economic satisfactions. Because left-liberalism and socialism share related evaluative resources, it may be that the long leftward swing that fed the growth of the modern state will be replaced by another decades-long trend. A leading indicator of a new tilt would be a shift in the distribution of elite opinions among new generations in the battle of ideas. This trend may presage a renewed basis of presumptive electoral advantage. If so, the change will occur hesitantly and unevenly, extending over lifetimes.

These speculations are, of course, preliminary, indicating the kinds of further analysis that would follow from the conception of democracy presented here. Once we have the basic understanding of democracy right, we can begin a proper empirical investigation of long-term trends both within nations and internationally. Meanwhile, the intellectual contest of democracy will continue with new generations of thinkers. The advantage will go to those who best understand it.

Notes

Chapter 2: What Is the People?

1 Ernest Barker, trans., *The Politics of Aristotle* (London: Oxford University Press, 1958), 1.
2 Henry George Liddell and Robert Scott, *A Greek-English Lexicon* (Oxford: Clarendon, 1940), s.v. 'koinonia.'
3 Manfred Riedel, *Between Tradition and Revolution*, trans. Walter Wright (Cambridge: Cambridge University Press, 1984), 131.
4 Ibid., lxvi.
5 Benjamin Jowett, trans., *The Politics of Aristotle*, rev. ed. (New York: Colonial, 1900), 1.
6 Barker, *The Politics of Aristotle*, 7.
7 For an account of both senses of 'society' in its early meaning, see John Bossy, 'Some Early Forms of Durkheim,' *Past and Present* 95 (May 1982): 8-11.
8 See Raymond Williams, *Keywords: A Vocabulary of Culture and Society* (London: Fontana, 1976), 76-829.
9 The prologue begins:
Two households, both alike in dignity,
In fair Verona, where we lay our scene,
From ancient grudge break to new mutiny,
Where civil blood makes civil hands unclean.
10 Richard Hooker, *Of the Laws of Ecclesiastical Polity* (London: Dent, [c. 1593] 1907), vol. 1, 198.
11 Ibid., 187-8.
12 Thomas Hobbes, *Leviathan* (Harmondsworth, Middlesex: Penguin, [c. 1651] 1968), 186.
13 John Locke, *The Second Treatise of Government* (New York: Macmillan, [1690] 1952), sec. 4.
14 Ibid., 154-5.
15 Ibid., 159-60.
16 Locke, *Second Treatise*, sec. 13.
17 Isaiah Berlin, 'The Decline of Utopian Ideas in the West,' in *The Crooked Timber of Humanity* (London: Fontana, 1991), 36-7.
18 Isaiah Berlin, 'The Pursuit of the Ideal,' in *The Crooked Timber of Humanity* (London: Fontana, 1991), 7-10.
19 Berlin, 'Decline of Utopian Ideas,' 39.
20 Edward Tylor, *Primitive Society*, vol. 7 (London: Murray, 1871), 7.
21 Edmund Burke, *Reflections on the Revolution in France* (Oxford: Oxford University Press, [1790] 1993), 149; Adam Smith, *The Wealth of Nations* (New York: Modern Library, [1776] 1937), 423. See also Donald Winch, 'The Burke-Smith Problem and Late Eighteenth-Century Political and Economic Thought,' *Historical Journal* 28 (1985): 231-47.
22 For example, 'The third and last duty of the sovereign or commonwealth is that of erecting and maintaining those public institutions and those public works ... advantageous to a great society.' Ibid., 681. The other two duties are national defence and the administration of justice.

23 Adam Ferguson, *An Essay on the History of Civil Society*, facsimile ed. (New York: Garland, [1767] 1971).
24 Ibid., 98 ff.
25 Ibid., 51.
26 Ibid., 45.
27 Ibid., 208.
28 Ibid., 89.
29 Ibid., 423.
30 Frank N. Pagano, 'Burke's View of the Evils of Political Theory,' *Polity* 17 (1985): 446-62.
31 Burke, *Reflections*, 107.
32 Ibid., 8.
33 Ibid., 97 and 102.
34 Ibid., 108.
35 Ibid., 95.
36 Immanuel Kant, *The Metaphysics of Morals*, trans. Mary Gregor (Cambridge: Cambridge University Press, [1797] 1996), 34; G.W.F. Hegel, *The Philosophy of Right*, trans. T.M. Knox (London: Oxford University Press, [1821] 1952), 154; Karl Marx, 'On the Jewish Question,' *Collected Works*, vol. 3. (New York: International, 1975), 154-62.

Chapter 3: From Ancient Virtues to Modern Values

1 Peter Berger, 'On the Obsolescence of the Concept of Honor,' *European Journal of Sociology* 11 (1970): 339-47.
2 See, for example, John W. Chapman and William A. Galston, eds., *Virtue*, Nomos 34 (New York and London: New York University Press, 1992).
3 A.W.H. Adkins, *Moral Values and Political Behaviour in Ancient Greece: From Homer to the End of the Fifth Century* (London: Chatto and Windus, 1972), 12.
4 H.C. Baldry, *The Unity of Mankind in Greek Thought* (Cambridge: Cambridge University Press, 1965), 17.
5 Baldry, *Unity of Mankind*, 20 ff.
6 Ibid., 53.
7 Alasdair MacIntyre, *After Virtue: A Study in Moral Theory* (Notre Dame: University of Notre Dame Press, 1981), 147.
8 Quoted in George Brantl, ed., *Catholicism* (New York: Braziller, 1962), 141-2.
9 See Janine Marie Idziak, ed., *Divine Command Morality: Historical and Contemporary Readings* (New York and Toronto: Mellen, 1979).
10 Martin Luther, *On the Bondage of the Will* [1525], trans. Janine Marie Idziak, excerpted in Idziak, ed., *Divine Command Morality*, 95.
11 Alasdair MacIntyre, *A Short History of Ethics* (London: Routledge and Kegan Paul, 1962), 126-7.
12 Giovanni Pico della Mirandola, *Oration on the Dignity of Man*, trans. A. Robert Caponigri (Chicago: Henry Regnery, [1496] 1956), 7-8. The emphasis on self-creativity varies between translations, with some versions sounding more modern than others.
13 Patrick Riley, *The General Will before Rousseau: The Transformation of the Divine into the Civic* (Princeton: Princeton University Press, 1986).
14 Jean-Jacques Rousseau, *The Social Contract*, in Alan Ritter and Julia Conaway Bondanella, eds., *Rousseau's Political Writings*, trans. Bondanella (New York: Norton, [1755] 1988), 94-100.
15 Immanuel Kant, *Foundations of the Metaphysics of Morals*, trans. Lewis White Beck (Indianapolis: Bobbs-Merrill, [1785] 1959), [393-94] 9-10. Page numbers in square brackets refer to original pagination.
16 Isaiah Berlin, *The Sense of Reality: Studies in Ideas and Their History* (New York: Farrar, Straus and Giroux, 1996), 177.
17 Ibid., 178.
18 Isaiah Berlin, 'The Decline of Utopian Ideas in the West,' in *The Crooked Timber of Humanity* (London: Fontana, 1990), 36-7.
19 F.W. Nietzsche, *Beyond Good and Evil*, trans. R.J. Hollingdale (London: Penguin, [1886] 1990), 36.

20 Ibid., 195.
21 F.W. Nietzsche, 'Thus Spoke Zarathustra,' in *The Portable Nietzsche*, trans. Walter Kaufman (New York: Viking, [1883] 1968), 228.
22 Ibid., 135.
23 Ibid., 13.
24 John H. Hallowell and Jene M. Porter, *Political Philosophy: The Search for Humanity and Order* (Scarborough, ON: Prentice Hall, 1997), 619-26.
25 Risieri Frondizi, *What Is Value?: An Introduction to Axiology*, trans. Solomon Lipp (La Salle, IL: Open Court, 1963), 31-3.
26 The word as used here is taken from J.G. Merquoir, *Liberalism: Old and New* (Boston: Twayne, 1991), 12 ff., which he defines as 'self-realization.' However, his usage suggests that one's defining telos is self-contained, so that life is the process of fulfilling one's essential nature. By contrast, the usage here is meant to stress voluntarism, so that one's true ends are not discovered but creatively self-given.
27 Judith Shklar has described the essentially anti-political nature of the romantic movement. See Shklar, *After Utopia: The Decline of Political Faith* (Princeton: Princeton University Press, 1957), 96-7.
28 On postmodernists' debt to Nietzsche, see Cornel West, 'Nietzsche's Preconfiguration of Postmodern American Philosophy,' in Daniel O'Hara, ed., *Why Nietzsche Now?* (Bloomington: Indiana University Press, 1981) 241-69.
29 The best discussion of the two ideals together is Isaiah Berlin, 'The Two Concepts of Liberty,' in *Four Essays on Liberty* (Oxford: Oxford University Press, 1969).
30 John Stuart Mill, *Utilitarianism, On Liberty, Considerations on Representative Government*, 3rd ed. (London: Everyman, 1993), 78.
31 John Rawls, *A Theory of Justice* (Cambridge, MA: Harvard University Press 1971), 60.

Chapter 4: The Teleology of Modern Time
1 René Descartes, 'Discourse on Method,' in *Descartes: Philosophical Writings*, trans. Elizabeth Anscombe and Peter Thomas Geach (London: Nelson, 1966), 41.
2 René Descartes, 'Principles of Philosophy,' in *Descartes: Philosophical Writings*, 190, 194.
3 Descartes, 'Discourse,' 41.
4 René Descartes, *Meditations on First Philosophy*, trans. Laurence J. Lafleur (Indianapolis: Bobbs-Merrill, [1641] 1960), 15. The quote is from the synopsis, which is not included in the Anscombe and Geach translation.
5 Descartes, 'Principles,' 189.
6 Thomas Hobbes, *Leviathan* (Harmondsworth, Middlesex: Penguin, [1651] 1968), 170.
7 Ibid.
8 Ibid., 88.
9 Ibid., 86, 94.
10 Ibid., 113.
11 Ibid., 160.
12 Ibid., 82-3.
13 Ibid., 189.
14 Ibid., 262.
15 A.W.H. Adkins, *Moral Values and Political Behaviour in Ancient Greece: From Homer to the End of the Fifth Century* (London: Chatto and Windus, 1972), 68.
16 Hobbes, *Leviathan*, 428-9.
17 As James Gibson was right to note, 'Without the influence of the Cartesian view of knowledge and the Cartesian conception of self-consciousness, it is not too much to say that the *Essay*, as we know it, would never have been written.' Gibson, *Locke's Theory of Knowledge and Its Historical Relations* (Cambridge: Cambridge University Press, 1960), 207.
18 John Locke, *An Essay Concerning Human Understanding*, 4th ed. (Oxford: Clarendon, [1700] 1975), I:iii:3.
19 Ibid., II:xxi:4.
20 Ibid., II:xxii:11.
21 Ibid., II:xx:3.
22 Ibid., II:xxvii:9.

23 Descartes, 'Principles,' 192-3.
24 Locke, *Essay*, II:xiii:3.
25 Ibid., II:xiv:1.
26 Ibid., II:xiv:1.
27 Ibid., II:xv:12.
28 Ibid., II:xxvii:11.
29 Ibid., II:i:19.
30 Ibid., II:x:1.
31 Ibid., II:xxvii:24-5.
32 Ibid., II:xv:9.
33 Ibid., II:i:4.
34 'They are the successive perceptions only, that constitute the mind.' David Hume, *A Treatise of Human Nature* (Oxford: Clarendon, [1740] 1978), I:iv:4
35 Locke, *Essay*, II:xv:12.
36 Ibid., II:xxi:47.
37 C.B. Macpherson, *The Political Theory of Possessive Individualism: Hobbes to Locke* (Oxford: Oxford University Press, 1962).
38 Hobbes, *Leviathan*, 217-8.
39 Locke, *Essay*, II:xxvii:17-8.
40 Ibid., II:xxvii:26.
41 Locke, *The Second Treatise of Government* (New York: Macmillan, [1960] 1952), secs. 27, 44.
42 Ibid., sec. 27.
43 Alexis de Tocqueville, *Democracy in America*, vol. 1 (New York: Vintage, [1835] 1990), I:iii, 48-50.
44 Locke, *Second Treatise*, I:iv.

Chapter 5: Splitting the Individual

1 John Locke, *The Second Treatise of Government* (New York: Macmillan, [1960] 1952), sec. 151.
2 Thomas Hobbes, *Leviathan* (Harmondsworth, Middlesex: Penguin, [1651] 1968), 122.
3 John Locke, *An Essay Concerning Human Understanding*, 4th ed. (Oxford: Clarendon, [1700] 1975), II:vii:3.
4 Ibid., II:xxviii:5.
5 Ibid., II:xxi:71.
6 John Stuart Mill, 'Coleridge,' in *Essays on Politics and Culture*, ed. Gertrude Himmelfarb (Garden City, NY: Anchor, [1840] 1962), 144.
7 Jeremy Bentham, *An Introduction to the Principles of Morals and Legislation* (London: University of London, [1789] 1970), II:vii.
8 Ibid., I:iv.
9 See, especially, Chapter 2 of Mill's *Considerations on Representative Government* in Mill, *Utilitarianism, On Liberty, Considerations on Representative Government*, 3rd ed. (London: Everyman, [1861] 1993)
10 Mill, 'Coleridge,' 136-41.
11 Mill, *Considerations*, chap. 16.
12 Isaiah Berlin, 'John Stuart Mill and the Ends of Life,' in *Four Essays on Liberty* (Oxford: Oxford University Press, 1969), 199.
13 John Stuart Mill, *Autobiography* (New York: Penguin, [1873] 1989), 95.
14 Ibid., 113-5.
15 Ibid., 118.
16 John Stuart Mill, *On Liberty*, in *Utilitarianism, On Liberty, Considerations on Representative Government*, 3rd ed. (London: Everyman, [1859] 1993), 79.
17 Mill, *Autobiography*, 118.
18 Ibid., 134-5.
19 John Stuart Mill, *A System of Logic*, 8th ed. (London: Longmans, [1843] 1959), 550.
20 Mill, *On Liberty*, 81.

21 Steven Lukes, 'Individualism,' in David Miller, ed., *The Blackwell Encyclopaedia of Political Thought* (Oxford: Blackwell, 1991), 239-40. For a similar discussion in longer form, see Lukes, *Individualism* (Oxford: Blackwell, 1973), 3-32.
22 Wilhelm von Humboldt, *The Limits of State Action*, trans. J.W. Burrow (Indianapolis: Liberty Fund, [1854] 1993), 10-2. These words must have been read by Mill as a kind of personal call to arms, especially the penultimate phrase quoted here.
23 Koenraad W. Swart, '"Individualism" in the Mid-Nineteenth Century (1826-1860),' *Journal of the History of Ideas* 23 (1962): 77-90.
24 Humboldt, *Limits of State Action*, 71.
25 Ibid., 12.
26 Ibid., 38, 106.
27 Ibid., 91.
28 Ibid., 84.
29 Mill, *On Liberty*, 98, 117, 130, 134.
30 Value pluralism was a theme throughout Berlin's writing. For a concise statement, see 'The Pursuit of the Ideal,' in *The Crooked Timber of Humanity* (London: Fontana, 1991), 1-19. In his best known book, *Four Essays on Liberty* (Oxford: Oxford University Press, 1969), see especially, x, xlix-li, lv-lviii, 39, 125, 128, 145-54, and 167-172.
31 For example, Christopher Lasch, *The Revolt of the Elites and the Betrayal of Democracy* (New York: Norton, 1995), 232.
32 Robert Nozick, *Anarchy, State and Utopia* (New York: Basic, 1974), 30-3.
33 On Stirner's egoism, see Lukes, *Individualism*, 19. On Nietzsche, see Chapter 3 above.
34 John Rawls, *A Theory of Justice* (Cambridge, MA: Harvard University Press, 1971), 302.
35 Ibid., 256.
36 Ibid., 254-6.
37 Ibid., 202.
38 Nozick, *Anarchy, State and Utopia*, 153 ff.
39 Ronald Dworkin, *A Matter of Principle* (Cambridge, MA: Harvard University Press, 1985), 4.
40 Ibid., 196.
41 Nozick, *Anarchy, State and Utopia*, 42-5, 50-1.
42 Will Kymlicka, *Liberalism, Community, and Culture* (Oxford: Clarendon, 1989), 241-2.
43 Ibid., 172.
44 Ibid., 175.

Chapter 6: Conservatism and the Temporal Order

1 David Hume, *A Treatise of Human Nature* (Oxford: Clarendon, [1740] 1978), II:iii:3.
2 Edmund Burke, 'Letter to a Member of the National Assembly,' in L.G. Mitchell, ed., *Reflections on the Revolution in France* (Oxford: Oxford University Press, [1791] 1993), 273.
3 David Hume, *An Enquiry Concerning Human Understanding* (Oxford: Clarendon, [1777] 1975), V:i.
4 'This operation of the mind, by which we infer like effects from like causes [is] essential to the subsistence of all human creatures.' Ibid., V:ii.
5 Ibid., V:i.
6 Ibid., III:i:1.
7 Donald W. Livingston, *Hume's Philosophy of Common Life* (Chicago: University of Chicago Press, 1984), 342.
8 This claim appears at the beginning of his anonymously published *Abstract of a Book Lately Published, Entitled, A Treatise of Human Nature* in Hume, *A Treatise of Human Nature* (Oxford: Clarendon, [1740] 1978).
9 Hume, *Treatise*, III:iii:1.
10 Ibid., III:ii:1.
11 Ibid., III:ii:9.
12 Ibid., III:ii:6.
13 Adam Smith, *An Inquiry into the Nature and Causes of the Wealth of Nations* (New York: P.F. Collier and Son, [1776] 1901), IV:ix.

14 Adam Smith, *The Theory of Moral Sentiments*, 6th ed. (Indianapolis: Liberty Fund, [1790] 1984), I:i:5.
15 Ibid., III:iii:11-14.
16 Ibid., III:iv:8-9.
17 Ibid., I:iii:3:5-6.
18 *Moral Sentiments*, IV:i:10; *Wealth of Nations*, IV:ii.
19 Hume, *Treatise*, II:ii:5; Smith, *Moral Sentiments*, I:iii:2.
20 *Encyclopaedia Britannica*, 1st ed. (Edinburgh: 1768-71), s.v. 'Moral Philosophy.'
21 Edmund Burke, 'Reform of Representation,' in Burke, *Works* (London: Bohn 1854-7), vol. 6, 147.
22 Edmund Burke, *Reflections on the Revolution in France* (Oxford: Oxford University Press, [1790] 1993), 98, 154.
23 Ibid., 60.
24 Ibid., 77.
25 Ibid., 96.
26 Ibid., 35.
27 Ibid., 185, 87.
28 Ibid., 185.
29 Quoted ibid., 65.
30 Ibid., 26, 93-4.
31 Ibid., 245.
32 Ibid., 96-7.
33 Hume, *Treatise*, III:ii:8.
34 Burke, *Reflections*, 37; cf. Smith, *Moral Sentiments*, III:iii:30-1.
35 Burke, *Reflections*, 76.
36 Ibid., 50-51, 49.
37 Ibid., 51.
38 Melvin J. Thorne, *American Conservative Thought since World War II: The Core Ideas* (New York: Greenwood, 1990).
39 James Q. Wilson, *The Moral Sense* (New York: Free Press, 1993), 71.
40 David Hume, *An Enquiry Concerning the Principle of Morals* (Oxford: Clarendon, [1777] 1975), II:ii.
41 'Like Adam Smith before him, [Alfred] Marshall ... refer[red] to the natural order arising in both ecological and economic systems ... An economic system, be it an industry, a set of interrelated markets, or an economy, is made up of a large number of interacting agents. Coordinating the decisions and activities of independent agents (designers, producers, marketers, distributors, financiers, and consumers) is the complex task "solved" by the market process. The result is a coherent socio-economic order.' See John C. Moorhouse, 'Economic Theory: An Ecological Perspective,' *PERC Reports* 14, 4 (Winter 1996): 17.
42 Isaiah Berlin, *The Crooked Timber of Humanity* (London: Fontana, 1991), 227.
43 The term comes from Mary Ann Glendon, *Rights Talk: The Impoverishment of Political Discourse* (New York: Free Press, 1991).

Chapter 7: Socialism and the Power of Social Unity

1 Immanuel Kant, *Political Writings*, 2nd ed., ed. Hans Reiss and trans. H.B. Nisbet (Cambridge: Cambridge University Press, 1991), 91. Consistent with the practice here, no emphases have been added to this quotation. The distinction was one that Kant wanted us to notice.
2 Ibid., 79.
3 Ibid., *Political Writings*, 191.
4 Immanuel Kant, 'Critique of Teleological Judgment,' in *Critique of Judgment*, trans. James Creed Meredith (Oxford: Clarendon, [1790] 1952), 109.
5 So certain was Kant about the conceptual structure and built-in limitations of human understanding that he denied that a Darwin could possibly arise. 'It is, I mean, quite certain that we can never get a sufficient knowledge of organized beings and their inner

possibility, much less get an explanation of them, by looking merely to mechanical principles of nature. Indeed, so certain is it, that we may confidently assert that it is absurd for
men even to entertain any thought of so doing or to hope that maybe another Newton
may some day arise, to make intelligible to us even the genesis of but a blade of grass from
natural laws that no design has ordered. Such insight we must absolutely deny to mankind.' Ibid., 54.

6 Ibid., 99.
7 Ibid., 93-5.
8 Charles Larmore summarized Kant's 'distinction between the negative freedom of spontaneity or mere empirical unconditionedness (*Willkür*) and the positive freedom of autonomy
in the strict sense of imposing the moral law upon oneself (*Wille*).' See Charles Larmore,
Patterns of Moral Complexity (Cambridge: Cambridge University Press, 1987), 82.
9 Immanuel Kant, *Foundations of the Metaphysics of Morals*, trans. Lewis White Beck
(Indianapolis: Bobbs-Merrill, [1785] 1959), [445-6] 64. Page numbers in square brackets
refer to the original pagination.
10 Ibid., [446] 64-5.
11 Ibid., [395] 10.
12 Ibid., [399] 16.
13 Ibid., [396] 12.
14 Ibid., [442] 61.
15 See Ronald Beiner, 'The Moral Vocabulary of Liberalism,' in John W. Chapman and William
A. Galston, eds., *Virtue*, Nomos 34 (New York and London: New York University Press,
1992), 146-7.
16 Kant, *Foundations*, [421] 39.
17 Immanuel Kant, *Critique of Practical Reason*, trans. Lewis White Beck (Indianapolis: Bobbs-
Merrill, [1788] 1956), 32. Both terms had appeared in the *Foundations* but not in contrast to
each other.
18 Kant, *Foundations*, [393] 9.
19 Ibid., [430] 49.
20 Ibid., [435] 53.
21 Immanuel Kant, 'What is Enlightenment,' in *Foundations of the Metaphysics of Morals*, trans.
Lewis White Beck (Indianapolis: Bobbs-Merrill, [1785] 1959) 89.
22 Kant, *Political Writings*, 41-53.
23 Ibid., 52.
24 Ibid., 50-51.
25 Ibid., 181.
26 Rousseau wrote, 'Anyone who dares to undertake the founding of a people should feel
himself capable of changing human nature, so to speak, of transforming each individual,
who by himself is a perfect and solitary whole, into part of a greater whole ... He must, in
a word, take away man's own forces in order to give him new ones which are alien to him
... [I]f the force acquired by the whole is equal or superior to the sum of the natural forces
of all the individuals, it can be said that legislation has reached the highest level of perfection.' See Jean-Jacques Rousseau, *The Social Contract*, in Alan Ritter and Julia Conaway
Bondanella, eds., *Rousseau's Political Writings*, trans. Bondanella (New York: Norton, [1755]
1988), 108.
27 Anthony Quinton, 'Spreading Hegel's Wings,' *New York Review of Books*, 29 May 1975,
34.
28 G.W.F. Hegel, *Reason in History*, trans. Robert S. Hartman (Indianapolis: Bobbs-Merrill, [1837]
1953), 23; Hartman has 'Spirit' for *Geist*.
29 Ibid.
30 G.W.F. Hegel, *Philosophy of Right*, trans. T.M. Knox (London: Oxford University Press, [1821]
1952), para. 5.
31 Hegel, *Reason in History*, 54.
32 Ibid., 25.
33 Hegel, *Philosophy of Right*, para. 33.

34 Hegel, *Reason in History*, 21-2.
35 Robert C. Tucker, 'Introduction,' in Tucker, ed., *The Marx-Engels Reader*, 2nd ed. (New York: Norton, 1978), xxxiii.
36 Karl Marx, 'Economic and Philosophic Manuscripts of 1844,' trans. Martin Milligan, in Robert C. Tucker, ed., *The Marx-Engels Reader*, 2nd ed. (New York: Norton, 1978), 112-21.
37 Ibid., 76.
38 Ibid., 92.
39 Karl Marx, *Capital*, trans. Samuel Moore and Edward Aveling, abridged in Robert C. Tucker, ed., *The Marx-Engels Reader*, 2nd ed. (New York: Norton, 1978), 316.
40 Karl Marx, *The Grundrisse*, trans. Martin Nicolaus, in Robert C. Tucker, ed., *The Marx-Engels Reader*, 2nd ed. (New York: Norton, 1978), 279.
41 Marx, *Capital*, 436.
42 Marx, *Capital*, 388.
43 Ibid., 327.
44 Carole Pateman, *Participation and Democratic Theory* (Cambridge: Cambridge University Press, 1970), 36, 42.
45 Benjamin R. Barber, *Strong Democracy: Participatory Politics for a New Age* (Berkeley: University of California Press, 1984), xv, 91.
46 Benjamin R. Barber, 'Liberal Democracy and the Costs of Consent,' in Nancy L. Rosenblum, ed., *Liberalism and the Moral Life* (Cambridge, MA: Harvard, 1989), 59-60.
47 Charles Taylor, 'Interpretation and the Sciences of Man' *Review of Metaphysics* 25, 1 (1971): 31-2.
48 Charles Taylor, 'What's Wrong with Negative Liberty,' in Alan Ryan, ed., *The Idea of Freedom* (Oxford: Oxford University Press, 1979), 176.
49 Charles Taylor, *The Malaise of Modernity* (Concord, ON: Anansi, 1991); also published as *The Ethics of Authenticity* (Cambridge, MA: Harvard University Press, 1992).
50 Ibid., 28-9.
51 Ibid., 32-3.
52 Ibid., 73, 79.
53 'The politics of resistance [against social fragmentation] is the politics of democratic will-formation.' Ibid., 118.
54 As Taylor pointed out, 'There is something in Hegel's philosophy which is irresistibly reminiscent of Baron Munschausen. The baron, it will be remembered, after falling from his horse in a swamp, extricated himself by seizing his own hair and heaving himself back on his horse. Hegel's God is a Munschausen God.' See Charles Taylor, *Hegel and Modern Society* (Cambridge: Cambridge University Press, 1979), 39.
55 Barber, 'Liberal Democracy,' 65.
56 Ibid., 63.
57 'The fundamental sense of freedom is freedom from chains, from imprisonment, from enslavement by others. The rest is extension of this sense, or else metaphor.' See Isaiah Berlin, *Four Essays on Liberty* (Oxford: Oxford University Press, 1969), lvi. This excerpt may belong to the tradition of J.S. Mill's extension of negative liberty towards the romantic ideal, as described in Chapter 5. Berlin was warm to romanticism, yet worried about the universalistic cooptation of positive liberty by thinkers like Kant.
58 Charles Taylor, *Reconciling the Solitudes* (Montreal and Kingston: McGill-Queen's University Press, 1993), 183.
59 For example, 'The goal that unborn people, say, my great-grandchildren, should speak Cree or French or Athabaskan, is not one that ... liberalism can endorse.' See Charles Taylor, 'Can Liberalism Be Communitarian?' *Critical Review* 8, 2 (1994): 260. For the survival of the culture, individuals' language options must be curtailed. This may seem unacceptably coercive to liberals but only because of their individualistic precommitments. Taylor seems to suggest that cultures have inherent value, too, and should be allowed to survive. Collectivities may have rights *over* their respective members as this becomes necessary in order to flourish.
60 Taylor, 'The Diversity of Goods,' 144, 142.
61 Taylor, *Sources of the Self*, 512.

62 Charles Taylor, 'Reply and Re-articulation,' in James Tully, ed., *Philosophy in an Age of Pluralism: The Philosophy of Charles Taylor in Question* (Cambridge: Cambridge University Press, 1994).
63 Paul Q. Hirst, *Associative Democracy* (Amherst, MA: University of Massachusetts Press, 1994).
64 Paul Q. Hirst, *Representative Democracy and Its Limits* (Cambridge: Polity, 1990), 9.

Chapter 8: Democracy as a Pattern of Disagreement

1 Values may be thought of as memes. See Richard Dawkins, *The Selfish Gene*, 2nd ed. (Oxford: Oxford University Press, 1989), chap. 11. As genes are to species, memes are to cultures. If this is so, then values are the packages of information that cultures pass on from generation to generation in order to replicate themselves. A caveat: 'Good' cannot be defined as 'that which survived.' Unlike genes, memes must be considered and then accepted, which is to say that they survive by virtue of their continued reasonableness. Memes survive because they are judged reasonable; they are not reasonable because they survive. The question of survival depends on the worthiness of an idea, upon which its future survival depends. Dawkins's imagery leaves the question of the relative worth of ideas untouched. It is useful mainly in suggesting that culture, like nature, tends towards complexity rather than uniformity. Values may compete without replacing each other.
2 For arguments in favour of the continued relevance of the left-right continuum, as well as a useful overview of attempts to define it, see Norberto Bobbio, *Left and Right: The Significance of a Political Distinction* (Chicago: University of Chicago Press, 1996). However, Bobbio's own definition of the continuum, in which the essential difference is between equality and inequality, is a partial one.
3 The term is associated with the postmaterialism thesis of Ronald Inglehart. See, for example, Inglehart, *The Silent Revolution: Changing Values and Political Styles among Western Publics* (Princeton: Princeton University Press, 1977); and *Culture Shift in Advanced Industrial Society* (Princeton: Princeton University Press, 1990).
4 Scott Flanagan, 'Value Cleavages, Economic Cleavages, and the Japanese Voter,' *American Journal of Political Science* 24 (1980): 177-206; Flanagan, 'Value Change in Industrial Society,' *American Political Science Review* 81 (1987): 1,303-19.
5 Herbert Kitschelt and Staf Hellemans, 'The Left-Right Semantics and the New Politics Cleavage,' *Comparative Political Studies* 23 (1990): 210-38.
6 Cees P. Middendorp, 'Models of Predicting the Dutch Vote along the Left-Right and the Libertarian-Authoritarianism Dimensions,' *International Political Science Review* 10 (1989): 279-308.
7 Oddbjørn Knutsen, 'Value Orientations, Political Conflicts and Left-Right Self-Identification,' *European Journal of Political Research* 28 (1995): 63-93.
8 Anthony Heath, Geoffrey Evans, and Jean Martin, 'The Measurement of Core Beliefs and Values: The Development of Balanced Socialist/Laissez Faire and Libertarian/Authoritarian Scales,' *British Journal of Political Science* 24 (1993): 113-32.
9 Knutsen, 'Value Orientations.'
10 John Stuart Mill, *On Liberty*, in *Utilitarianism, On Liberty, Considerations on Representative Government*, 3rd ed. (London: Everyman, 1993), 72.
11 Tom Flanagan, *Waiting for the Wave: The Reform Party and Preston Manning* (Toronto: Stoddart, 1995).
12 Michael Sandel, ed., *Liberalism and Its Critics* (New York: New York University Press, 1984).
13 Alasdair MacIntyre, 'The Virtues, the Unity of a Human Life, and the Concept of a Tradition,' in Sandel, ed., *Liberalism and Its Critics*, 141.
14 Ibid., 144-5.
15 Ibid., 145.
16 Ibid., 144.
17 Peter Berger, 'On the Obsolescence of the Concept of Honour,' in Sandel, ed., *Liberalism and Its Critics*, 156.
18 Ibid., 155.
19 Robert N. Bellah, et al., *Habits of the Heart: Individualism and Commitment in American Life*, 2nd ed. (Berkeley: University of California Press, 1996), 303.

20 Frances Fox Piven and Richard A. Cloward, *Regulating the Poor: The Functions of Public Welfare* (New York: Vintage, 1971).
21 Marvin Olasky, *The Tragedy of American Compassion* (Washington: Regnery, 1992).
22 Reprinted in Isaiah Berlin, *Against the Current* (London: Hogarth, 1979).
23 Ibid., 284.
24 Excerpted in Hans Kohn, *Nationalism: Its Meaning and History*, 2nd ed. (Princeton, NJ: D. Van Nostrand, 1965), 171.
25 Alan Ryan, 'National Socialism,' in David Miller, ed., *The Blackwell Encyclopaedia of Political Thought* (Oxford: Blackwell, 1991), 351.
26 Berlin, *Against the Current*, 298.
27 Lane W. Lancaster, *Masters of Political Thought: Hegel to Dewey* (Boston: Houghton Mifflin, 1959), 296.
28 David Cameron, *Nationalism, Self-Determination and the Quebec Question* (Toronto: Macmillan, 1974), 117-8.
29 Berlin makes this argument throughout his work. For a concise statement, see 'The Pursuit of the Ideal,' in *The Crooked Timber of Humanity* (London: Fontana, 1991), 1-19. In his best known book, *Four Essays on Liberty* (Oxford: Oxford University Press, 1969), see especially x, xlix-li, lv-lviii, 39, 125, 128, 145-54, and 167-72.
30 Ibid., xxxi-xxxii.
31 Michael Ignatieff, 'Understanding Fascism,' in Edna and Avishai Margalit, eds., *Isaiah Berlin: A Celebration* (London: Hogarth, 1991), 138.
32 Reprinted in *Four Essays on Liberty*, 118-72.
33 Ibid., lviii, fn. 1.
34 Ibid., 155-60.
35 Charles Taylor, 'What's Wrong with Negative Liberty?' in Alan Ryan, ed., *The Idea of Freedom* (Oxford: Oxford University Press, 1979).
36 Paul M. Sniderman, Joseph F. Fletcher, Peter H. Russell, and Philip E. Tetlock, *The Clash of Rights: Liberty, Equality, and Legitimacy in Pluralist Democracy* (New Haven: Yale University Press, 1996), 24-5.
37 For a discussion of this issue from an iconoclastic Native point of view, see *Isinamowin: The White Man's Indian* (Toronto: CBC Ideas Transcripts, 1992).
38 Michael Foley, *The Silence of Constitutions: Gaps, 'Abeyances' and Political Temperament in the Maintenance of Government* (London and New York: Routledge, 1989); see also David M. Thomas, *Whistling Past the Graveyard: Constitutional Abeyances, Quebec, and the Future of Canada* (Toronto: Oxford University Press, 1997). I am indebted to Roger Gibbins for pointing out the relevance of these works to this one.
39 Ibid., 9-10.
40 Benedict Anderson, *Imagined Communities: Reflections on the Origin and Spread of Nationalism*, 2nd ed. (London: Verso, 1991).
41 Foley, *Silence of Constitutions*, 117 ff.

Bibliography

Adkins, A.W.H. *Moral Values and Political Behaviour in Ancient Greece: From Homer to the End of the Fifth Century*. London: Chatto and Windus, 1972.

Ajzenstat, Janet, and Peter J. Smith. 'Liberal-Republicanism: The Revisionist Picture of Canada's Founding.' In *Canada's Origins: Liberal, Tory or Republican?* ed. Ajzenstat and Smith. Ottawa: Carleton University Press, 1995.

Anderson, Benedict. *Imagined Communities: Reflections on the Origin and Spread of Nationalism*, 2nd ed. London: Verso, 1991.

Aristotle. *The Nicomachean Ethics*, trans. David Ross. Oxford: Oxford University Press, 1980.

–. *Politics*, trans. Benjamin Jowett. New York: Colonial, 1900.

–. *Politics*, trans. Ernest Barker. London: Oxford University Press, 1958.

Ashcraft, Richard. *Revolutionary Politics and Locke's Two Treatises of Government*. Princeton: Princeton University Press, 1986.

Baldry, H.C. *The Unity of Mankind in Greek Thought*. Cambridge: Cambridge University Press, 1965.

Barber, Benjamin R. *Strong Democracy*. Berkeley: University of California Press, 1984.

–. 'Liberal Democracy and the Costs of Consent.' In *Liberalism and the Moral Life*, ed. Nancy L. Rosenblum. Cambridge, MA: Harvard, 1989.

Barker, Ernest, trans. *The Politics of Aristotle*. London: Oxford University Press, 1958.

Beiner, Ronald. 'The Moral Vocabulary of Liberalism.' In *Virtue*, Nomos 34, ed. John W. Chapman and William A. Galston. New York and London: New York University Press, 1992.

Bejczy, István. 'Tolerantia: A Medieval Concept.' *Journal of the History of Ideas* 58 (1997): 3.

Bellah, Robert N., et al. *Habits of the Heart: Individualism and Commitment in American Life*, 2nd ed. Berkeley: University of California Press, 1996.

Berger, Peter. 'On the Obsolescence of the Concept of Honor.' *European Journal of Sociology* 11 (1970): 339-47; reprinted in Michael Sandel, ed., *Liberalism and Its Critics*. New York: New York University Press, 1984.

Berlin, Isaiah. *Four Essays on Liberty*. Oxford: Oxford University Press, 1969.

–. *Against the Current*. London: Hogarth, 1979.

–. *The Crooked Timber of Humanity*. London: Fontana, 1991.

–. *The Sense of Reality: Studies in Ideas and Their History*. New York: Farrar, Straus and Giroux, 1996.

Bloom, Allan. *The Closing of the American Mind*. New York: Simon and Schuster, 1987.

Bobbio, Norberto. 'Gramsci and the Concept of Civil Society.' In *Civil Society and the State*, ed. John Keane. London: Verso, 1988.

–. *Left and Right: The Significance of a Political Distinction*. Chicago: University of Chicago Press, 1996.

Bossy, John. 'Some Early Forms of Durkheim.' *Past and Present* 95 (May 1982): 3-18

Brantl, George, ed. *Catholicism*. New York: Braziller, 1962.

Broce, Gerald. 'Herder and Ethnography.' *Journal of the History of the Behavioral Sciences* 22 (April 1986): 150-70

Bronowski, Jacob, and Bruce Mazlish. *The Western Intellectual Tradition*. New York: Harper, 1960.

Burke, Edmund. *Reflections on the Revolution in France*. Oxford: Oxford University Press, [1790], 1993.

–. 'Letter to a Member of the National Assembly.' In *Reflections on the Revolution in France*. Oxford: Oxford University Press, [1790], 1993.

–. 'Reform of Representation.' In Burke, *Works*. Vol. 6. London: Bohn, 1854-7.

Cameron, David, *Nationalism, Self-Determination and the Quebec Question*. Toronto: Macmillan, 1974.

Campbell, T.D. *Adam Smith's Science of Morals*. London: Allen and Unwin, 1971.

Chapman, John W., and William A. Galston, eds. *Virtue*, Nomos 34. New York and London: New York University Press, 1992.

Cohen, Jean L., and Andrew Arato. *Civil Society and Political Theory*. Cambridge, MA: MIT Press, 1992.

Conniff, James. 'Burke on Political Economy: The Nature and Extent of State Authority.' *Review of Politics* 49 (1987): 490-514.

Dahl, Robert A. *A Preface to Democratic Theory*. Chicago: University of Chicago Press, 1956.

–. *Democracy and Its Critics*. New Haven: Yale University Press, 1989.

Darwin, Charles. *The Descent of Man*. Amherst: Prometheus Books, [1871] 1998.

Davidson, Donald. 'On the Very Idea of a Conceptual Scheme.' In *Post-Analytic Philosophy*, ed. John Rajchman and Cornel West. New York: Columbia University Press, 1985.

Dawkins, Richard. *The Selfish Gene*, 2nd ed. Oxford: Oxford University Press, 1989.

Descartes, René. *Meditations on First Philosophy*, trans. Laurence J. Lafleur. Indianapolis: Bobbs-Merrill, [1641] 1960.

–. *Descartes: Philosophical Writings*, trans. Elizabeth Anscombe and Peter Thomas Geach. London: Nelson, 1966.

Deth, Jan W., and Peter A.T.M. Geurts. 'Value Orientation, Left-Right Placement and Voting.' *European Journal of Political Research* 17 (1989): 17-34

DeWiel, Boris. 'The Politics of Ideological Diversity.' In *Mindscapes: Political Ideologies towards the 21st Century*, ed. Roger Gibbins, et al. Toronto: McGraw-Hill Ryerson, 1996.

Ding, X.L. 'Institutional Amphibiousness and the Transition from Communism: The Case of China.' *British Journal of Political Science* 24 (July 1994): 293-318.

Donner, Wendy. *The Liberal Self: John Stuart Mill's Moral and Political Philosophy*. Ithaca, NY: Cornell University Press, 1991.

Dryzek, John S. *Discursive Democracy: Politics, Policy, and Political Science*. Cambridge: Cambridge University Press, 1990.

Dunn, John. *Locke*. Oxford: Oxford University Press, 1984.

Dworkin, Ronald. *A Matter of Principle*. Cambridge, MA: Harvard University Press, 1985.

Ferguson, Adam. *An Essay on the History of Civil Society*. Facsimile ed. 1767. Reprint, New York: Garland, 1971.

Fischer, Mary Ellen, ed. *Establishing Democracies*. Boulder, CO: Westview, 1996.

Flanagan, Scott. 'Value Cleavages, Economic Cleavages, and the Japanese Voter.' *American Journal of Political Science* 24 (1980): 177-206.

–. 'Value Change in Industrial Society.' *American Political Science Review* 81 (1987): 1,303-19

Flanagan, Tom. *Waiting for the Wave: The Reform Party and Preston Manning*. Toronto: Stoddart, 1995.

Flew, Antony. *David Hume: Philosopher of Moral Science*. Oxford: Basic Blackwell, 1986.

Flew, Antony, ed. *A Dictionary of Philosophy*, 2nd ed. New York: St. Martin's, 1984.

Foley, Michael. *The Silence of Constitutions: Gaps, 'Abeyances' and Political Temperament in the Maintenance of Government*. London and New York: Routledge, 1989.

Forbes, Duncan. *Hume's Philosophical Politics*. Cambridge: Cambridge University Press, 1975.

Frondizi, Risieri. *What Is Value?: An Introduction to Axiology*, trans. Solomon Lipp. La Salle, IL: Open Court, 1963.

Gibson, James. *Locke's Theory of Knowledge and Its Historical Relations.* Cambridge: Cambridge University Press, 1960.

Glendon, Mary Ann. *Rights Talk: The Impoverishment of Political Discourse.* New York: Free Press, 1991.

Goldsmith, M.M. *Hobbes's Science of Politics.* New York: Columbia University Press, 1966.

Grant, Ruth W. *John Locke's Liberalism.* Chicago: University of Chicago Press, 1987.

Habermas, Jurgen. *The Theory of Communicative Action,* 2 vols., trans. Thomas McCarthy. Boston: Beacon, [1984] 1987.

Halliday, R.J. *John Stuart Mill.* London: Allen and Unwin, 1976.

Hallowell, John H., and Jene M. Porter. *Political Philosophy: The Search for Humanity and Order.* Scarborough, ON: Prentice Hall, 1997.

Hegel, G.W.F. *Philosophy of Right,* trans. T.M. Knox. London: Oxford University Press, [1821] 1952.

–. *Encyclopedia of the Philosophical Sciences in Outline.* 1827; reprint, New York: Continuum, 1990.

–. *Reason in History,* trans. Robert S. Hartman. Indianapolis: Bobbs-Merrill, [1837] 1953.

Held, David. *Models of Democracy.* Stanford: Stanford University Press, 1987.

Hirst, Paul Q. *Representative Democracy and Its Limits.* Cambridge: Polity, 1990.

–. *Associative Democracy: New Forms of Economic and Social Governance.* Amherst, MA: University of Massachusetts Press, 1994.

Hobbes, Thomas. *Leviathan.* Harmondsworth, Middlesex: Penguin, [1651] 1981.

Hooker, Richard. *Of the Laws of Ecclesiastical Polity.* London: Dent, [c. 1593] 1907.

Horowitz, Gad. 'Liberalism, Conservatism, and Socialism in Canada: An Interpretation.' *Canadian Journal of Economics and Political Science* 20 (1966): 143-71.

Huber, John D. 'Values and Partisanship in Left-Right Orientations: Measuring Ideology.' *European Journal of Political Research* 17 (1989): 599-621.

Humboldt, Wilhelm von. *The Limits of State Action,* trans. J.W. Burrow. Indianapolis: Liberty Fund, [1854] 1993.

Hume, David. *A Treatise of Human Nature.* Oxford: Clarendon, [1740] 1978.

–. *Abstract of a Book Lately Published, Entitled, A Treatise of Human Nature.* In Hume, *A Treatise of Human Nature.* Oxford: Clarendon, [1740] 1978.

–. *An Enquiry Concerning Human Understanding.* Oxford: Clarendon, [1777] 1975.

– *An Enquiry Concerning the Principle of Morals.* Oxford: Clarendon, [1777] 1975.

Huntington, Samuel P. *The Third Wave: Democratization in the Late Twentieth Century.* Norman, OK: University of Oklahoma Press, 1991.

Idziak, Janine Marie, ed. *Divine Command Morality: Historical and Contemporary Readings.* New York and Toronto: Mellen, 1979.

Ignatieff, Michael. 'Understanding Fascism.' In *Isaiah Berlin: A Celebration,* ed. Edna and Avishai Margalit. London: Hogarth, 1991.

Inglehart, Ronald. *The Silent Revolution: Changing Values and Political Styles among Western Publics.* Princeton: Princeton University Press, 1977.

–. *Culture Shift in Advanced Industrial Society.* Princeton: Princeton University Press, 1990.

Isinamowin: The White Man's Indian. Toronto: CBC Ideas Transcripts, 1992.

Ismail, Salwa. 'The Civil Society Concept and the Middle East: Questions of Meaning and Relevance.' Paper presented at the Canadian Political Science Association Annual Meeting, Calgary, Alberta, 13 June 1994.

Johnson, Paul. *Modern Times: The World from the Twenties to the Nineties,* rev. ed. New York: Harper Collins, 1991.

Jowett, Benjamin, trans. *The Politics of Aristotle.* Rev. ed. New York: Colonial, 1900.

Kant, Immanuel. *Foundations of the Metaphysics of Morals,* trans. Lewis White Beck. Indianapolis: Bobbs-Merrill, [1785] 1959.

–. 'What Is Enlightenment.' In *Foundations of the Metaphysics of Morals,* trans. Lewis White Beck. Indianapolis: Bobbs-Merrill, [1785] 1959.

–. *Critique of Practical Reason,* trans. Lewis White Beck. Indianapolis: Bobbs-Merrill, [1788] 1956.

–. *Critique of Judgement,* trans. James Creed Meredith. Oxford: Clarendon, [1790] 1952.

–. *Political Writings*, 2nd ed., ed. Hans Reiss and trans. H.B. Nisbet. Cambridge: Cambridge University Press, 1991.

–. *The Metaphysics of Morals*, trans. Mary Gregor. Cambridge: Cambridge University Press, [1797] 1996.

Keane, John. *Democracy and Civil Society*. London: Verso, 1988.

–. 'Despotism and Democracy.' In *Civil Society and the State*, ed. John Keane. London: Verso, 1988.

Keane, John, ed. *Civil Society and the State*. London: Verso, 1988.

Kitschelt, Herbert, and Staf Hellemans. 'The Left-Right Semantics and the New Politics Cleavage.' *Comparative Political Studies* 23 (1990): 210-38.

Knopff, Rainer, and F.L. Morton. *Charter Politics*. Scarborough, ON: Nelson, 1992.

Knox, T.M., trans. *Hegel's Philosophy of Right*. London: Oxford University Press, 1967.

Knutsen, Oddbjørn. 'Value Orientations, Political Conflicts and Left-Right Identification: A Comparative Study.' *European Journal of Political Research* 28 (1995): 63-93.

Kohn, Hans. *Nationalism: Its Meaning and History*, 2nd ed. Princeton: Nostrand, 1965.

Kroner, Richard. 'Hegel's Philosophical Development.' In *On Christianity: Early Theological Writings by Friedrich Hegel*, ed. Kroner. New York: Harper, 1961.

Kumar, Krishan. 'Civil Society: An Inquiry into the Usefulness of an Historical Term.' *British Journal of Sociology* 44 (September 1994): 375-95

Kymlicka, Will. *Liberalism, Community, and Culture*. Oxford: Clarendon, 1989.

Lancaster, Lane W. *Masters of Political Thought: Hegel to Dewey*. Boston: Houghton Mifflin, 1959.

Larmore, Charles. *Patterns of Moral Complexity*. Cambridge: Cambridge University Press, 1987.

Lasch, Christopher. *The Revolt of the Elites and the Betrayal of Democracy*. New York: Norton, 1995.

Laslett, Peter. 'Introduction.' In John Locke, *Two Treatises of Government : A Critical Edition*, 2nd ed. Cambridge: Cambridge University Press, 1967.

Leff, Gordon. *The Dissolution of the Medieval Outlook: An Essay on Intellectual and Spiritual Change in the Fourteenth Century*. New York: Harper and Row, 1976.

Lenin, V.I. *State and Revolution*. New York: International, 1932.

Liddell, Henry George, and Robert Scott. *A Greek-English Lexicon*. Oxford: Clarendon, 1940.

Lipset, Seymour Martin. 'The Sociology of Politics.' In *Political Man: The Social Bases of Politics*. Baltimore: Johns Hopkins University Press, [1960] 1981.

–. 'The Social Requisites of Democracy Revisited.' *American Sociological Review* 59 (February 1994): 1-22.

Lipset, Seymour Martin, et al. 'The Psychology of Voting: An Analysis of Political Behavior.' In *Handbook of Social Psychology*, vol. 2, ed. Gardner Lindzey. Cambridge: Addison-Wesley, 1954.

Listhaug, Ola, Stuart Elaine Macdonald, and George Rabinowitz. 'A Comparative Spatial Analysis of European Party Systems.' *Scandinavian Political Studies* 13 (1990): 227-54

Livingston, Donald W., *Hume's Philosophy of Common Life*. Chicago: University of Chicago Press, 1984.

Locke, John, *A Letter Concerning Toleration*. Indianapolis: Bobbs-Merrill, [1689] 1955.

–. *The Second Treatise of Government*. New York: Macmillan, [1690] 1952.

–. *An Essay Concerning Human Understanding*, 4th ed. Oxford: Clarendon, [1700] 1975.

Lowe, E.J. *Locke on Human Understanding*. London: Routledge, 1995.

Lukes, Steven. *Individualism*. Oxford: Blackwell, 1973.

–. 'Making Sense of Moral Conflict.' In *Liberalism and the Moral Life*, ed. Nancy L. Rosenblum. Cambridge, MA: Harvard, 1989.

–. 'Individualism.' In *The Blackwell Encyclopaedia of Political Thought*, ed. David Miller. Oxford: Blackwell, 1991.

Luther, Martin. *On the Bondage of the Will*, trans. Janine Marie Idziak, excerpted in Idziak, ed., *Divine Command Morality: Historical and Contemporary Readings*. New York and Toronto: Mellen, [1525], 1979.

MacIntyre, Alasdair. *A Short History of Ethics*. London: Routledge and Kegan Paul, 1962.

–. *After Virtue: A Study in Moral Theory*. Notre Dame: University of Notre Dame Press, 1981.

–. 'The Virtues, the Unity of a Human Life, and the Concept of a Tradition.' In *Liberalism and Its Critics*, ed. Michael Sandel. New York: New York University Press, 1984.

Macpherson, C.B. *The Political Theory of Possessive Individualism: Hobbes to Locke*. Oxford: Oxford University Press, 1962.

–. *The Life and Times of Liberal Democracy*. Oxford: Oxford University Press, 1977.

Mansbridge, Jane. *Beyond Adversary Democracy*. New York: Basic, 1980.

Marx, Karl. 'Preface to A Contribution to the Critique of Political Economy.' In Marx and Engels, *Basic Writings on Politics and Philosophy*, ed. Lewis S. Feuer. Garden City, NY: Doubleday, 1959.

Marx, Karl, and Friedrich Engels. *Collected Works*, vol. 3. New York: International, 1975.

–. *Werke, Band 3*. Moscow: Progress, 1975.

–. *The Marx-Engels Reader*, 2nd ed., ed. Robert C. Tucker. New York: Norton, 1978.

Merquoir, J.G. *Liberalism: Old and New*. Boston: Twayne, 1991.

Middendorp, Cees P. 'Models of Predicting the Dutch Vote along the Left-Right and the Libertarian-Authoritarianism Dimensions.' *International Political Science Review* 10 (1989): 279-308

Mill, John Stuart. 'Bentham.' In *Essays on Politics and Culture*, ed. Gertrude Himmelfarb. Garden City, NY: Anchor, [1838] 1962.

–. 'Coleridge.' In *Essays on Politics and Culture*, ed. Gertrude Himmelfarb. Garden City, NY: Anchor, [1840] 1962.

–. *A System of Logic*, 8th ed. London: Longman, [1843] 1959.

–. *Autobiography*. 1873. New York: Penguin, [1873] 1989.

–. *Utilitarianism, On Liberty, Considerations on Representative Government*, 3rd ed. London: Everyman, [1963, 1859, 1861] 1993.

Miller, Arthur, and Ola Listhaug. 'Ideology and Political Alienation.' *Scandinavian Political Studies* 16 (1993): 167-92.

Miller, David. *Philosophy and Ideology in Hume's Political Thought*. Oxford: Clarendon, 1981.

Moorhouse, John C. 'Economic Theory: An Ecological Perspective.' *PERC Reports* 14, 4 (Winter 1996): 16-7.

Nietzsche, F.W. *Beyond Good and Evil*, trans. R.J. Hollingdale. London: Penguin, [1886] 1990.

–. *The Portable Nietzsche*, ed. and trans. Walter Kaufman. New York: Viking, 1968.

Nisbet, Robert. *Conservatism*. Minneapolis: University of Minnesota Press, 1986.

Nozick, Robert. *Anarchy, State and Utopia*. New York: Basic, 1974.

Oakeshott, Michael. 'Introduction.' In Hobbes, *Leviathan*. Oxford: Blackwell, 1946.

Olasky, Marvin. *The Tragedy of American Compassion*. Washington: Regnery, 1992.

Pagano, Frank N. 'Burke's View of the Evils of Political Theory.' *Polity* 17 (1985): 446-62.

Pateman, Carole. *Participation and Democratic Theory*. Cambridge: Cambridge University Press, 1970.

Pico della Mirandola, Giovanni. *Oration on the Dignity of Man*, trans. A. Robert Caponigri. Chicago: Regnery, [1496] 1956.

Piven, Frances Fox, and Richard A. Cloward. *Regulating the Poor: The Functions of Public Welfare*. New York: Vintage, 1971.

Popper, Karl R. *The Open Society and Its Enemies*, 2 Vols., 5th rev. ed. Princeton: Princeton University Press.

Putnam, Robert D. *Making Democracy Work: Civic Traditions in Modern Italy*. Princeton: Princeton University Press, 1993.

Quinton, Anthony. 'Spreading Hegel's Wings.' *New York Review of Books*, 29 May 1975, 34-7; 12 June 1975, 39-42.

Raphael, D.D. *Hobbes: Morals and Politics*. London: Allen and Unwin, 1977.

–. *Adam Smith*. Oxford: Oxford University Press, 1985.

Rawls, John. *A Theory of Justice*. Cambridge, MA: Harvard University Press, 1971.

–. 'The Idea of an Overlapping Consensus.' *Oxford Journal of Legal Studies* 7, 1 (1987): 1-25.

Raz, Joseph. 'Multiculturalism: A Liberal Perspective.' *Dissent* 41 (Winter 1994): 67-79.

Riedel, Manfred. *Between Tradition and Revolution: The Hegelian Transformation of Political Philosophy*, trans. Walter Wright. Cambridge: Cambridge University Press, 1984.

Riker, William H. *Liberalism Against Populism*. Prospect Heights, IL: Waveland, 1982.

Riley, Patrick. *The General Will before Rousseau: The Transformation of the Divine into the Civic*. Princeton: Princeton University Press, 1986.

Robinson, Daniel N. 'The Scottish Enlightenment and Its Mixed Bequest.' *Journal of the History of the Behavioral Sciences* 22 (April 1986): 171-7

Robson, John M. *The Improvement of Mankind: The Social and Political Thought of John Stuart Mill*. London: Routledge and Kegan Paul, 1968.

Rorty, Richard. *Objectivity, Relativism and Truth*. Cambridge: Cambridge University Press, 1991.

Rousseau, Jean-Jacques. *Rousseau's Political Writings*, ed. Alan Ritter and Julia Conaway Bondanella, trans. Bondanella. New York: Norton, [1755] 1988.

Ryan, Alan. *The Philosophy of John Stuart Mill*. London: Macmillan, 1970.

–. 'National Socialism.' In *The Blackwell Encyclopaedia of Political Thought*, ed. David Miller. Oxford: Blackwell, 1991.

Sabine, George. 'The Two Democratic Traditions.' *Philosophical Review* 61 (1952): 451-74.

Sandel, Michael, ed. *Liberalism and Its Critics*. New York: New York University Press, 1984.

Schmidt, James. 'Recent Hegel Literature.' *Telos* 46 (1980-1): 113-47.

Schumpeter, Joseph A. *Capitalism, Socialism and Democracy*, 6th ed. London: Unwin, 1987.

Seligman, Adam B. *The Idea of Civil Society*. New York: Free Press, 1992.

Shapiro, Leonard. *The Origin of the Communist Autocracy*, 2nd ed. Cambridge, MA: Harvard University Press, 1977.

Shils, Edward. 'The Virtue of Civil Society.' *Government and Opposition* 26 (Winter 1991): 3-20.

Shklar, Judith. *After Utopia: The Decline of Political Faith*. Princeton: Princeton University Press: 1957.

–. 'Hegel's Phenomenology: An Elegy for Hellas.' In *Hegel's Political Philosophy: Problems and Perspectives*, ed. Z.A. Pelczynski. Cambridge: Cambridge University Press, 1971.

Smith, Adam. *An Inquiry into the Nature and Causes of the Wealth of Nations*. New York: P.F. Collier and Son, [1776] 1901.

–. *The Theory of Moral Sentiments*, 6th ed. Indianapolis: Liberty Fund, [1790] 1984.

Smith, Steven B. *Hegel's Critique of Liberalism*. Chicago: University of Chicago Press, 1989.

Sniderman, Paul M., Joseph F. Fletcher, Peter H. Russell, and Philip E. Tetlock. *The Clash of Rights: Liberty, Equality, and Legitimacy in Pluralist Democracy*. New Haven: Yale University Press, 1996.

Strauss, Leo. *The Political Philosophy of Hobbes: Its Basis and Its Genesis*, trans. Elsa M. Sinclair. Chicago: University Of Chicago Press, 1952.

Swart, Koenraad W. '"Individualism" in the Mid-Nineteenth Century (1826-1860).' *Journal of the History of Ideas* 23 (1962): 77-90.

Taylor, Charles. 'What's Wrong with Negative Liberty.' In *The Idea of Freedom*, ed. Alan Ryan. Oxford: Oxford University Press, 1979.

–. *Hegel and Modern Society*. Cambridge: Cambridge University Press, 1979.

–. 'The Diversity of Goods.' In *Utilitarianism and Beyond*, ed. Amartya Sen and Bernard Williams. Cambridge: Cambridge University Press, 1982.

–. *Sources of the Self*. Cambridge, MA: Harvard University Press, 1989.

–. 'Modes of Civil Society.' *Public Culture* 3 (Fall 1990): 95-118.

–. *The Malaise of Modernity*. Concord, ON: Anansi, 1991. Also published as *The Ethics of Authenticity*. Cambridge, MA: Harvard University Press, 1992.

–. *Reconciling the Solitudes*. Montreal and Kingston: McGill-Queen's University Press, 1993.

–. 'Can Liberalism Be Communitarian?' *Critical Review* 8 (1994): 257-62.

–. 'Reply and Re-articulation.' In *Philosophy in an Age of Pluralism: The Philosophy of Charles Taylor in Question*, ed. James Tully. Cambridge: Cambridge University Press, 1994.

Thomas, David M. *Whistling Past the Graveyard: Constitutional Abeyances, Quebec, and the Future of Canada*. Toronto: Oxford University Press, 1997.

Thorne, Melvin J. *American Conservative Thought since World War II: The Core Ideas*. New York: Greenwood, 1990.

Tocqueville, Alexis de. *Democracy in America*, 2 vols. New York: Vintage, [1835, 1840] 1990.

Tylor, Edward. *Primitive Society*, vol. 7. London: Murray 1871.

Waszek, Norbert. *The Scottish Enlightenment and Hegel's Account of 'Civil Society.'* Dordrecht: Kluwer, 1988.

West, Cornel. 'Nietzsche's Preconfiguration of Postmodern American Philosophy.' In *Why Nietzsche Now?* ed. Daniel O'Hara. Bloomington: Indiana University Press, 1981.

Whelan, Frederick G. *Order and Artifice in Hume's Political Philosophy*. Princeton: Princeton University Press, 1985.

–. 'Hume on the Development of English Liberty.' *Political Science Reviewer* 16 (1986): 127-83.

Williams, Howard. *Kant's Political Philosophy*. Oxford: Basic Blackwell, 1983.

Williams, Raymond. *Keywords: A Vocabulary of Culture and Society*. London: Fontana, 1976.

Wilson, James. Q. *The Moral Sense*. New York: Free Press, 1993.

Winch, Donald. *Adam Smith's Politics: An Essay in Historiographic Revision*. London: Cambridge University Press, 1978.

–. 'The Burke-Smith Problem and Late Eighteenth-Century Political and Economic Thought.' *Historical Journal* 28 (1985): 231-47.

Wokler, Robert. 'Situating Rousseau in His World and Ours.' *Social Science Information* 34 (1995): 521-2.

Wood, Neal. *The Politics of Locke's Philosophy*. Berkeley: University of California Press, 1983.

Yolton, John W. *Locke: An Introduction*. Oxford: Basic Blackwell, 1985.

Index

abeyances, constitutional (Foley), 176-7
Alexander the Great, 27
alienation: of Disraeli and Marx (Berlin),
  161; due to individualism, 88-9, 91, 142,
  172; of labour (Marx), 130-2
Arianism, 29
Aristotle, 9, 12, 13, 14, 18, 25-7, 31-2, 35,
  43-8, 50, 51-2, 54, 58, 72, 75, 126, 149,
  151
art, 18, 35, 38
atomism, 82-3, 88-9, 91, 96, 100, 134
Augustine of Hippo, Saint, 26, 28-35, 40,
  67
autonomy, 23, 37, 38, 41, 43, 80, 81, 86,
  88, 91, 115, 120-3, 127-8, 133, 134, 151,
  167, 187; compared to autotelic power,
  121, 123, 151
autotelic power, 41, 71, 82-3, 87, 89,
  115-16, 119, 128, 134; compared to
  autonomy, 121, 123, 151
Averröes, 31

Bacon, Francis, 45
Bacon, Roger, 45
Barber, Benjamin, 13-14, 136-7
belonging, value of, 46, 88, 91-2, 110,
  113, 116, 133, 139-40, 159, 161, 166-8,
  176
Bentham, Jeremy, 74-6, 88, 94
Berger, Peter, 160
Berlin, Isaiah, 17, 38, 76, 84, 114, 137-8,
  161, 162, 163, 164-7, 188
Bible, 34, 35, 40,
Bildung (Humboldt), 80, 82
Bonald, Louis-Gabriel-Ambroise, vicomte
  de, 104
Burke, Edmund, 18, 20, 92, 93, 98, 104,
  106-11, 117, 155

Calvin, John, 31, 34-5
capital, 129-32; social, 110; as value-
  creating, 131-2
capitalism, 114, 129-32, 171
Cartesianism, 18, 36
categorical imperative (Kant), 37-8, 39,
  86, 122-3
Catholic Church, 17, 29-32, 35, 44, 48, 50
causality, 9, 43, 47, 50-9, 62, 63, 64, 66,
  69, 73-5, 78-9, 81, 95, 119-21, 127, 139,
  151
character formation (Mill), 76-9
Charter of Rights and Freedoms, 175, 177
Christianity, 16, 28-31, 34, 39, 44, 50, 82
Cicero, 32
civil society, 11-21, 39, 76, 95, 100, 107,
  110, 128, 138, 150
civilization, 9, 16, 18, 20, 21, 96, 105,
  110, 111; Greek, 24-5, 27
communitarianism, 153, 158-60, 166,
  188
community, 12, 13, 22, 75, 84, 88-92,
  115-16, 117, 118, 123, 133, 134-7, 140,
  152, 153, 157-60, 163-4, 167-8, 171. See
  also belonging, value of
consciousness: Descartes, 49, 56, 183;
  Locke, 55-69, 183
consent, tacit, 109
consent and consensus, 177
conservatism, 83, 87-8, 90-116, 126, 127,
  129, 137, 140, 145, 152-3, 157-63, 171-2
Constantine the Great, 28-9
constitutional abeyances (Foley), 176-7
constitutions, 118, 143, 175-8
Copernicus, Nicholas, 45
cultural knowledge, 6, 18, 92, 95-7, 99,
  108-9
cultural pluralism, 39, 170-1

culture, 4, 6, 7, 8, 9, 11-13, 16-22, 91, 92, 95-7, 99, 103, 106-9, 146, 158; of authenticity (Taylor), 135; of democracy, 7-9, 84, 90, 146, 158, 163, 174; of modernity, 4-6, 9, 63, 84, 146, 150, 169; Tyler's definition of, 18
custom (Hume), 95-9

Darwin, Charles, 50, 111, 186
deep diversity (Taylor), 137, 144
Deism, 50, 51, 58, 72, 74, 94, 151
democracy, 3-10, 11, 21-2, 23, 24, 41-2, 83-4, 85, 90, 91, 113, 115-16, 136, 137, 139, 148-50, 153-9, 167-79; associative (Hirst), 138; culture of, 7-9, 84, 90, 146, 158, 163, 174; defined, 3, 11, 149, 150, 171, 172, 173; participatory, 42, 82, 133-4, 137, 140; and solidarity, 90, 91, 115, 123, 133-4, 156, 169, 171
Descartes, René, 43, 45, 47-50, 53-7, 59, 60, 62, 67, 72, 99, 134, 183
determinism, 47-9, 63, 66, 78, 81, 120
Diderot, Denis, 36-7
Disraeli, Benjamin, 161-2
divine-command morality, 28, 30-1, 35, 37, 40, 44, 55, 72, 148, 150-1
dualism, Cartesian, 47, 49, 54, 55, 57, 59
Duns Scotus, John, 31, 44
Dworkin, Ronald, 87, 133, 170

economic libertarianism, 5, 85, 145, 154, 156, 158, 159, 171-2
egalitarian plateau (Dworkin), 133, 170
egalitarianism, 7, 87, 106, 111, 112, 113, 123, 125, 129, 133, 135, 140, 155, 157, 161, 170-2. *See also* equality
Einstein, Albert, 56
elitism, anti-democratic, 171, 175, 178
emanationism, 28-30, 40, 119, 140, 150
empiricism, 45-66, 70, 73-9, 80-1, 92-9, 100, 101, 103, 104, 117, 120, 122, 134, 151
Encyclopaedia Britannica, 105
Encyclopédie, 36
energy, 51, 58, 59, 61, 63, 66
Enlightenment, 35, 36, 117, 118, 123; French, 16, 17, 20, 36, 38, 74-5; Scottish, 18, 92, 94, 95, 99, 105, 111
Epicureanism, 75
equality, 5, 7, 14, 38, 41, 42, 87, 89, 106, 110, 111, 123, 129, 133, 135, 154-6, 170-1, 189; vs. excellence, 7-8, 9, 110
Erasmus, 32, 34
extension, 49, 54, 55-62, 66-7

fact-value dichotomy, 96, 122
fascism, 83, 159, 162-3, 167
Ferguson, Adam, 18-20, 21
Ficino, Marsilio, 33
Foley, Michael, 176-7
freedom. *See* liberty
freedom of choice, 91, 109, 147-8

Galileo, 44-7, 50, 52, 55, 59, 75, 151
Gassendi, Pierre, 75
Geist (Hegel), 126-30
Geneva, 35, 36
Gentile, Giovanni, 162
God, 28-40, 47-52, 62, 72-3, 128, 188. *See also* Deism; divine-command morality; emanationism; prime mover; unmoved mover
good, the, 3-10, 22-31, 35-6, 39, 42, 43-4, 46, 51, 71, 75, 76, 79, 86, 88-91, 93, 96, 104, 110, 113, 143, 150, 163
goodness: quality of, 8, 141; source of, 23, 28-9, 37-8, 39, 40, 44, 72, 93, 95, 97, 108, 110, 121-4, 163
goods, conflicts of, 4-5, 7-8, 84, 137, 141, 147, 149, 179. *See also* value pluralism
Greece, ancient, 12, 22-8, 32, 53, 146

habit, 92, 96, 107-8, 112
happiness, pursuit of, 9, 43-6, 67, 70-2, 85, 92, 96, 153-4; Hobbes, 52; Locke, 59, 63, 70, 74, 151; Mill, 77; Smith, 100
Hegel, Georg Wilhelm Friedrich, 20-1, 124-32, 136, 188
Helvétius, Claude-Adrien, 74
Herder, Johann Gottfried von, 17, 19, 20, 21, 39, 129, 134
Hirst, Paul Q., 138-9
history of ideas, 6, 50, 146, 148
Hitler, Adolf, 144, 162
Hobbes, Thomas, 11, 14, 15, 18, 45, 47, 49-55, 57, 59, 65, 67-70, 72, 73, 75, 82, 86, 92-4, 104, 107, 170
Homer, 24, 26
Hooker, Richard, 13-16
human nature, 14, 44-6, 50-5, 65, 67, 69, 73-5, 77-80, 85, 92-4, 96-8, 100-1, 103, 105-8, 110-13, 117-25, 127, 133-4, 139-40, 143, 152, 154-5, 187
humanism, 28, 32-6, 115
Humboldt, Wilhelm von, 76-7, 79-82, 86, 104, 107, 118, 124, 129, 134, 165
Hume, David, 61, 76, 92-3, 95-9, 101, 103-4, 107, 109, 111, 114, 117-18, 121-3
Hutcheson, Francis, 93-4, 101

ideas, 6, 61, 146; absorbed by Natives, 177, 190; innate, 49, 54, 74. *See also* history of ideas
identity: vs. character (Mill), 79; cultural, 16-17, 20; derived from community, 60-1, 88, 91-2, 135, 161, 167-8; personal (Locke), 54-7, 59, 67-8, 74, 106, 167, 168
ideologies, 3-6, 20, 150, 152-63, 166, 168, 172, 173, 178, 179; diversity of, 42, 84, 149, 157-9, 172-9; holistic, 159, 160-3; liberalism as dominant, 88-9, 153, 168; stipulative definition, 5
impartial spectator (Smith), 101, 105
individualism, 22, 32, 72-3, 75-7, 79-87, 90, 100, 104, 114-16, 118, 134-7, 151-6, 158-63, 167-8, 171-3
individuality, 80-2, 85, 92, 107, 132, 140
inertia, 45-6, 50-2, 55, 59, 75, 92, 95, 97, 151
Inglehart, Ronald, 155-6
innate ideas, 49, 54, 74
institutions, social, 34-5, 83, 88, 92, 95-100, 103-6, 110-11, 113, 117, 121, 152-3, 155-6
invisible hand (Smith), 9, 18, 98, 103
Islam, 16, 31

Jansen, Cornelius, 35
Judaism, 30, 31, 161
judgment, 63-5, 67, 74, 102, 120, 147, 161
justice, 14, 18, 36, 68, 87, 95-6, 98-100, 105, 108

Kant, Immanuel, 20-1, 23, 33, 37-9, 43-4, 46, 63, 72, 81, 86, 93, 117-25, 127-9, 137, 150-1, 154, 155, 186, 187, 188
knowledge, 6, 18, 28, 47, 49, 51, 54, 76, 93-5, 134, 147, 177; as cultural, 6, 18, 92, 95-7, 99, 108-9
Kymlicka, Will, 88, 133, 170

labour: dignity of, 114; division of (Smith), 99-100; Locke, 69; as value-producing (Marx), 129-32
left-liberalism, 85, 87, 89, 96, 153, 158, 172, 179
left-right continuum, 3, 9, 149-50, 152-6, 159, 163, 172, 189
liberalism, 32, 42, 72, 80, 82-92, 94, 114-15, 133-7, 152-3, 157-63, 166-8, 179, 188. *See also* individualism; left-liberalism; right-liberalism
libertarianism. *See* economic libertarianism
liberty: ancient idea of, 53; system of natural (Smith), 100-3. *See also* negative liberty; positive liberty

Locke, John, 13-16, 44, 46-7, 49, 53-70, 72-7, 79-82, 86, 92-5, 99, 104, 106, 109, 122, 134, 151, 170, 183
logos (reason), 25-6, 28, 32
Luther, Martin, 31-2, 34-5, 49, 51

MacIntyre, Alasdair, 27, 32, 160
Maimonides, 31
Maistre, Joseph de, 104
Marx, Karl, 20-1, 42, 100, 117, 119, 125, 129-34, 136, 154, 161
Marxism, 100, 125, 129, 133
materialism: Cartesian, 47-8, 56, 125, 129; economic, 46, 85, 114, 133; Marxist, 125, 129, 139. *See also* mechanicism vs. materialism
mechanicism, 43, 47, 50-1, 57, 99, 107, 187; vs. materialism, 51, 55, 57, 63
memes (Dawkins), 188
memory: cultural, 92; Locke, 56-7, 59-62, 66-8; Helvétius, 74
merit, 68, 102-3, 106, 110, 112, 115
Mill, James, 76
Mill, John Stuart, 73-82, 86, 94, 104, 107, 124, 157, 185, 188
mind, 47-50, 53-7, 59-68, 70, 94, 97, 135, 184
Minkowski, Hermann, 56
modernity. *See* culture of modernity
moment, 59-64, 67; vs. instant, 60
momentum. *See* inertia
monism, 137-8, 166-7, 174, 175, 178
moral sense, 93-5, 101, 111
morality, 23, 35-40, 63-71, 84, 92-106, 111-15, 121-5, 140, 147-51, 155; teleological, 44, 51, 92, 120. *See also* divine-command morality; utilitarianism
More, Thomas, 34
Mussolini, Benito, 162

nationalism, 16-17, 83, 129, 163
Native Canadians, 174-5, 178, 190
natural law, 13-14, 16, 28, 44, 99, 122
natural rights, 16, 36, 53
naturalism, 43-4, 50-1, 69, 81, 122, 151
nature, 27, 44-5, 49-59, 65-7, 69, 81, 119, 120-4, 126-7, 151, 187, 189; second (Burke), 98, 107-9. *See also* human nature
negative liberty, 41-3, 52, 58, 72, 79-85, 87, 103-4, 114, 134-7, 140, 143-4, 151-4, 158, 164-7, 172, 188; vs. positive liberty, 41-2, 46, 55, 67, 70-1, 100, 119-21, 165, 188. *See also* economic libertarianism
new politics (Inglehart), 155
Neoplatonism, 28-31, 50-1, 72, 150

Nietzsche, Friedrich, 39-41, 79, 82, 86, 113, 138, 183
Nozick, Robert, 87

Ockham, William of, 31, 44
Orphic beliefs, 26, 30, 67

passions, 48, 50-5, 72, 74, 92-9, 101-7, 112, 117-19, 121, 127
Pateman, Carole, 133
Petrarch, 32-3
Pico della Mirandola, Giovanni, 33, 34, 182
Plato, 9, 18, 25-30, 48-9, 67, 119, 141
political parties, 163-4, 172-3
political theory, 5, 8, 145
politics, 3-11, 38, 41-2, 83-4, 142-50, 155-7, 159, 166-79
positive law, 14, 16, 18, 122
positive liberty, 24, 37, 41-6, 66, 78, 84-7, 92, 100, 103, 107, 115-29, 131, 135, 138, 142-6, 148, 150-5, 158, 164-7, 171, 173, 188; vs. negative liberty, 41-2, 46, 55, 67, 70-1, 100, 119-21, 165, 188. *See also* self-creativity; self-sufficiency
postmaterialism (Inglehart), 155-6. *See also* new politics
postmodernism, 41, 158, 183
poverty, 114, 148, 161
Price, Richard, 104, 108
Priestley, Joseph, 104
prime mover, 31, 44, 50-2, 54, 72, 74, 95, 120, 121, 151. *See also* unmoved mover
process, 43-7, 50-70, 72-5, 77, 79, 87, 89, 92-3, 95-6, 104-7, 110-12, 119, 151, 154, 174, 186; vs. status, 55, 56, 69, 75, 87, 104, 106, 112
Protagoras, 11, 25
Protestantism, 51, 114
psyche, 25-6

Quebec nationalism, 163

racism, 111-12, 143
rationalism, 16-20, 74-6, 97, 99, 104, 129, 162; constitutional, 176-7
Rawls, John, 86-7
relativism, 4, 18, 23, 25-6, 46, 84, 164-5
religion, 12-13, 16-17, 94, 100, 104, 108, 110, 140
resonance of passions (Hume), 97-8, 101, 105
right, prior to the good, 86, 122
right-liberalism, 85, 96, 153, 172
rights, 16, 20, 44, 68, 88, 115, 174, 175, 178; collective, 88

rights-talk (Glendon), 115, 174
romanticism, 20-1, 35, 38, 40-1, 76-80, 85-7, 129, 155, 158, 167, 174, 183, 188
Rousseau, Jean-Jacques, 21, 23, 34-9, 41, 72-5, 86, 93, 117-19, 124-5, 133-4, 154-5, 182, 187

scholasticism, 9, 31-5, 47-8, 50, 53
second nature (Burke), 98, 107-9
self-creativity, 24, 36-7, 43, 55, 66-7, 73-4, 79, 80, 85, 92, 112-18, 125, 127, 131-3, 135-40, 145, 150-55
self-ownership, 54, 67-70, 89, 92, 149, 170-1
self-sufficiency, 37, 38, 40-1, 63, 66, 115, 123, 126-7, 129, 135, 150, 153, 158
Shaftesbury, Anthony Ashley Cooper, third earl of, 15, 94
slavery, 38, 70
Smith, Adam, 18, 93, 99, 100-4, 109, 111, 129
social capital, 110
social unity, 92, 94, 97, 100-1, 124, 154
socialism, 42, 80, 83, 87, 90, 116-19, 124-5, 129, 131, 133-41, 143, 152, 154, 157-63, 172. *See also* solidarity
Socrates, 11, 25-6, 30
solidarity, 42, 90, 115, 123, 132-4, 137-9, 153-6, 163, 166-71
Sophists, 11, 25-6
Sorel, Georges, 162-3
soul, 26, 30, 32-6, 47-54, 67, 69, 80-3, 126
space-time continuum, 56-7, 66
spiritualism, 32, 139-40
status vs. process, 55, 56, 69, 75, 87, 104, 106, 112
Stirner, Max, 86
Stoicism, 27-8, 30, 32, 44, 50, 102
Strauss, Leo, 41
surplus value (Marx), 129-31
sympathy, 92-3, 95, 97-106, 121, 123

tabula rasa (Locke), 54, 76, 94
Taylor, Charles, 42, 134-9, 171, 188
teleology, 9, 26, 43-59, 69-70, 77, 82, 92-3, 96-7, 104, 120, 122, 150-1
telic security, 71, 82-3, 88-9, 115-16, 151
theodicy (problem of evil), 29, 76
Thomas Aquinas, Saint, 13, 44, 48, 50, 53, 54
time, 45, 54-70, 74-5, 87, 92-3, 95-7, 104, 106, 108, 110-11, 126; and space, 56-7, 66
Tocqueville, Alexis de, 70, 72
tolerance, 42, 72, 94

tradition, 14-15, 20-1, 23, 40, 82, 85, 88, 92, 110, 135, 152, 155-6, 160-1
Tylor, Edward, 18

universalism, 16-18, 25-9, 33, 36-9, 118, 121-4, 128-9, 188
unmoved mover, 44, 50
utilitarianism, 73-7, 93-4, 104

value pluralism, 3-10, 42, 84, 88-91, 138, 141, 143, 145-9, 150, 152, 154-6, 163-79, 185
value, surplus (Marx), 129-31

values vs. virtues, 23, 29-30, 35, 150
vis viva, 51, 58, 59

Weber, Max, 114
will: creative, 9, 20, 23, 26, 28-9, 33-5, 37-43, 67, 72-3, 106, 108, 118, 119, 121-4, 127-9, 133, 139, 148; general (Rousseau), 35-7, 73, 118, 134; God's, 28-38, 40, 150; human, 9, 23, 26, 30-4, 37, 43, 63-7, 72-3, 78, 93, 106, 109, 117-29, 139, 144, 150; pure vs. holy (Kant), 123; rational (Kant), 121, 123, 125
Wilson, James Q., 111